THE LIFE AND TIMES OF

MARY ANN McCRACKEN

1770—1866

MARY McNEILL

A BELFAST PANORAMA

THE
BLACKSTAFF
PRESS

BELFAST

First published in 1960 by
Allen Figgis & Company Limited
This Blackstaff Press edition is a photolithographic facsimile
of the first edition printed by Cahill and Company Limited

This edition published in June 1988 by
The Blackstaff Press
3 Galway Park, Dundonald, Belfast BT16 0AN, Northern Ireland
Reprinted October 1988

Printed by The Guernsey Press Company Limited

British Library Cataloguing in Publication Data
McNeill, Mary
The life and times of Mary Ann McCracken,
1770–1866: a Belfast panorama.
1. Belfast. McCracken, Mary Ann, 1770–1866.
Biographies
I. Title
941.6′707′0924

ISBN 0-85640-403-9

CONTENTS

ILLUSTRATIONS

FOREWORD

At the close of the eighteenth and beginning of the nineteenth centuries the North of Ireland was profoundly influenced by the American, the French and the Industrial Revolutions. Mary Ann McCracken's long life spanned this great era of upheaval and creative change. A woman of strong character and generous sympathies, with a ready pen and a forthright mind, she was solidly embedded in that vigorous, industrious, intellectually alert middle class which played such a decisive part in moulding British and Ulster life. She suffered deeply from the tragic consequences of rebellion. But she was unbroken, and after the saddening days of 1798 and 1803 she threw herself with enthusiastic energy into living a many-sided life dominated by family affection and humanitarian zeal. Mary McCracken and her circle were keen letter writers and fortunately much of what they wrote has survived. This mass of correspondence has been used by Miss McNeill in composing her account of Mary McCracken's life. Miss McNeill brings to her task not only industry but also a sympathetic understanding of her subject's ideals and feelings and keen awareness of Belfast, the growing city, pulsating with energy, in which Mary Ann McCracken's life was spent.

R. B. McDowell.

Trinity College,
Dublin.
18.9.1959.

INTRODUCTION

Mary Ann McCracken is known to many as the devoted sister of Henry Joy McCracken, most famous of the Northern leaders in the Irish Rebellion of 1798. Few, however, are aware of the other activities of her long career and of the charm and forthrightness of her personality. Except for the short monograph included in *Historical Notices of Old Belfast* [1896] by R. M. Young, no story of her life has been written. Yet from contemporary sources and from her own letters and writings it is possible to get a complete picture of the sort of person she was, and of her varied and outstanding achievements during one of the most fascinating periods of Irish life.

In a great age of letter-writers Mary McCracken was herself a fluent correspondent, and the series of letters that passed between her and her two brothers while the latter were prisoners in Kilmainham Gaol throws a vivid light on their authors and on the history they helped to make. Only a small part of this correspondence has previously been published. At the end of her life another series of letters shows her as the friend and collaborator of Dr. R. R. Madden, author of *The Lives of the United Irishmen*. In the years between come her close association with Edward Bunting and the renaissance of Irish Harp Music ; the successful muslin business that she established in conjunction with her sister ; and her work for the women and girls in the Belfast Poor House, recorded in the Minute Book of the Ladies Committee of the Belfast Charitable Society of which, for a quarter of a century, Mary McCracken was Honorary Secretary. I am greatly indebted to Dr. R. W. M. Strain for unearthing this treasure and bringing it to my notice, and to the Belfast Charitable Society for permission to use it.

Any one of these activities would have marked Mary McCracken as an interesting and unusual woman. In 1792 her contemporary, Mary Wollstonecraft, regarded with despair the fashionable young women of her day spending their time " going they scarcely care where for they cannot tell what." Why, she asks in *The Vindication of the Rights of Women*, would they not study politics, enter business, or take up " the art of healing " ? One such occupation per person would have satisfied that most progressive of eighteenth century writers ; yet, as Mrs. Wollstonecraft was penning her words, there was in the growing town of Belfast a young woman of twenty-two who herself would achieve all three distinctions, for Mary Ann McCracken was already a student of politics, had already embarked on a business enterprise and was preparing herself to be a healer of physical and social ills.

For the historical and social background against which Mary's life was lived I have drawn largely from contemporary sources. To all students of the period the correspondence, known as the *Drennan Letters*, between Dr. William Drennan in Dublin and his sister Mrs. McTier in Belfast, is an inexhaustible mine of information and delight. Both were deeply involved in the political affairs of the day. Mrs. McTier's husband—Samuel—was President of the 1st Belfast Society of United Irishmen, and Dr. Drennan, eminent physician and author of the *Test* to which all United Irishmen subscribed, held office in one of the Dublin societies when, in 1794, he was charged with sedition and successfully defended by John Philpot Curran—" that marmoset of genius "—to use Drennan's own description of the renowned counsellor.

While *Historical Collections relating to the town of Belfast* and *Belfast Politics* were published anonymously, it is known that they were compiled by Mary McCracken's cousin, Henry Joy, junior. They, with the files of the *Belfast News-Letter*, the newspaper which his family founded and owned for many years, are invaluable sources of local information, as are, from another angle, the volumes of Wolfe Tone's incomparable *Journal*. Dr. Madden's *Lives of the United Irishmen*, though not actually contemporary, is based on information gathered from those who had been intimately connected with the Rebellion. It is in the *Madden Papers*, now in Trinity

College, Dublin, that most of Mary McCracken's letters are to be found.

Though it is true that Mary McCracken lived her life in Belfast and was deeply implicated in matters that, at a first glance, appear to be primarily of Irish interest, she was very definitely a product of two great movements, originating, the one in France and the other in Britain, viz. the Enlightenment and the Industrial Revolution; and there are few records of a single life that responded with such vigour to both these influences. In the first half of her life Mary is a glowing example of the Ulster middle-class liberalism that flourished in the short hey-day of Belfast's Georgian brilliance at the close of the eighteenth century. With the opening of the nineteenth century she sets herself to discover the only valid answer to the challenge about to be presented by the new industrial age. Her life is, therefore, of interest to students of these two distinctive eras.

In quoting from her own and other letters I have as far as possible retained the original spelling, punctuation, etc., adding only an additional comma and full-stop when otherwise the sense is difficult to discover on the first reading.

In the course of my investigations I have sought help and information from many individuals, some already known to me, others, till then, strangers. In all instances I have been struck by the sense of something akin to family pride that has been evoked by my queries, and which has brought an added pleasure to my work. To all who have ransacked their book-cases, their old letters and their memories, I am most grateful. In one instance only have I talked with someone who herself had known Mary Ann McCracken. Just a few weeks before her death in her 101st year Mrs. Adam Duffin, granddaughter of Dr. William Drennan, related to me how as a small child she had, with her grandmother, visited Miss McCracken. It is perhaps a reflection of Mary's understanding of little children that Mrs. Duffin's memories of that visit centred round exciting jelly in little glasses, enjoyed while her elders discussed matters that were no concern of hers.

I am much indebted to the Misses Duffin for permission to use their typescript copy of the *Drennan Letters* and to quote from them, and for much incidental help and encouragement.

To the following I express my thanks for permission to consult original documents and to quote from them : The Board of Trinity College, Dublin; Queen's University of Belfast ; the Keeper, State Paper Office, Dublin ; the Deputy Keeper, Northern Ireland Public Record Office ; the Governors, Linenhall Library, Belfast ; Belfast Public Libraries ; Belfast Museum and Art Gallery ; Presbyterian Historical Society, Belfast ; and the Belfast Charitable Society. I am indebted to members of Staff in these institutions for advice and help. Of these I must mention by name Mr. J. W. Vitty, Librarian of the Linenhall Library, the successor in office of one of the characters of my story. I am grateful to Mrs. R. M. Beath for permission to use letters in her possession, and to Dr. R. W. M. Strain for permission to quote from *The History and Associations of the Belfast Charitable Society*. Also to Dr. Constantia Maxwell for permission to use the quotations on p. 50; to Messrs. John Murray & Co., for those on pages 58, 78, 79, 80, 82, 83 ; and to the Talbot Press for that on p. 102.

For the illustrations on frontispiece and facing pages 48, 49, 54, 65, 80, 106, 288 I am indebted to the Belfast Museum, for that on page 272 to the Belfast Charitable Society, and for those on pages 38 and 112 to Mr. H. C. Aitchison, of Blomfontein, South Africa, who with extreme kindness had these miniatures photographed for me and gave me permission to use them.

It remains for me to thank Prof. T. W. Moody, Prof. J. E. Beckett, Dr. R. B. McDowell and Mr. John Hewitt for reading the manuscript and for much valuable help and advice, and Mr. A. H. George for reading the proofs. I alone am responsible for any errors that remain.

BELFAST, 1959.

CHAPTER I

FRANCIS JOY

1697–1790

> I hope the present era will produce some women of sufficient talent to inspire the rest with a genuine love of Liberty and a just sense of [its] value . . . for where it is understood it must be desired . . . I therefore hope it is reserved for the Irish nation to strike out something new and to show an example of candour, generosity and justice superior to any that have gone before.[1]

So wrote Mary Ann McCracken to her brother in a Dublin prison. The date was 1797, she was twenty-six years of age and standing on the threshold of a long career of public interest in which she herself would strike out something new.

While there are some who reach fulfilment unaided by family tradition, and some who achieve it in actual antagonism to such influences, Mary Ann was one of those in whom all the various streams of inherited tendencies converge in strength, to produce a personality true to type but of greater vitality and excellence. So, in order to appreciate the ingredients that went to the making of her character, it is necessary to commence with her forebears and with a brief outline of the historical background of the town in which she lived.

After years of political, religious and economic upheaval following the Irish Rebellion of 1641, the Commonwealth, and the Williamite wars, Belfast, in the first half of the eighteenth century, was entering on a period of comparative calm. Though on a smaller scale inevitably than in Britain, prospects of mercantile expansion were taking shape in the minds of her citizens, primarily in the trades and industries connected with an agricultural economy. By 1715 the town had developed from the small fortified ford of James I's reign to take its place, after Dublin and Cork, as the third port in Ireland. Great quantities of beef, hides, tallow and corn were exported, and imports arrived from the northern ports of Europe as well as from France, Spain and Portugal. Indeed by the beginning of the century Belfast was not only well known on the continent as a place of considerable trade but, in a scale of credit appended by the Exchange at Amsterdam to the names of various commercial towns of Europe, its place was in the first rank.[2] The possibilities of this increasing commerce were obvious to the enterprising townsfolk, but it was no less obvious that Irish trade and industry could never be fully expanded so long as the English parliament controlled Irish affairs and continued its policy of strangling any mercantile development that threatened to compete with English interests.

As the century progressed, all the constructive political thought in Ireland centred on freeing, by constitutional methods, the parliament in Dublin from the shackles that bound it to Westminster, viz. Poynings' Law and the more recent enactment of George I, and in this struggle Ulster gave the lead to the whole country. Not only were the Belfast merchants, by reason of their distance from the capital, more independent of the ruling oligarchy than were the traders of Dublin, but their ideas and convictions had prepared them for just such a situation. Countless were the meetings, declarations and addresses asserting the sole right of the King, Lords and Commons of Ireland to legislate for Ireland, and in all this the family of Francis Joy was to occupy a position of increasing influence.

Francis Joy, the maternal grandfather of Mary Ann McCracken, was born in Killead, Co. Antrim, in 1697, of prosperous farming stock.[3] In due course he settled in Belfast as an attorney, and, while still a young man of twenty-four, married Margaret Martin, granddaughter of George Martin, Sovereign [or chief Burgess] of the town in the early days of the Commonwealth. Francis was an able and enterprising person. By his own exertions and by inheritance he was comparatively wealthy, and he and his wife must have occupied a prominent place in the growing professional and mercantile community of the little town. Both of them sprang from strongly Calvinist stock. The Joys had, in all probability, fled to England from religious persecution in France, coming to Ireland with the armies of James I.[4] With the same armies came the Martins who settled near Belfast, but in 1649 Margaret's uncompromising grandfather had had to seek refuge in Britain for refusing to billet Commonwealth troops in Belfast.[5] Later he aroused the displeasure of the Lady Donegall* of the day by retiring on the Sabbath to his Presbyterian place of worship, after fulfilling his duties as Sovereign by attending her to her seat in the Parish Church.[6] No doubt Francis and his wife had decided views on the stirring "New Light" controversy centring round subscription to the Westminster Confession of Faith, and just then agitating profoundly the Presbyterian community in Ulster. These were also the years of the Test Act when Presbyterians as well as Roman Catholics were debarred from holding public office. But, in spite of controversies and disabilities, the law business prospered, family life was happy, and in due course Henry, Robert and Ann were born.

It was not, however, till he was forty years of age that the incident occurred which gave Francis Joy the opportunity to exert his enterprising ability far beyond the confines of his legal profession. In 1737, as a result of a bad debt,[7] he found himself the owner of a small printing business, and, with no other preparation for a journalistic career, he decided to start the publication of a newspaper. On September 1st of that year there appeared from the sign of "The Peacock" in Bridge Street the first issue of The *Belfast News-Letter* which, as his grandson briefly but proudly remarks, was "the first newspaper printed in this town."[8] The full title of the paper was The *Belfast News-Letter and General Advertiser* and undoubtedly its function was to provide not only news, but a medium through which shippers and merchants might announce their goods, an indication of the growing importance of the trade of the town. We know nothing of the immediate motives which prompted the undertaking, but at the very

*Family name Chichester, the wealthy landowners of Belfast and neighbourhood.

moment when Belfast was awakening to a realisation of its importance Francis Joy provided the organ which welded its thought and proclaimed its views. He was too much of a lawyer to be rash and foolhardy, but if wisdom and foresight directed him towards certain action then obstacles were noticed only to be overcome.

Francis threw himself enthusiastically into the demands of his journal, but no sooner was the venture well started than a paper shortage had to be faced. Previously paper had been imported from France,[9] now war on the Continent made this increasingly difficult, so a paper mill was bought in Ballymena. This in turn opened up fresh possibilities, and in 1745 Francis left Belfast and settled in Randalstown, not so far from his early home, where he opened a larger mill, installing with the aid of a government subsidy of £200 some up-to-date machinery hitherto unknown in Ireland. The following description of this undertaking appeared in the *Dublin Journal* shortly after Francis' death.

> A laudable example of spirit and active enterprise in the late Mr. Francis Joy, of the County of Antrim, deserves to be recorded : This person was one of the first who brought to any perfection in Ireland the manufacture of printing and writing papers ; after the erection of his paper engines Mr. Joy found himself at a great loss for fine rags in making fine paper, which even that part of the kingdom had not been accustomed to preserve; to remedy this Mr. Joy, at considerable pains and expense, for many years, made and distributed in all the towns and villages in the counties of Antrim, etc. great numbers of strong paper bags, to be affixed to walls in houses, in order to preserve *rags*—he published advertisements in the Belfast paper, intreating the public to save such *rags*—and not only gave a generous price for them, but encouraged, by considerable premiums, the gathering of such—he was in consequence, enabled to make annually large quantities of printing paper, clothier's pressing paper, of from 11/6 to 14/- per ream, a great price at that time. But what deserves to be particularly noticed is the following fact, because it shews how far the intelligence and activity of a single man may promote the manufacturing interests of Ireland : Mr. Joy made ordinary

> writing paper and good printing paper from the *backings* or refuse of flax or tow, which article had, for many years, been exported in vast quantities from the North of Ireland to foreign parts.
>
> The quantity and value of the paper made at one time by this truly patriotic man, was more than was made at that period through the whole kingdom, Dublin excepted, in which a Mr. Slater had most laudably distinguished himself in the manufacture of very fine papers, almost equal to Dutch, which at this time was generally used by merchants and others.[10].

At Randalstown this enthusiast for machinery erected also a flax dressing mill with some new and ingenious appliances—probably not unconnected with the supply of *backings* for his paper mill.

Though he had moved to the country, Francis kept in close touch with his children in town. His sons and his daughter married, there was an ever growing collection of grandchildren, and he watched the activities of these three families with loving interest. Only two letters written by him have escaped destruction and they are addressed to members of his family circle,—this to his son-in-law, the captain of a merchant vessel and the father of Mary Ann, is on paper bearing the watermark F. Joy :

> Treehoge, 26th May 1760.
>
> Son McCrackan
>
> I congratulate you on your safe arrival: it gave me much ease and pleasure, after my reading a Paragraff in the newspaper, of sev^{l} ships from the West Indies being taken by the French, on the coast of this Kingdom, finding the account of your arival inserted: Such good Providences demand our reasonable and religious acknowledgments. I am with affectionate Compliments to your kind and good Mother, my Daug^{r} yr Wife and Child
>
> Yr. Affect father
>
> Frans. Joy[11]

" Reasonable and religious "—there could be no truer description of his way of life and of the attitude that he bequeathed to his children. Owing to the war with France there was constant danger of attack at sea, and

Captain McCracken had already been a prisoner in the hands of the French. Earlier in the very year in which this letter was written, Thurot, with three French frigates, had entered Belfast Lough, captured the Castle at Carrickfergus and held it for several days. So this joyous welcome was indeed heartfelt, especially as the Captain's wife was at this time expecting her second baby.

The other letter was occasioned by sorrow :

Treehoge.
1 Dec. 1762.

Son Robert

I do sincerely join in your griefe, for the death of so good a wife and Mother of your young children. Had I thought I would have been usefull I would infalibly have gon to Belfast, on receipt of your brothers short Letter, even over all the obstructions which was in my way. I hope rational religious consideration will in time meetigate and abate your griefe and sorrow. She having lived a pious life of well doing, and tho now absent from the body is present with the Lord, enjoying immortal happyness, which, as you loved her, you ought not to grudge her of, as in case you spend your life as I hear she did, it will be the best preparation for dying the death of the Riteous, as I believe she did; and you may meet again in a state of purity and uninterupted happyness. And I rely on the Divine Providence for the well being of your young Children, and you know it is appointed for us all to die, which ought to be ever in remembrance. I am sensible that your case is piteous, and no doubt perilous, your best way to take [it] is, to set the Lord always before you, and to acknowledge him in all your ways, and he is faithfull, who has promised to care for you and yours and hold up your goings by directing your paths in the way of Riteousness and Peace and Happyness which is, and always shall be, my earnest desire while I continue in the this world. But being now advanced in the sixty sixth year of my age during which time I have gone through many troubles and nevertheless have experienced much of the goodness of the Divine Providence: and tho I shun not fatague, I find a weekness growing upon me, which are the symptoms of mortality. I therefore conclude, that the time of my departure is not far of. Happy, thrice happy are they who having the Sting of Death removed are arived in safety and happyness beyond the dangers and troubles of this present State. I would say more but you have and can have better help than I can give you which I hope you will not fail to have due recourse unto and so conclude

Dear Son your
affect father
Frans Joy.[11]

In spite of his forebodings Francis Joy had still many years before him—indeed he outlived both his sons. In the course of his long life much history had been enacted—Marlborough's victories had resounded through Europe, two Jacobite risings had collapsed and the Hanoverian dynasty sat firmly on the English throne and, most significant of all, the American colonies had wrested independence from a domineering and unsympathetic British government. News would have reached him too, just before his death, of that other great movement for liberty—the Revolution in France.

In Ireland, the aim for which he had striven had, seemingly, been achieved. The Volunteers, so closely identified with his own family—as will be shown—had firstly guarded the shores of Ireland from invasion, and then by the pressure of their support had enabled Grattan to win in 1782 the independence of her parliament. One wonders if the old man, advocate to the end of constitutional reform, was ever troubled by the thought of where that armed force might lead. We do not know, and at any rate, even at ninety-three, there was still a public duty to perform. Parliamentary independence had been won, but parliamentary reform was urgent, for the great landowners and their reactionary influence still dominated the Irish Parliament in Dublin. The election of 1790 was in full swing, and in County Antrim the contest was a trial of strength between the independent candidates sponsored by the merchants and the freeholders, and the representatives of the party in power. Every vote would be needed. Francis was infirm and suffering greatly from his leg, but, he who had never "shunned fatigue" gathered up his ebbing strength and, in spite of all "obstructions", had himself transported from Randalstown to the polling booth at Antrim town, every jolt on the rough road inflicting still more pain. When his astonished grandson from Belfast met him and exclaimed in amazement "What brought you here, Sir?", the characteristic answer was instantly forthcoming: "The good of my country."[12] The Independent candidates, the Hon. John O'Neill and the Hon. Hercules Rowley, were triumphant by a small majority,* but within three weeks, on June 10th 1790, Francis Joy died.

By a curious coincidence the brief paragraph in the *Belfast News-Letter* modestly announcing the death of its founder, is immediately followed by a more lengthy notice of the death of Dr. Benjamin Franklin in Philadelphia,—two men whose sympathies in their separate spheres were closely akin.

His remains were brought back to the town that owed him so much, and Francis Joy lies buried where once was the graveyard of the Parish of Belfast.

It is not without significance that the story of the Antrim election was remembered and recorded by his granddaughter Mary Ann McCracken.

*In the county of Down the election was still more momentous. There, after a terrific struggle, one of the seats was wrenched from the clutches of the wealthy and powerful Downshire family, by Robert Stewart, a handsome lad of barely twenty-one. When, in the following January, the newly elected Parliament assembled it included also another young man—Capt. Arthur Wellesley. Eight years later John O'Neill was to meet his death in tragic circumstances in Antrim town, while the other two were well on their way to the fame that awaited them as Viscount Castlereagh and the Duke of Wellington respectively.

CHAPTER II

HENRY AND ROBERT JOY

1720–1785

THE first authentic glimpse of Francis Joy's sons is found in a letter from Henry to Robert, written in 1745 from Carrickfergus. The Young Pretender had lately raised his forces in Scotland and there were rumours of an attempted invasion of the Antrim coast. As in previous warnings of danger, hundreds of stalwart young men from the neighbouring counties rushed to augment the garrison at Carrickfergus, at that time a place of far greater strategic importance than Belfast, making " a handsome appearance, and going through their exercise with great regularity and exactness "[1] when they were reviewed by the Earl of Antrim, Lord Lieutenant of the county. Henry Joy was one of these, and, full of importance and excitement, he wrote to his brother on October 30th, less than six weeks after Charles Edward's victory at Preston Pans :

> Dear Bro.
>
> We are sent down here to keep Garrison, how long we are to remain I cannot tell . . . I dont believe this place was better garrisoned these many years. The reasons of our coming here you will find in our Paper enclosed. There is no getting furloes and I dont know how we'll get our business managed and my Father begs you may come down—there are four out of our house viz Father, I, Michael and Billy Dunn, and the other people have published two papers and design to continue it, but meet with no manner of encouragement, I believe they'll be obliged to drop it. You must excuse my seldom writing, we are so prodigiously hurried and in continual alarms.
>
> Yours in great haste,
>
> Henry Joy.[2]

The rival publication was almost certainly the short lived *Belfast Courant*,[3] and there is more than a suggestion of professional rivalry in its appearance. *The Courant* was started in 1745, printed by John Magee on paper manufactured by James Blow, both men being already well-established printers in Belfast. Probably they resented the intrusion into their domain of the enterprising lawyer, and determined to retaliate. However, their effort met with little success and continued for only one year.

Brother Robert was in Dublin. Perhaps he was visiting Mr. Slator and his famous paper mills at Saggart and Clondalkin ; perhaps, too, he had been one of the vast number who during two days had filed past the coffin of the great Dean of St. Patrick's, for Jonathan Swift[4] had died just one week before the letter from Henry was written—Jonathan, who fifty years earlier, as the young prebend at Kilroot, had made his way so many times along the shore of the lough to Belfast in his ardent wooing of Jane Waring, his Varina.

Be all that as it may, the volunteering episode at Carrickfergus was to have its later far-reaching repercussions.

When their father moved from Belfast, Henry and Robert were twenty-five and twenty-three respectively. Henry took over the notary's office, and both brothers were responsible for editing and printing the *News-Letter*. The following years were predominantly a time of happy family life. Of Henry's wife, Barbara Dunbar, we know little, while the following note from Robert to his fiancée —and second cousin—Grizell Rainey of Magherafelt, suggests that he had had to be a patient and considerate wooer :

> My dear Miss Grizzey,
>
> Mr. Rankin has consented to oblige me, provided it be done with secrecy.
>
> And by this time I hope there remains nothing to protract any longer the happy crisis—But that you may not be in any degree disconcerted, I shall not set out till Thursday; when I hope to see you: and shall order it so as our Boy and horse will be with us the next day at Noon—Meantime (as we'll depend on the Portmantua from Antrim) his carriage may be ready
>
> I am, my Dearest
>
> Belfast Yrs. most affectionately
>
> Nov. 24. 1751. Robert Joy.[5]

The Rev. John Rankin was the recently ordained minister of the new Presbyterian congregation in Antrim. His insistence on secrecy is an interesting reminder that at that date, and until 1847, marriages solemnized by Presbyterian clergymen were illegal. "Miss Grizzey" was greatly admired and loved by all her friends, she and Robert were to be very happy and in the eleven years of their short married life they had six children, but only two of them reached maturity.

Meanwhile the firm of Henry & Robert Joy extended its connections. A considerable amount of printing and publishing other than the *News-Letter* was undertaken, and it is still possible to pick up books with its imprint. In 1767 the site at Cromac, then outside the confines of Belfast, was acquired on which the Joy paper mill was to be built.

The *News-Letters* of the period form a fascinating commentary on the growing Belfast. As well as carefully written editorials and occasionally an article in lighter vein, the paper carried detailed reports of proceedings in the Dublin and London Parliaments, news from Europe, Asia and the New World, descriptions of social functions at the Court of George III, and a little legitimate gossip about London society in general. Shipping intelligence was of the greatest importance, and the arrival of vessels in the port of Belfast, and the cargoes they carried were carefully reported: sugar, rice, mahogany and molasses from the West Indies; brandies, wines, fruits and spices from France, Spain and Portugal; timber from Memel and other Baltic ports; as well as the more general trade with London, Liverpool and Scotland. All these imports came in exchange for the salted meat and fish, hides, butter, tallow and linen, produced throughout the province, truly the beginning of Belfast's seaborne trade. Merchants and shopkeepers in their turn used the paper to advertise their wares—whalebone for stays, hams and cheeses in great variety, velvets and velveteens, serges and sateens, silks and satins—and we read names so soon to become notable in the history of the town: Mr. Getty and his timber, teas and wines; Mr. Neilson and his drapery ; Mr. Cunningham displaying all the riches of the West Indies ; Mr. Emerson his tobacco and snuff, and so on. There were announcements, too, of local social events,—the coteries in Belfast, the coteries in Ballymena, Dromore and elsewhere, not to speak of cock fights and travelling menageries with their attendant shows. Mr. McGrath the dancing master from Dublin notified the public of his return to town for some weeks, as did the dentist who, also for a few weeks, would be found—strangely enough—at the timber merchant's at Hanover Key ; the peruke maker and the ladies hair-dresser were also there, and there is a familiar ring about the constant advertisements for domestic servants, who need not apply unless they can furnish reliable " characters ".

This, and much more, went to make up the bi-weekly issues of the *News-Letter* and through it all ran the serious purpose of Francis Joy and his sons—the provision of reliable information and the dissemination of the new and liberal ideas in political thought. So, when in 1775 the American colonies embarked on what was to be their momentous struggle for freedom, the proprietors were ready to advocate their cause " with the most undaunted zeal "[6] to the great annoyance of their contemporary the *Dublin Mercury* which burst into the following scurrilous verse :

On the accounts published in the Belfast Journal, relative to the present state of America.

The puritan-Journal, Impress'd at Belfast,
Exhibits the printer's complexion and cast:
Whose partial accounts of each public transaction
Proclaim him *the infamous tool of a faction.*
From worthy old Faulkner,* to give him his due,
Nought issues, but what is authentic and true;
Each foreign report and domestic relation
Approv'd and admitted on good information.
But . . . .† the low scribe of a party quite frantic

**Faulkner's Journal*, Dublin.
†Joy.

With zeal for their brethern across the Atlantic
Discreetly and piously chuses to tell
No tidings, but such as come *posting from hell.*
Thence furnished with news, it is easy to guess,
Why nothing but falsehoods proceed from his press;
Of which *he* is sure to have constant supplies,
Who still corresponds with the *father of lies.*[7]

That the *News-Letter* was voicing the growing opinion in the town is evident from the report of a meeting held on Nov. 9, 1775

> when a motion was made and seconded (and passed unanimously) that an humble address be presented to His Majesty from the merchants, traders, and other principal inhabitants of the town of Belfast, stating their grievances and apprehension resulting from the present unnatural state of things: their concern, as members of the British empire, for its present disturbed and endangered state: their feelings, as men, for the horrors of civil war now in America: their hopes in the royal mercy for a speedy termination of these: and their prayers for a restoration of the old constitutional system.*[8]

Henry Joy was one of the 240 signatories to this address.

There were many in Belfast who appreciated the deep issues involved, and as the American struggle continued and political independence was finally achieved, the effect on the minds of the rising mercantile class was very great.

Ulster sympathy in the American struggle was aroused, in part by commercial interests. Her people had already suffered from the self-centred policies that Britain was now inflicting on the colony, and, furthermore, the extensive linen business that Ulster had developed with the eastern seaboard of America was now threatened with dislocation and possible ruin.

But alongside of these commercial ties the people of the North of Ireland had a strong human connection with N. America. Throughout the 18th century as England, in her own interests, successively destroyed

*A reference to the Massachusetts Government Act.

the Irish woollen, silk and glass industries, which, in point of fact, were almost exclusively in the hands of English and Scottish settlers, emigration had been continuous and thousands of workers from Ireland were forced to find new homes in America.

Moreover, as the century wore on large sections of the employing classes were forced, by continued economic and financial distress, to leave the country. A report published by the *Belfast News-Letter* in 1773 deplores this increasing emigration, stating that in the previous two years over 17,000 persons had departed, and estimates that " the North of Ireland has in the last five or six years been drained of one fourth of its trading cash and the like proportion of the manufacturing people. Where the evil will end remains only in the womb of time to determine."[9]

Such disruption of industry resulted in continuous suffering amongst the poor in town and country. Lack of work in the country districts—and practically all the spinning and weaving was done in rural areas—meant a ceaseless drift of labourers into the town in search of employment, and beggars and destitute people roamed the streets of Belfast. Early in the century provision had been made by act of Parliament for the erection of work houses from public funds in Dublin and Cork, but elsewhere in Ireland the care of the poor, entirely dependent on voluntary initiative, was extremely haphazard.

In 1752 steps had been taken by the Sovereign and leading citizens of Belfast to form the Belfast Charitable Society and to inaugurate a fund to build " a poor House and Hospital and a new Church in or near the town of Belfast,"[10] an ambitious scheme for the still small community. Lotteries, then as now hailed as a means of producing quick money, were found in this instance to have disappointing results, indeed to have landed the promoters in serious financial complications, partly owing to the skilful manipulation of the lottery market by Dr. Mosse who was at that moment building the Rotunda Hospital in Dublin. Not until 1767 were the members of the Society in a position to set out their plans and to request Lord Donegall, to whom all the town belonged, to make over to them the site already promised " on the North West side of the road leading to Carrickfergus . . . the most convenient place for erecting the intended Buildings, and where they will be most ornamental to the Town of Belfast."[11] By now the care of the destitute was so urgent that the idea of a hospital and church had been abandoned.

Henry and Robert Joy were leading members of the Charitable Society from its early days. Henry's name is constantly found in connection with the raising of funds —during one gloomy period he was asked to send a messenger every morning and evening to wait upon certain subscribers until outstanding sums were produced —and, when the time came, the lease from Lord Donegall was made out in his name as representing the Society. Later he was appointed one of the " Key Carriers " entrusted with the three keys necessary to open the Society's chest, the Board directing that the chest itself should be kept in his house " in the small closet adjoining his dining room."[12] The firm of H. & R. Joy undertook the printing and distribution of lottery tickets.[13]

Meanwhile Robert worked in other directions. Plans of poorhouses and infirmaries were sought from Liverpool, Birmingham, Manchester and Glasgow but failed to give satisfaction. Robert, as he pondered on the requirements of the new institution, set about drawing a plan for himself, though, with the reticence of an amateur, he would not produce it to the committee. Nevertheless some members, seeing it privately, were much impressed. It was then decided that an " Architect of Eminence " should be consulted, and " resolved that Mr. Robt. Joy be requested to take with him to Dublin the three plans now delivered in, & such other drawings as are now in his possession, and lay the same before Mr. Cooley, for his examination, with directions to choose out of those four the Plan which he shall most approve of."[14]

Thomas Cooley, then at the height of his fame, received Mr. Joy, studied the plans and amended one of them—at a cost to the Society of six guineas. But doubts persisted and were finally resolved by the unanimous adoption of Robert Joy's own drawing. We may perhaps regret that a great master of Irish Georgian architecture was not permitted to leave his mark on this northern town, and that his design for the Poorhouse has long since passed into oblivion ; but as we survey Robert Joy's simple but beautiful building, the front of which remains exactly as he conceived it, we stand amazed at the extraordinary ability, versatility and public-spirited endeavour of its originator. In the words of David Boyd, later a schoolmaster in the institution,

All labour'd freely in the bless'd employ,
  But the most active Mr. Robert Joy;
He took to Dublin with th' utmost respect,
  The various plans, [that] the skilled Architect
Might one approve—the work of choosing past ;
  His was the plan they voted best at last.
Through the whole business still the active man ;—
  Here stand the Poorhouse built on Robert's plan.[15]

It is even more creditable when one recalls that all this was accomplished at the very time when the brothers were building the great paper mill at Cromac which necessitated the damming of the Blackstaff River to insure an adequate supply of water power, and in which, no doubt, the most up-to-date machinery was being installed ; to say nothing of the day to day work of the *Belfast News-Letter*.

It was sad for Robert that the year 1771 that witnessed the auspicious ceremony of laying the foundation stone of the Poorhouse building was the year in which his second son died at the age of 15—another Robert, a lad greatly loved and of much promise.

All through the building operations Henry and Robert were continually active, Henry concerned with funds and " debentures ", Robert interviewing workmen, buying materials and keeping his eye on every detail of the rising walls ; both of them spending apparently hours of time at long and frequent meetings of committee. To the end of his days the Poorhouse and the people in it occupied a foremost place in Robert's thoughts. His niece, Mary Ann McCracken, remembered with affection how, as a dying man, he was taken to visit it for the last time in a sedan chair.[16] Indeed it was his great practical concern for the welfare of the poor both inside and outside "the House" that caused him to embark on another far reaching achievement, for, writes his son Henry:

> no sooner were any of his various plans for public utility brought to perfection than the activity of his mind led him to new Objects; which he never failed to prosecute to completion. So early as the year 1777*, on a tour through North Britain, he conceived the scheme of introducing into this then desponding Kingdom, the most intricate Branches of the Cotton Manufacture which had proved unfailing sources of Industry and Opulence to our sister country. In this he was principally prompted by a desire to serve the lower orders of the working poor, particularly linen weavers and spinners whose livelihoods are often precarious, where a nation depends, as ours *did*, almost solely on a single manufacture sometimes as much depressed as at others prosperous. He possessed himself of the rudiments of a business foreign from any former pursuit of his life. He traced it through its remotest parts at a time when no incentive presented itself in the commercial prospects that have since opened upon Ireland, unaided by that protection which was shortly to be given by the legislature to those very springs of wealth of which indeed he may be called the parent and which he lived to see brought to considerable degree of Perfection.[17]

Robert Joy inspired his friend Thomas McCabe and together, at their own expense, they installed in the Poorhouse the machinery necessary to teach the children in the House to spin and weave cotton, so that they could later be employed, without further apprenticeship, in the mills that he hoped would soon be started in the town. Young Mr. Nicholas Grimshaw was also interested, and though the mill that he built in Whitehouse in 1779 for spinning cotton thread was actually the first in the

*Hargreaves and Arkwright had patented their spinning inventions in 1764 and 1769 respectively.

country, it was followed in 1784 by that of Messrs. Joy, McCabe & McCracken which included weaving also and was the first mill in Ireland to be operated by water power.[18]

Thus the spectacular era of cotton manufacture in the North of Ireland was started. So rapid was its development that in 1790, only thirteen years after Robert Joy's tour in Scotland, 500 looms were working in Belfast as against 130 looms for weaving linen and cambric, and it is estimated that eight thousand people were employed in the various branches of the trade within a radius of fifteen miles of the town.[19] Fortunes were quickly made and many were as quickly lost. By the 1830's, largely owing to recurring war with America, the industry had virtually died, but to the original promoters belongs the credit of introducing mechanised spinning and weaving, thus making possible the revival of linen manufacture on a factory basis.

Lest Robert Joy be accused by the cynical of merely exploiting child labour for his own ends it must be added that he and McCabe paid reasonable rates for work done and arranged the hours to be spent at spindles and looms.

So we come to the last public achievement. Already a newspaper proprietor and co-editor by profession, a paper manufacturer by trade, by interest and inclination an architect and industrial engineer, Robert now turned his attention to military affairs, for it was none other than he, with that directness and foresight that characterised all his projects, who inaugurated the 1st Belfast Volunteer Company—the pattern for the Volunteer movement. War with France had already caused alarm and throughout the country groups of young men had, as formerly, banded themselves together for local protection. When, on April 13th 1778, Paul Jones the American privateer sailed into Belfast Lough fears for the safety of the town increased. Three days later, the anniversary of the Battle of Culloden, sixteen survivors of the hastily collected volunteers who manned the fortress at Carrickfergus in 1745 [see p. 21,] dined together at the Donegall Arms. No doubt it was an occasion for convivial remembrance, and we are told that the toasts were expressive of "loyalty and constitutional liberty", but the intention of the diners was "to give their countenance and approbation to the spirit now springing up in the place for self-defence, similar to that which appeared here . . . in the year, 1745."[20].

Henry and Robert Joy were certainly there and Robert, immersed though he was in his cotton schemes, realised that the present grave danger demanded a defence force far more carefully organised than previous efforts had been, more especially as the country was denuded of military forces, army headquarters in Dublin being able to provide no more than 60 troopers for the protection of Belfast. He set to work and by the last Sunday in June

> the 1st Belfast Volunteer Company paraded, and marched to church in their uniform, which is scarlet turned up with black velvet, white waistcoat and breeches. After the sermon, which was delivered by the Rev. Mr. Graham, a very sensible and polite address was made from the pulpit, in commendation of that laudable spirit which had so early occasioned the formation of the company, and pointing out the very valuable purposes it was calculated to promote.—The clothing of the majority of the Company was of IRISH MANUFACTURE;* and the whole made a brilliant and pleasing appearance.[21]

Amongst the first rush of recruits to this famous company was Robert Joy's nephew, young Francis McCracken, Mary Ann's eldest brother. Some weeks later the Chief Secretary wrote from Dublin Castle, seat of the Irish government, that His Excellency the Lord Lieutenant "very much approves of the spirit of the Inhabitants of Belfast who have formed themselves into companies for the defence of the town."[22] And so the great Irish Volunteer movement was established.

The remaining years of Robert's life must have been crowded with incident. Though the fear of invasion receded, trade continued to decline: "We think our-

*An illusion to the widespread movement in the North to support home industry.

selves most loudly called upon," declared the Sovereign and Burgesses in 1779, " by the present crisis, to express our sense of the distresses and calamities in which this ill-fated country is involved, by the decay of trade, by the want of manufactures, and by the impolitic restrictions on our commerce, under which we labour."[23] Such agitation, and the influence that the Volunteers were beginning to wield, induced the British Parliament in 1780 to revoke some of the restrictions previously imposed on Irish trade, and these concessions were welcomed by illuminations and demonstrations in the town, and a long address of thanksgiving was sent to George III. In the same year the Test Act was repealed so that Presbyterians were no longer debarred from holding official positions. Nevertheless uneasiness and distrust continued, " and an opinion daily gained ground, that without a LEGISLATURE TOTALLY INDEPENDENT of the British parliament, the privileges of a commerce granted to this country would be quite precarious."[24] The subsequent spectacular progress of the Irish Volunteers—the reviews in Belfast, Lord Charlemont's stirring message: " Go on—Persevere—Oppression is impossible, and Ireland must be happy " ; their meetings, their addresses, their dinners and toasts ; the great convention at Dungannon in 1782 and, finally, independence and " Grattan's Parliament "—belongs in detail to the general history of Ireland, though in spirit to this story. The Volunteer movement grew from Robert's plan, its political triumph—four years after its inception—was in no small measure due to the constant support of the " Principal Inhabitants of Belfast ", and it constituted the milieu in which the next generation grew up.

We have no record of Robert Joy's personal feelings at the achievement of Irish freedom : probably, in his wisdom, he realised that much would still need to be done before all the benefits could be reaped, but even he could not foresee that in less than four years after his death a revolution in France would turn his world upside down, and that because of it, the next generation would use to such different purpose the tool that he had fashioned.

At the end of his full but not long life [he was sixty-three when he died in 1785] the Rev. J. T. Bryson, Minister of the 2nd Presbyterian Congregation and Chaplain to the Belfast Volunteers, wrote these words :

> Sunday night last died Mr. Robert Joy, one of the proprietors of the Belfast News-Letter. His character was uniformly marked with striking characteristics of unaffected Piety, and extensive Goodness. Possessed of an imagination capable of conceiving largely ; of an understanding capable of digesting minutely ; and of a Heart capable of attempting and promoting liberally the designs of public and private good—his life is a fitter subject of History than of Description. The extensive share he had in designing, *promoting* and *bringing into use* the Establishment in the Town in favour of the young and aged poor ; his attempt to preserve Industry among the old, and the knowledge of useful Arts among the young ; his being the Introducer of *the Cotton Manufacture* into this Province, and the Father—the Venerable Father of the *Volunteer Army* in it—are sufficient Illustrations of his worth and the Writer's sincerity. His Modesty as a man, his *Kindness* as a neighbour, and his exalted *Sensibilities* as a Parent and Friend, need no praise among those who knew him well, and by those who did not know him, a just picture would be deemed flattery. In his *Public Character* he was bold and wise in his designs, persevering and circumspect in their execution. It may be truly said of this good man, that he lived more for his Country than for himself or Family, but he possessed the happy Talent of putting great machines in motion without material injury to his own Fortune, which others might continue with great improvement of theirs. *Thus* without hurting himself in any Thing, he became the Instructor of the Province in many things. May that God who sent him as an Instrument and Example of Industry and Goodness bless this country with many successors to his Virtue in both.[25]

Robert's brother, Henry, survived him by some four years. From 1759 to 1772 he was deputy Town Clerk of Belfast, the designation of " deputy " being in all probability a convenient method of by-passing the prohibitions of the Test Act; certainly there is no suggestion that Henry Joy was merely a second in command. He was one of the group of merchants who established in 1783 the Belfast Chamber of Commerce, following "the plan which has been adopted by our Worthy and Highly Respected Brethren, the Merchants of Dublin."[26] The Belfast Chamber must rank among the oldest in the three Kingdoms, and it is of interest that one of its first public acts was to petition the Irish House of Commons for assistance in developing the harbour, by substituting for the difficult "meandering line" of deep water connecting the Pool of Garmoyle [where it was necessary for ships to await the high tide] with the Quay, a "straight cut which would for ever be kept open by the Waters of the River Lagan running therein", [27] and which would enable vessels of large burthen to pass conveniently up and down,—the first of the engineering feats that have resulted in the great Port of Belfast.

The provision of facilities for marketing white linens in Belfast was one of Henry's projects. Lisburn and Lurgan were at this time the principal linen markets of the North, and it was only in 1773 that the Marquis of Donegall had given Belfast its Brown Linenhall. Brown or unbleached linens were bought by bleachers and, after being treated, were taken to Dublin where the central market for white linen was attended by buyers from England and the Continent. Naturally it would be most beneficial if some of this trade could be diverted to Belfast, and no doubt the enterprising owners of the extensive bleach greens that were being set up around the town—for example the Sinclaires—welcomed such a scheme. Henry's efforts resulted in the building, by a group of citizens, of the White Linenhall in 1783 to the cost of which he and Robert made generous contributions, and which remained one of the dignified landmarks of the city until it was demolished at the close of the 19th century to make way for the present City Hall.[28]

On May 1st 1781 Henry was elected a burgess of the town. This had no particular democratic significance, for the electoral roll was confined to the Sovereign and the Burgesses whose doings were closely scrutinized by Lord Donegall, but his election, coming a year after the repeal of the Test Act, testifies to the high regard in which this uncompromising Whig was held. For such were Henry's political views, and as he trained his nephew, another Henry, in the *News-Letter* office, strong Whig principles were anchored in the young man's mind. This second Henry is known always as Henry Joy, jun., and on his uncle's death he assumed sole responsibility for the paper.

Once again Henry senior was honoured by his fellow-citizens when, just a few months before his death, they expressed to him their " gratitude for the innumerable services rendered by him in a long series of years to his fellow-citizens : as a promoter of concord, by preventing litigious suits, as an able and upright Counsellor, an impartial Arbitrator—and an Honest Man."[29] He was much pleased by this recognition. In his will he left to his son Henry, known for many years as Counsellor Joy, the cup and cover " lately presented to me by the principal inhabitants of Belfast, in the hope that his conduct through life may be such as to entitle him to be as honourably remembered by his fellow-citizens."[30] Henry's wife had predeceased him many years. In this same will he charges his two youngest daughters, Harriet and Grizell, " to pay all respect and obedience to their Aunt Dunbar who has behaved to them as an affectionate parent since the death of my dearly beloved wife." and he bequeaths to this lady " thirty guineas and a ring as a token of my gratitude, respect and esteem."[31]

For, however notable were his public achievements, Henry Joy was essentially a family man. His children loved him, and he must have watched with pride his young son Henry embark on a career that was to end as Chief Baron of the Irish Court of Exchequer. It is an interesting sidelight on the rising financial status of the Joy brothers that Henry, as well as providing liberally for his other children, was able to educate this son in Dublin, London and Paris.

To his sister Ann McCracken Henry was a constant friend and adviser, especially during the long absences from home of her sea-faring husband; the two families lived side by side in High Street. He was always sociable—in the early days when, perhaps, life was not quite so full, he had time to go round to Tim's Coffee House in Bridge Street, to listen to old Dominick Mangan playing his harp,—he considered Dominick a good harpist; and when that interesting young man David Manson opened his little brewery Henry Joy would turn in for a mug of ale and long discussions on politics and education.

He died in January 1789. An obituary notice, long and formal, emphasises the affection with which he was regarded " Too modest to court the attentions of any he was beloved by all ". " He was the blessing of the town and neighbourhood " for, professional lawyer though he was, " he prevented law suits, composed differences and gave opinions which were received with almost unbounded confidence, because they were known to proceed from enlarged ideas, and inflexible integrity. While every other person admired his prudence and revered his knowledge, he alone beheld them with diffidence . . . he lived the wise, the kind, the invaluable friend of all, and dies without the enmity of any."[32]

CHAPTER III

CAPTAIN AND MRS. McCRACKEN

1745–1770

ANN, the youngest of Francis Joy's children by his first wife, was still a child when her mother died. About the time of the move to Randalstown [1745] her father married again and there is no indication that his daughter accompanied him to the new home; probably she remained in Belfast to keep house for her, as yet, unmarried brothers. But housekeeping was not to occupy all her energies, and, while in her early twenties, she opened a milliner's shop in High Street.[1] This enterprise cannot have been prompted by necessity, for Francis Joy was in a position to provide his daughter with every comfort; rather, it was an expression of that independent, practical outlook later to be so characteristic of her own two girls. One's imagination plays with the thought of the little shop; the wide-brimmed bonnets and the great feathered hats, the straws, the beavers and the velvets, the ribbands and other trimmings; and the young woman with her clever fingers taking pride and pleasure in making her customers look their best. In due course the hat shop was abandoned for Ann met and married a sea-captain, John McCracken. In contrast to the Joys he was tall; he was also handsome, a widower and ten years her senior. We know nothing whatever of the romance, but their sincere and happy attachment ended only with his death.

Generations earlier the McCrackens had settled at Hillhall near Lisburn in County Antrim, having been driven from Scotland during the persecution of the Covenanters by Claverhouse.[2] Possibly the family was related to the Rev. Alexander McCracken, Presbyterian minister in Lisburn from 1688–1730, whose strong views against the Oath of Abjuration forced him to fly the country and eventually landed him in prison. Certainly John McCracken had been trained in the Covenanting tradition, and in the new family that started from his marriage the stern, fiery, uncompromising characteristics of the Scot are evident alongside the calmer, more orderly tendencies of the French-English roots of the Joys.

John McCracken, himself, was a man of deep spiritual convictions and unbending integrity, and yet withal, of so kind and lovable a nature that " his particular gentleness " was long remembered as one of his most endearing qualities. On matters of principle he was adamant : for example—in an age when, as a matter of course, every ship's captain and, to a lesser degree, every member of the crew, augmented their earnings by smuggling, Captain McCracken would have none of it, either for himself or for his men. He regarded, it was said, his Custom House oath to be as binding as any other ; furthermore, he considered that smuggling was unfair to the honest trader. In spite of this, and other, strict interpretations of duty his men loved him, for he had all the qualities of a leader.[3]

The Captain and his wife set up house in High Street next door to Henry Joy and close to the quay where his ship would berth. It was an anxious early married life for Ann. She must have been separated from her husband for long periods, and communications were woefully uncertain. In addition to the perils from nature, there was, as we have seen by the letter from her father, constant danger from the enemy, and once, at any rate, Captain McCracken was taken prisoner by the French. The fact that her husband's mother lived with her may have made the young wife less lonely, but Mrs. McCracken senior, was not an altogether easy companion. A fierce, uncompromising old lady, she was regarded by her grandchildren with awe, due in part to a belief that any threat she might utter would surely come to pass. Her granddaughter, Mary Ann, related one such family experience. In the spring of 1763 it was necessary for Captain McCracken to spend some time in Liverpool supervising the building of two vessels for his employer, George Black, a substantial Belfast wine merchant. Supposing that his mother would readily undertake the care of the

MRS ANN JOY McCRACKEN

CAPTAIN JOHN McCRACKEN

two small children, he arranged to take his wife with him. But the old lady had other views. Feeling, perhaps, that the wife's place was in the home, and having no sympathy for the Joy delight in a new experience, she declared most vindictively that " she wished she [her daughter-in-law] might get a scare before coming back." The stay in Liverpool was highly successful, the new ships were completed, but Captain McCracken, not wishing to expose his wife to the risk of a maiden voyage, decided that she should travel home before him. The vessel in which she sailed, encountering bad weather, was wrecked off Ballywalter on the County Down coast, and as the small boat into which the passengers clambered was unable to reach land because of shallow water, it was necessary to wade ashore. In addition to the effects of fright, fatigue and cumbersome clothing, Mrs. McCracken was only too conscious of the 200 golden guineas carefully concealed about her person, which her husband had entrusted to her safe keeping.[4] Altogether an alarming outcome of Grandmother's threat! The old lady held tenaciously to her Covenanting ideas, and, in protest against the iniquity of set-days and holydays, would sit ostentatiously in the window on a Christmas Day busily engaged at her spinning wheel. But there must have been a more attractive side to her rugged nature, for, as we have seen, she had succeeded in winning the respect of old Mr. Joy.

A letter written by George Black to John McCracken at the time of the Liverpool visit is interesting :

Belfast, 3rd May, 1763.

Dear Jack,

I suppose last week's very bad weather has retarded Mr. Oakall's launching the two Vessells, so that you have got little or nothing done yet, excepting the draft and the moulds, which, no doubt are finished by Mr. Sutton ere this ; and who knows but that the bad weather might induce him to make the small model we spoke of, as he could do no work without doors. Tom Black will tell you what great matters we have been doing here, haveing, on a quarter of an Hour's deliberation, bought a ship of 200 Tons and freighted one of 70. This was on receiving

> an order from London for the transporting the french prisoners here and at Castle Dawson, in number abt 420, to france, and finding M. Auld was not lyke to appear, we freighted Bob Moore to go to Bordeaux in his place, and he is to carry about 90 or 100 prisrs. The ship we bought of Ts Greg, and is the 'Prince of Wales' from Boston, Capt. Trail, which you saw. She cost us above one thousand Britt: but this is her first Voyage, tho' but indiffly found. She is a course, stout, full-built carrier. Capt. Eager goes in her to Bordeaux, when she may be sold . . .[5]

The Black family [to which the famous chemist, Joseph Black of Edinburgh, belonged] had an extensive wine business in Bordeaux, and presumably McCracken was the principal captain of their fleet of trading vessels. Later he was constantly engaged in the shipment of linens to the West Indies and America. As a result of the Bordeaux voyages he acquired a life long interest in France and French ways which he communicated to his children. Indeed, so anxious was he that they should learn the French language accurately, that he engaged an old weaver, the only native speaker he could find in Belfast, to give them lessons. Little could he guess in what direction admiration of the French would later lead them.

This French connection, and his own experiences as a prisoner there, would account for John McCracken's association with Robert Joy and other prominent citizens in a movement to alleviate the lot of French prisoners of war quartered in Belfast in 1759.[6] The unfortunate prisoners were being cruelly exploited by a dishonest local agent, and these gentlemen suggested to the government in London that a committee of townspeople should be appointed to look after their welfare.

However, neither a stern mother-in-law nor the long dreary absences of her dear husband, clouded the happiness of Ann's growing family. High Street then was a bright, safe playground, and with the cousins next door, the Templeton family nearby, and other neighbours, there was ample scope for fun and high spirits. Many, many years after, Mary Ann was able to remember "hopping three times across High Street without stopping" the height of ambition for an active little girl, holding her own against older competitors. Though there was a garden at the rear of their house, Captain McCracken rented a larger plot out of the town beside Uncle Robert's Poorhouse, and in Mary Ann's own words "as soon as I was able to walk my mother took me with her to the garden, and we often visited the Poorhouse."

During his periods at home John McCracken started various projects of importance. In 1758 he established a ropewalk. No doubt rope of some kind had already been made in connection with the port, but McCracken's affair was on a much larger scale. It was situated on the County Antrim shore of the Lough [as indeed was all the town in those days,] and ran along the east side of the Fore Plantation, a district now entirely covered by docks.*

McCracken also started the first factory for the manufacture of sail cloth and canvas, and we have seen how he combined with his brother-in-law in the cotton firm of Joy, McCabe and McCracken; indeed it was he who shipped the first cargo of raw cotton from Liverpool to Belfast.[7] Later he built a cotton factory of his own in Francis Street, said to have been named after his eldest son, and when, as the family grew up, Mrs. McCracken once again turned her attention to business, it was to start a small muslin industry. Indeed the McCracken family was to be associated with the cotton trade in Belfast much longer than the other original partners,—long enough to make and lose in three generations a very considerable fortune.

As well as his many business concerns John McCracken had time and thought for other interests: he established the Marine Charitable Society,[8] a benevolent undertaking to which sailors paid regular contributions and received benefits in sickness and old age. This society continued to function till the beginning of the 19th century, when, at the request of Captain McCracken's son Francis, the

*With the growth of the port several other ropewalks were started later, one of which eventually became the present world-famous Belfast Rope Works.

Belfast Charitable Society took over the funds and the consequent obligations.[9] He was also, with his brother-in-law Robert Joy, an active member of the Third Presbyterian congregation, and the Committee Minute Books of the period contain both their names as office bearers. In the baptismal records of that congregation are to be found the names of all his children.

We do not hear of him taking much part in politics, though he co-operated with others in calling a town meeting to consider the resolutions for the famous Dungannon Convention of 1782, and he was interested to some extent in the notable Antrim election of the following year.[10] Perhaps his frequent absences from home prevented him from taking a more prominent part in these affairs, or perhaps, as I think more likely, politics did not greatly interest him. An anonymous handwritten note, found in the Bigger collection of papers,[11] describes Captain McCracken as a man of comfortable means, who was a patron of the arts and kept open house, delighting to welcome any strangers to the town who were interested in music or painting.

This, then, was the home into which seven little children were born. The eldest died in infancy, as did Captain McCracken's son by his first wife. The rest grew up amid an atmosphere of rich family affection, spontaneous enjoyment, continual coming and going of friends and relations, wide interests and constant activity of one sort or another. Mary Ann, the youngest but one of this happy family, was born on July 8th, 1770, the year of Wordsworth's birth, and the year in which Goldsmith published *The Deserted Village*. At home she was generally called Mary, but the two names are always coupled in her signature, and it is as Mary Ann McCracken that she has lived in the annals of her town.

CHAPTER IV

CHILDHOOD AND ADOLESCENCE

1770–1790

ONE of the first unusual experiences in Mary McCracken's life came to her at school.

The main educational establishment in Belfast in the middle of the eighteenth century was the " Latin school " for boys, founded and maintained by the Donegall family. It was situated beside the Parish Church and provided a grounding in the three Rs and the classics. From time to time other masters in the town gave tuition in various subjects, pupils going from one to the other according to their requirements. Such competition irritated his Lordship, and in 1754 the following notice appeared :

> The Earl of Donegall, at the request of a great part of the inhabitants of the town of Belfast, has at a great expense put the School House in repair, and brought to town the Rev. Nich. Garnet and appointed him schoolmaster for the Town. The Earl and his Trustees have heard that some of the inhabitants do send their children to other schools. They have ordered me to acquaint the Inhabitants, as well as their other Tenants in the Neighbourhood, that they are not pleased with such treatment, and hope they will not be laid under the necessity of taking notice of any individual who shall continue to do so.
>
> John Gordon, Agent.[1]

For girls, the very elementary academic instruction provided by one or two impecunious ladies was augmented by classes in sewing, knitting and embroidery, and for both girls and boys of any social standing at all the dancing master was essential.

Into this situation came young David Manson. Born at Cairn Castle, County Antrim, he settled in Belfast in 1752, determined not merely to teach but to teach in a very particular manner. When as a child in the depth of the country David was recovering from a serious illness, his mother had taught him, by means of play, the first simple lessons, sowing in his mind at the same time the seeds of his future success. Before coming to Belfast he had prepared himself by study, and by practical experience of teaching in places so far apart as Ballycastle and Liverpool, to set up a school where children "will be taught to read and understand the English tongue without the discipline of the rod by intermingling pleasurable and healthful exercise with their instruction."

Meanwhile, in order to support himself and his wife, and to gain the acquaintance of citizens, Manson started a small home brewery.[2] His beer was good—about brewing also he had his own particular theories—and much talk and discussion must have taken place over the counter of the little shop, for such notions on education sounded novel to minds accustomed to normal 18th century schooling. Gradually a group of enthusiastic supporters emerged, foremost among them being Henry Joy, and in spite of all Mr. Gordon's warnings an advertisement appeared in the *Belfast News-Letter* of October 1755 to the effect that

> David Manson, at the request of his customers, having opened an evening school at his house in Clugston's Entry, teaches by way of amusement English grammar, reading and spelling, at a moderate expense.

This new venture was to be run on co-educational lines and Henry Joy's eldest child, Elinor, then about six years old, was one of the first pupils. Others followed from both the Joy families and from the McCrackens. There were also the Templeton children, Catherine and possibly Elizabeth Hamilton, Lord Templetown's son, a clever lad from Cushendall called James McDonnell, and many more. In due course Mary Ann McCracken herself appeared, and as the influence of her school days remained with her always it is necessary to give a brief sketch of this very unusual establishment.

At the time of Mary's arrival Manson was at the height of his fame and had moved to a large, specially built house in Donegall Street, an area recently developed and much sought after for its proximity to the country and fresher air. Here he took some boarders. Long before this, however, he had evolved a definite educational system. Each class-room was divided into two " companies ", based on the accepted grades of society, and every child was given a ticket of membership, bearing the letters F.R.S., to be retained or forfeited according to behaviour. Each company included a King, a Queen, Princes and Princesses, Dukes and Duchesses, Lords and Ladies, etc., rank being acquired by the satisfactory preparation of home-work. The actual amount of preparation was left to the discretion of each child, but if the royal crown was coveted upwards of 24 lines had to be memorised, the qualifications for other ranks being graded accordingly. Not everyone could attain nobility, and those who managed only eight lines or less were tenants and under-tenants. The school day began at 7 a.m., when repetition was heard and the children took the places they had earned. After the break for breakfast at 9 o'clock there was reading, spelling and grammar, and here a Chancellor and Vice-Chancellor officiated, the former being called upon to explain difficult words, and the latter to correct punctuation. Worked into this elaborate performance was a scheme whereby the children could help one another. After the lessons had been heard a successful landlord took in hand a less successful tenant, and every line learned by the latter constituted £1 of rent due to the landlord, who kept a note in his ledger of all rents due and paid. Whoever held the position of King and Queen for a week had the privilege of calling a Parliament on Saturday, when arrears were settled, and those tenants " who had nothing to give acceptable to the land-lord must plead poverty with their feet uncovered, their arrears being discharged out of the fund of toys which were taken from those who had used them at improper seasons."

It was indeed a novel school.

As for punishment—it was the hey-day of clubs, and at the back of the room an empty space was known as

" The Trifler's Club " to which idlers were relegated. Worse still : there was a large wooden figure called the Conqueror, and those who defied the stigma of the Club were obliged to have so many rounds of boxing with this unresponsive opponent. It was a first principle with Manson never to use the rod, hence this rather ingenious plan for self-inflicted corporal punishment.

Another feature of the school was the carefully prepared books and apparatus. Manson compiled spelling books, a grammar and a dictionary ; he had various unusual devices for teaching the younger children to spell phonetically and, seeing how constantly they played with the battered packs of cards rejected by their elders, he had " spelling, reading and memorial cards " specially printed, and used for the many games then in vogue. " Manson's cards " and his school books were in wide circulation for years after his death. The Bible and the newspaper were used by the older pupils for reading, as was also *The Lilliputian Magazine*, one of the recent publications for children emanating from Mr. Newbury's shop in St. Paul's Churchyard. In the Lilliput playground, situated at the edge of the town near the lough, was a well kept bowling green for the boys and also the Flying Chariot—a wonderful mechanical velocipede of Manson's invention—made for the enjoyment of the pupils, and, at stated times, of the public. For shorter spells of exercise the children were permitted to use the courtyard of the nearby Brown Linenhall.

Mechanisation was already in the air and outside his teaching hours Manson spent much time with his inventions, one of which was a spinning machine set in motion by one man and operating twenty spindles, thereby making it necessary for the spinner to use her hands only. He presented this model to the Poorhouse for the use of the girl inmates, and we can imagine how entranced he must later have been when Robert Joy's new spinning and weaving machinery was being set up. He was much concerned about the effect of these new methods on the traditional economy of the countryside, and published a pamphlet in which he maintained that the new industry should be built round agriculture and not centralized in towns. All these points of interest he would present to his pupils in simplified form, and one young mind at any rate was obviously stirred and set on its ultimate course. But before everything else Manson was a teacher :

> Every tutor, [he wrote] should endeavour to gain the affection and confidence of the children under his care ; and make them sensible of kindness and friendly concerns for their welfare ; and when punishment becomes necessary, should guard against passion and convince them 'tis not their *persons* but their *faults* which he dislikes . . . These things are easily comprehended ; but the great nicety lies in the execution : for *knowledge*, *diligence* and *sobriety* are not sufficient qualifications for this employment without patience, benevolence and a peculiar turn of mind, by which the Preceptor can make the course of education an entertainment to himself as well as to the children.[3]

His interest in the education of girls was remarkable. " Young ladies ", it was recorded after his death, " received the same extensive education as young gentlemen. He, and the schoolmasters taught by him were the great cause of infusing into their delicate and tender minds the rudiments of the good sense and erudition for which our ladies during this age have been remarkable."[4] Elinor Joy progressed so quickly that while still a child she was able to help her father in comparing manuscripts and " correcting the press ", and Mary Ann McCracken attained at an early age an unusual accuracy at figures.

This benevolent and much loved schoolmaster was made a freeman of the town in 1779, and when he died in 1792 he was given the honour of a funeral by torch light, his remains being laid in the parish graveyard at midnight.[5] Shortly afterwards, Elizabeth Hamilton, already arrived at literary fame, wrote of him thus :

> David Manson's extraordinary talents were exerted in too limited a sphere to attract attention. He consequently escaped the attacks of bigotry and envy ; but the obscurity which ensured peace, prevented his plans from obtaining the notice to which they were entitled ; nor did their

acknowledged success obtain for him any higher character, than that of an amiable visionary, who, in toys given to his scholars, foolishly squandered the profits of his profession. A small volume containing an account of the school, rules of English grammar, and a spelling dictionary, is, as far as the writer of this knows, the only memorial left to a man, whose unwearied and disinterested zeal in the cause of education, would, in other circumstances, have raised him to distinction.[6]

Such was the person from whom Mary Ann received her formal schooling, and the place where her subsequently advanced views on education were no doubt nurtured. Much, too, was learnt at home. Her practical mother would instruct her in all the skills of housekeeping, which included, in those days, spinning as well as sewing, knitting and cooking and the preparation of simple medicinal remedies. Like all the McCrackens Mary Ann was clever with her hands. It is said that while still a child she made dresses for the Poorhouse children, the stout homespun being purchased with money which she collected from her friends. Dancing would be fitted in somewhere, and in that musical family music lessons would be a matter of course.

As for the small compact town of Belfast in which she was growing up—it, too, was beginning to expand. The population in 1782 is given as 13,105, having risen from 8,549 thirty years earlier.[7] The High Street, with the Farset River flowing down the centre of it from Bridge Street to the " Key ", was still the main thoroughfare, flanked on either side by Waring Street and Ann Street and connected with them by Bridge Street and the Cornmarket and by numerous Entries then the home of the smaller shopkeepers. In Bridge Street, Samuel Neilson, the oncoming son of a presbyterian manse in County Down, was building up the woollen drapery business that was shortly to be one of the largest concerns in the town, and in the adjoining North Street was the goldsmith's shop of Robert Joy's friend Thomas McCabe. Many of the dwellings in these streets still had thatched roofs, but at the Four Corners—the junction of Bridge

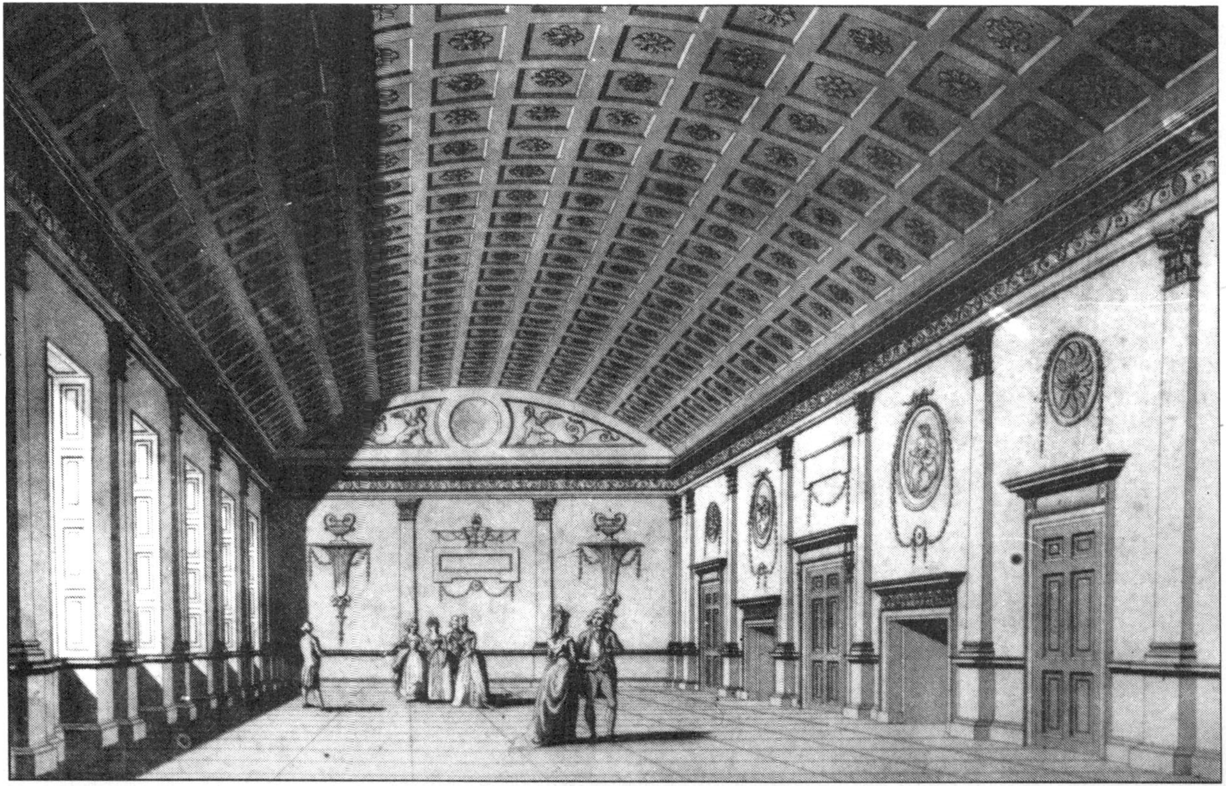

THE ASSEMBLY ROOM, BELFAST

DAVID MANSON

Street, Waring Street, North Street and Rosemary Lane—stood the imposing Exchange, to which was added in 1777, as the first storey, the beautiful Assembly Rooms, designed by Sir Robert Taylor, whose name is perpetuated in the Taylorian Museum at Oxford. For this lovely gift the town was indebted to the munificence of the Donegall family.

An extensive development scheme was taking shape at the southern end of the town, where New Street [later Linenhall Street and later still Donegall Place] was being laid out to accommodate the splendid houses of the few very wealthy families. Here the Lord Donegall of the day was to have his town residence, the early family castle in the centre of the town having been destroyed by fire in the beginning of the century. So exclusive was this street that when it was completed no horse drawn traffic was permitted to pass along it, and on Sundays it was the fashionable parade for the well-to-do. After 1783 Mary Ann must sometimes have been taken by Uncle Henry Joy to watch the building of the White Linenhall at the end of the long vista up New Street.

This was not the first ambitious scheme for developing Belfast. As early as 1671 George Macartney, the foremost citizen of his day, on returning from a visit to Italy planned to make it a second Venice by utilising the extensive water-front and the various rivers that entered the Lough at this point. His scheme, however, did not materialise.

The Mall and the Bank were other favourite walks, which blossomed into finery on Sunday afternoons. The former ran from the site on which the White Linenhall was to be built towards Joy's paper mill, along the pleasant Blackstaff, or Owen-varra, River, with trees and fields beyond. The Bank stretched from the present Arthur Square towards the Lagan, also amid rural surroundings. In Millfield corn was still being ground by the water wheel set up in the time of Elizabeth.

The older streets were ill-lighted and badly kept, and pigs from many styes wandered about at will. On market days the chief thoroughfares were crowded with booths and stalls. Second-hand clothing, imported from Glasgow and sold in the streets, was a profitable trade in times of depression and gave rise to many complaints from the more hygienically minded citizens. Samuel Foote might have included the beggars of Belfast when he remarked that " till he had seen the beggars in Dublin he could never imagine what the beggars in London did with their cast off cloaths."[8] In 1780 a gentleman travelling from Dublin to Scotland via Belfast wrote as follows to the *News-Letter* :

> I was vastly surprised and hurt to see a long string of falling cabins and tattered houses all tumbling down with a horrid aspect, and the seeming prelude to a pitiful village, which was my idea of Belfast until I got pretty far into the town, when I found my error, for indeed with some trifling improvements it might be made to vie with any town in Ireland, save Dublin and Cork.[9]

And in 1785 another correspondent in the same paper inquires

> if it is not inconsistent in the inhabitants to be daily giving proof of taste and increasing opulence in opening new streets, in public erections, etc. when they never once turn their eyes to shambles that for nastiness have not their equal in the meanest village in Ireland—tho' they have been noticed by travellers and by some of them recorded to our discredit ?

Leaving aside its beautiful situation, the Belfast of those days was a practical little town with few embellishments. By the 1790's Robert Joy's slender spire on the Poorhouse, the cupola of the new Parish Church in Donegall Street, and the belfry of the Market House alone broke the low sky line, and when Captain McCracken's ship was in port her masts, along with those of other vessels, were clearly visible from the opposite end of High Street.

In Rosemary Lane three Presbyterian Meeting-houses [two of them adhering to the " New Light " principles] clustered together, testifying to the growing numbers and differing views of that community, and in 1784 the first Roman Catholic chapel in the town was opened, an occasion made memorable by the attendance of the 1st Company of the Belfast Volunteers as a mark of their goodwill. As members of this company Francis and William McCracken were there and we can be sure that the event was much discussed in their household. So also would be the visits of John Wesley. Nine different times he came to Belfast on his journeyings through Ireland, preaching in the open air, or in the Market House, though on the last occasion, in 1789, the use of First Meeting-house was granted ' in the most obliging manner ".

> It is, [Wesley wrote in his Journal] the completest place of public worship I have ever seen . . . It is very lofty, and has two rows of large windows, so that it is as light as our new chapel in London. And the rows of pillars, with every other part, are so finely proportioned, that it is beautiful in the highest degree. The House was crowded both within and without (and indeed with some of the most respectable persons in the town) that it was with the utmost difficulty I got in ; but I then found I went not up without the Lord ; Great was my liberty of speech among them : Great was our glorying in the Lord, so that I gave notice contrary to my first design of my intending to preach there again in the morning ; but soon after the sexton sent me word it must not be, for the crowds had damaged the House, and some of them had broke off and carried away the silver which was on the Bible on the pulpit ; So I desired one of our Preachers to preach in our little House,* and left Belfast early in the morning.[10]

Behind a rather sober exterior the town provided a great deal of gaiety and sociability. Dances, balls and card parties were held in the beautiful Assembly Rooms. A coterie met regularly here, and another in the Donegall Arms. There was a great deal of card playing, sometimes for very high stakes, and hard drinking was regarded as

*The first Methodist chapel in Belfast was opened in 1787 in Fountain Street.

an accomplishment rather than a vice. A description of the festivities of "that old and very respectable meeting known as the Card Club of Belfast" at an anniversary celebration in 1784 of the Glorious Revolution, mentions no less than twenty-nine toasts and indicates that others followed: the toasts illustrate clearly the wide interest in liberal movements among the "respectable" citizens of the town.[11] Festivities of this kind were very popular, and commemorations and rejoicings were often accompanied by fireworks and illuminations, particularly on the King's birthday. The Adelphi Club, of which Amyas Gr ffith was a member, was a popular non-political affair.

Hospitality, lavish by modern standards, was dispensed in private houses, when guests were regaled with course after course of abundant food and drink. Indeed many a hostess in Belfast must have welcomed the arrival of Charles Frederick Schuller, "late cook to the Rt. Hon. John Foster, Speaker of the House of Commons", and read with interest his advertisement in a *News-Letter* of October 1792 in which he

> Begs leave to inform the Ladies ot Belfast & its Environs that he has opened a Pastry Cook & Confectionary Shop in Hercules Lane (a few doors from the corner of Rosemary Lane) where all sorts of Cakes, Jellies, Pies & Comfits may be had. He like-wise dresses Dinners or Suppers in the newest & most approved manner; & hopes from his long experience & abilities to give perfect satisfaction to those who may please to honour him with their Commands.

In the same year George Langtry, a general merchant, was advertising his wares as follows:

Alicant Barilla	Gunpowder
Starch and Hair Powder	Castor Oil
Indigo	Variety of Teas
Black Soap	Prunes & Walnuts
Liquorice Ball	Shovels

Nails & Iron & a few puncheons of Strong Jamaica rum.

The two theatres played an important part in social life.

Already Belfast audiences were renowned for their discerning taste. Mary Ann must have seen Mrs. Siddons in these early days, for the famous actress made the first of three visits to the town in June 1785. There were frequent concerts ; pantomimes, side-shows, wax works, and menageries were all enthusiastically enjoyed. There was hunting and cock fighting for those who favoured outdoor pastimes, and for the literary there was the Belfast Reading Society.

The social life of the town reached the height of its excitement when Lord and Lady Donegall were in residence. The Chichesters—to use their family name—loved gaiety; and dancing, riding, hunting, amateur theatricals and cards took much of their time and a great deal of their very considerable wealth.

But at the back of everything lurked the ever-present dread of " the fever ". Outbreaks of typhus became more and more frequent as contact, through shipping, with foreign lands increased ; frequently vessels had to lie out in Carrickfergus Bay for weeks of quarantine ; on one occasion at least we know that Mary Ann was a victim, and Mrs. McTier writes : " We have all been greatly shocked by the death of poor Getty, his fever was a dreadful one, and no creature yet ventures to the house ". And again : " A fever certainly prevails here—tho' its having been mostly among the better sort marks it perhaps more to us than at other times."[12] At last, in 1797, the Belfast Fever Hospital was opened, the first institution of its kind in Ireland.

Such was the general appearance of the town in which Mary Ann McCracken grew up. We do not hear of the Joys and McCrackens participating in the more riotous entertainments, but in their own circle of friends there was always time for mirth and gaiety and happy social intercourse. There were, no doubt, during Captain McCracken's seafaring days, visits to the Blacks at Stranmillis, that lovely elevated district a mile or two inland on the banks of the Lagan, and we may assume that Francis Joy's daughter would as often as possible take her children to see their grandfather at Randalstown,

—the old gentleman who left such an indelible impression on Mary Ann. Political events in America, on the Continent and in Ireland; the development of their cotton and other trading enterprises; the interests stimulated by their love of music and painting were matters for constant thought and discussion by all in the McCracken circle, and there is ample evidence that the female members were accustomed to take their full share in family doings.

By 1790 the third generation of Joys and McCrackens were grown-up. The deaths of Uncle Robert and Uncle Henry had cast dark shadows, but there had also been the happy occasions of the weddings of Elinor and Mary Joy to prominent Belfast merchants, and no doubt there were other love affairs of which no record has been left. The McCracken family had moved from High Street to Rosemary Lane, and it was to this welcoming roof that in due course William and John brought their young wives: the house indeed became known as "Noah's Ark," for neither stray animals nor dear friends were ever turned from its door.

Margaret, the eldest, did not marry. She was tall and good-looking, quiet and reserved, with a misleading hint of haughtiness, extremely capable and practical. Mary Ann records with deep affection how much she was guided by the wisdom of her only sister: "My sister and I" she says "had but one heart, though she always kept in the background and left me to act frequently on her suggestions, although considerably my senior in years and much my superior in understanding."[13]

Francis came next, also quiet and, one imagines, a sensitive and conscientious person. He was among the earliest recruits for the Belfast Volunteers in 1778, and later was to play an active if unspectacular part in the United Irishmen. He took over the management of his father's rope walk and the sail cloth factory, and was connected with them till the end of his life. William, too, was an early Volunteer, and was to be more conspicuously associated with subsequent developments, finding a most encouraging and resourceful wife in

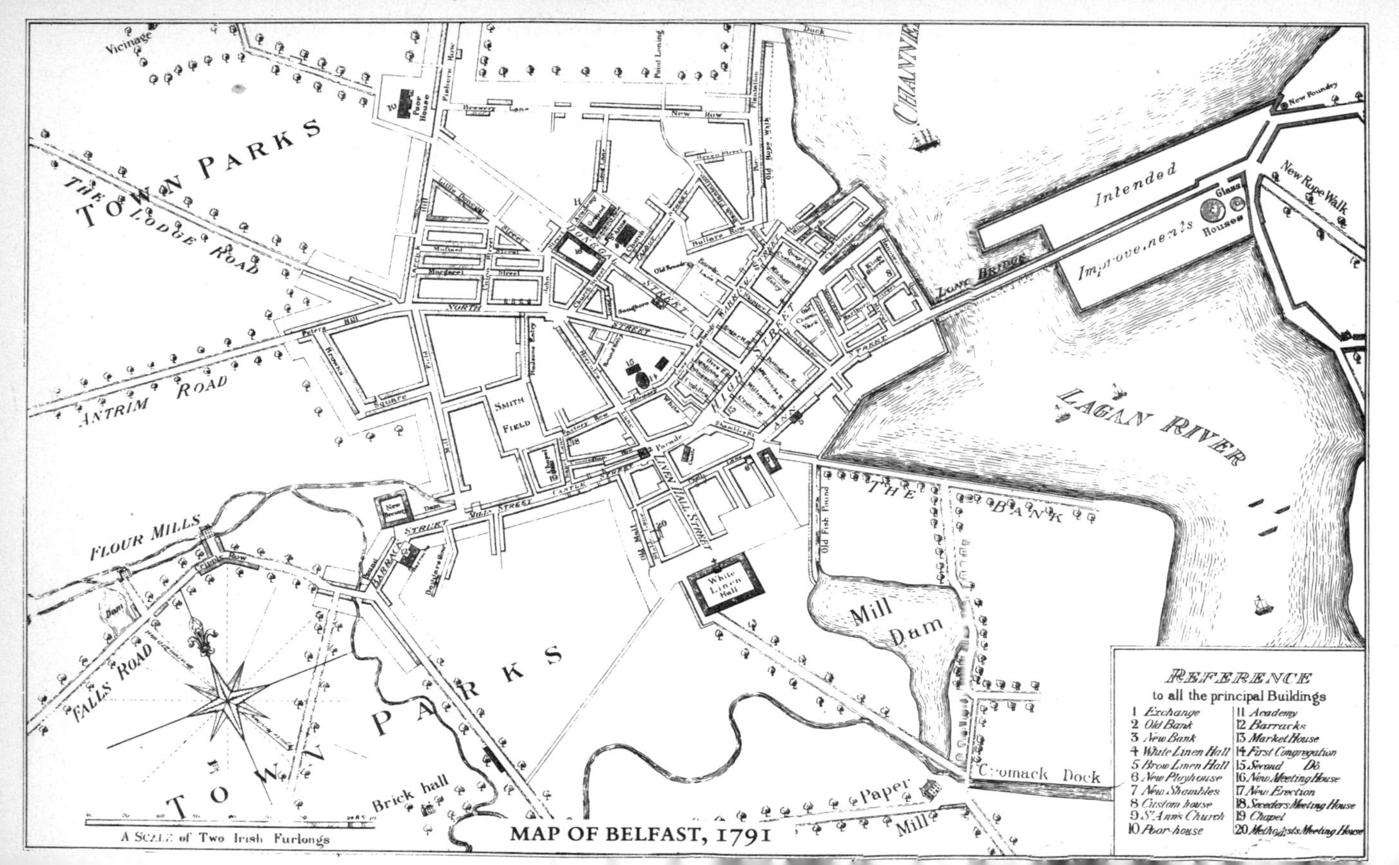

MAP OF BELFAST, 1791

Rose Ann McGlathery. He also was in the cotton business.

And next comes Henry Joy—Mary Ann's adored Harry, and as Harry he will be known in this story. Much has been written and sung about this romantic figure; here we are concerned with the part he played in the family and in his sister's life. Six foot all but an inch, extremely handsome, vivacious, intelligent and capable—life was almost too full of interests for Harry. From his schoolboy days he was noted for his quick powers of observation and his gift of mimicry: had he not, during Breslaw's* visit to Belfast, detected the secrets of the famous conjurer, reproducing his tricks with all the appropriate patter to the immense delight of his young friends? Many years later while a prisoner in Kilmainham Gaol, he disguised himself as a clergyman and dilated with such vigour and realism to one of his faltering fellow-prisoners on the eternal punishments awaiting informers, that the unfortunate young man was reduced to abject terror. Everything that Harry touched drew from him a whole-hearted response—be it political discussion, family merriment, friendships, or the welfare of those suffering from injustice or poverty—everything, that is, but business. His courage [he was noted for the alacrity with which, in days of thatched roofs and poor water supplies, he answered every alarm of fire] and personal charm made him a natural leader, but behind all the high spirits there was in his sister's words, "a deeply contemplative character which afterwards developed."[14]

Captain McCracken was anxious to settle all his sons in the cotton industry and at the age of seventeen Harry began work at one of the mills; soon he was sent to Scotland to recruit skilled workers. Humdrum routine bored him, but he revelled in close contact with the working people. For them he started the first Sunday School in Belfast, finding a room in the old Market

*One of Breslaw's turns, advertised in Dublin, was "to cut off the heads of two horses, and the head of a postilion, and make the horses draw a post chaise round St. Stephen's Green, dexterously whipped and flogged by the headless postilion". [Young MSS. Queen's University, Belfast.]

House and collecting some of his friends as teachers. Girls, men and boys were his pupils : " Writing as well as reading was taught. They did not presume to impart religious knowledge, but they taught their scholars how to obtain it for themselves, by which every sect might equally profit. It was afterwards found to be practised in England ;* and then Mr. Bristow [the Sovereign] came to the place of meeting with a number of Ladies, with rods in their hands as badges of authority, which put to flight the humble pioneers."[15] Thus did Mary Ann describe this early attempt at social service, which included also a lending library. How different from Hannah More's statement to the Bishop of Bath and Wells that she taught in her schools only " such coarse works as may fit them [the working class] for servants. I allow of no writing for the poor. My object is . . . to train up the lower classes in habits of industry and piety."[16]

John, the youngest of the family, united great business ability with an infinite capacity for enjoying the leisured accomplishments of life. " Designed by nature to be a painter,"[17] — so Mary Ann described this brother —drawing and music delighted him, and his father's love of the sea became in him a passion for sailing and yacht-racing. Politics meant nothing to him, or rather, an activity to be most carefully avoided as likely to lead one into nasty and difficult situations : there was nothing, absolutely nothing, of the social reformer in John's make-up. He married young and his wife was very beautiful, and he became one of the most successful cotton manufacturers in the town.

Mary Ann's character will unfold itself as her story is told. Physically she was slight of build and lacked the commanding presence that others of the family had inherited from their father. No early portrait of her exists, but from the miniature [see plate facing p. 112], painted about 1801, we can derive some idea of what she looked like in her early twenties. Of all the family she seems to have most resembled her mother in appearance—the same round face, full lower lip and dark eyes set wide apart, eyes that

*Probably a reference to Robert Raikes.

gave some indication of the powerful will and strong emotions that inhabited her slender frame. She had been a delicate child and retained the fragile appearance that often accompanies tubercular tendencies. She gathered up in herself the outstanding qualities of all the others so that each of them found in her companionship and understanding. Very early she showed a marked interest in figures and book-keeping, and when barely out of her teens persuaded her sister Margaret to join her in starting a small muslin business in order, so she said, that she might have a little money to use as she pleased.

These apparently light-hearted ventures into industry, undertaken first by Mrs. McCracken and now by her daughters, sound formidable to us with twentieth century notions of factory regulations, trade unions and so forth. For Mary Ann, however, it would be a case of distributing cotton yarn to hand-loom weavers who worked in their own homes. But, comparatively simple though the venture may have been, it demanded much from the proprietors: a knowledge of weaving; a variety of patterns always available, for trends of fashion were fickle then as now; the marketing of finished goods; an adequate system of book-keeping; some financial outlay; and the continual correspondence that such transactions would demand. Mary Ann was responsible for the office end of the undertaking, and recalled years afterwards how she revelled in the daily errand to the post office, which had to be accomplished before breakfast.

It remains only to mention young Edward Bunting. Sometime in 1784 a fatherless lad of eleven arrived in Belfast to take up his duties as assistant to Mr. Ware, organist of the new parish church of St. Anne. The child had shown unusual talent and for two years had been trained by his brother Anthony, an organist of some repute in Drogheda. We know nothing of the introductions or the circumstances that led young Edward to Mrs. McCracken's home, but there he was received as one of the family, and there he was to live for the next thirty years. Very shortly after his arrival Mr. Ware was obliged to travel to England and he left his juvenile assistant not only to deputise for him at the organ but also to undertake the instruction of his pupils. The deputy was much more exacting than his master, and Bunting afterwards recorded with amusement that one of these pupils—Miss Stewart of Wilmont—was so taken aback by the audacity of her young instructor that, on being reproved a second time " she indignantly turned round upon him and well boxed his ears."[18]

Such a youthful genius cannot have been a simple addition to Mrs. McCracken's family. " Atty " as he was called [probably a corruption of Eddy] was, naturally enough, a self-opinionated boy; he had a biting tongue that remained with him to the end of his life and, except in his professional work, he was self-indulgent and lazy. He was the same age as young John. Mary Ann was two years his senior.

This then is the picture of her family circle and her home surroundings. Next comes the political background.

CHAPTER V

THE UNITED IRISHMEN

1783–1791

PARLIAMENTARY independence, won so dramatically with Volunteer support in 1782, had proved a bitter disappointment to those who looked to it as a first step towards essential and radical reform. In the very year of its achievement William Drennan declared that " the collars of the Knights of St. Patrick will in time strangle the freedom of this nation " and his warning was swiftly justified. The armed forces, the appointment of judges, and all patronage in Church and State was still controlled by Britain ; the landed interest remained supreme at College Green,* to be exploited by the Westminster government when desirable ; parliamentary reform was strenuously opposed ; and in 1785 Britain refused, in spite of Pitt's efforts to the contrary, to modify her crippling import duties on most Irish manufactures, except on terms destructive to the newly won independence. These were serious blows to those constitutionalists who sincerely hoped that the political achievements of '82 would prepare the way for happier relations between the two Kingdoms.

Nowhere in Ireland was the disappointment more keenly felt than by the enterprising mercantile community in Belfast. While the sole foundation of its new found prosperity was trade it was virtually unrepresented in Parliament, for Belfast was a pocket borough, its two members being returned by the handful of burgesses who were nominees of Lord Donegall. Of the 300 members of the Irish House of Commons 124 were returned by fifty-three peers, 91 were returned by fifty-two commoners, 13 were returned mainly by individual influence, and only 72 were freely elected.[1] Shocking as this was for the Protestant interest, the Roman Catholics, numbering approximately 9/10ths of the total population

*Where the Irish Houses of Parliament were situated.

of the Kingdom, were not represented at all. Little wonder, then, that parliamentary reform was the constant preoccupation of the Belfast citizens. Early in 1784 they set out their case in a long petition, forwarded to the independent members for County Antrim for presentation to the Irish House of Commons, and opening thus :

> Your Petitioners in the most humble and respectful manner, take leave to represent to your Hon. House,
>
> That Belfast is a large and populous town, containing above 15,000 inhabitants, carrying on a very extensive foreign commerce, as well as inland trade, and paying annually upwards of £80,000 towards the public revenue.
>
> That this numerous body of people not being represented in your Hon. House, are, contrary to the fundamental principle of the constitution, governed by laws to which they give no assent ; for although the borough of Belfast sends two Members to Parliament, yet those members are returned (under the immediate direction of a noble peer) by five or six Burgesses, in the appointment of whom your Petitioners have no share, and therefore the Members so returned cannot in *any* sense, be deemed the Representatives of your Petitioners.[2]

In the National Convention held in Dublin in 1784, "to press for a more equal representation of the Commons of Ireland", Belfast was represented by Henry Joy, jun., the McCrackens' cousin ; the Rev. Sinclaire Kelburn of the third Presbyterian congregation — the McCrackens' minister ; the Earl Bishop of Derry—strange bed-fellow for such staunch Presbyterians—and two others. Indeed, so intent were these reformers on exploring every avenue which might assist their cause that in 1783 a Volunteer convention meeting in Lisburn had appointed a committee under the chairmanship of Colonel Sharman to communicate with

> persons in England, most distinguished for their talents, and their zeal in the cause of liberty, requesting their advice and opinion on this important subject : among these were the Duke of Richmond, Lord Effingham, Mr. Pitt, Dr. Price, Dr. Jebb, Rev. Christopher Wyvill . . . and Major John Cartwright.[3]

Of this enterprising committee Henry Joy, jun., then a young man of 30, was secretary. He and his committee, the national conventions, and all that the volunteer movement represented, were the Irish counterpart of the movement for parliamentary reform then so vociferous in Britain. Native and independent though both movements were, their influence on each other was considerable, and they represent a period of " stirring " in the development of the British system of parliamentary government. It is significant that the McCracken family had, through their cousin, this close contact with the leaders of the Yorkshire Association movement, and the names of Joy and McCracken occur in the lists of the prominent citizens who concerned themselves with calling Town Meetings, composing petitions, and generally directing public opinion towards parliamentary reform.

The National Conventions had little practical result. Already some " among the volunteers were sensible, that . . . an attempt to gain their object by compulsion must be hopeless, without the co-operation of the Romanists, and that in case of success by this assistance, the *Protestant interest in Ireland would be annihilated.* The Convention saw clearly the dilemma to which it was reduced; but they chose what appeared to them the least of two evils, and rather than call in the aid of the great body of Romanists . . . they submitted quietly and tamely to the chastisement of that government whose authority they had insulted, and in a manner defied; incurring by this means the censure of the moderate for their violence, and of the violent for their moderation."[4] It was this dilemma that, very quickly, " annihilated " the moderate party, and there were those in the North who would not tolerate such a choice.

In Belfast the Volunteers were dominated by the progressive element and were enthusiastically sympathetic to Catholic enfranchisement. This was the year, 1784, in which the 1st Belfast Company attended the opening of the first Roman Catholic Church to be built in the town—a gesture of goodwill considered by the more cautious reformers to be unnecessarily cordial.[5] Throughout the country Protestant support for Catholic enfranchisement was partial and prompted generally by considerations of expediency, but in Belfast it was directed by genuinely altruistic motives ; here, for the first time were Irishmen prepared to struggle not only for their own liberty, but for that of their Catholic brothers, who since the Penal enactments had enjoyed no legal status in the country at all.

Until the reign of Anne all sections in Ireland had enjoyed the franchise to the same limited extent, but on account of the insecurity of the Protestant succession after the Revolution and the supposed Stuart sympathies of the Catholics in Ireland, legislation of the utmost severity was enacted against the Catholics from time to time between 1697 and 1746. These laws made it extremely difficult for Catholics to practise their religion and severely restricted their freedom to acquire land ; they were forbidden to have their own schools and heavy penalties were inflicted on those who sent their children to be educated abroad ; they were debarred from the professions [except medicine], from parliament and all public offices and from the franchise. Such abuse of power naturally encouraged the practice of every kind of evasive deception by the Catholics, and fostered the abominable system of proselytising and informing among the Protestants. It should be remembered that Dissenters, practically all Presbyterians, suffered also, though to a lesser extent. The Test Act of 1704 made it necessary for all persons holding public appointments to take Communion in the Established Church within three months of their assuming office. As a result, of the twelve aldermen of the city of Derry, ten Presbyterians were dismissed, as were fourteen of the twenty-four burgesses. In Belfast eight of the thirteen burgesses were Presbyterians and had to forfeit their seats. There were similar dismissals from the Bench and other official bodies ; no Presbyterians could legally conduct a school, in many instances land would not be let to Presbyterian tenants[6] and if magistrates so wished, church services could be declared illegal and the building of churches prohibited.

The position of the presbyterian ministers had been further complicated by the refusal of some to take the Oath of Abjuration, not wishing to be bound to the heirs of the House of Hanover, thus laying themselves open to a charge of Jacobitism, with which they had no sympathy at all.

As the years went by and fears of Jacobite risings diminished, penal legislation against both Dissenters and Catholics tended to fall into abeyance. In 1780 the Test Act was repealed and two years earlier the first considerable Catholic Relief Bill was passed: but, while the plight of the Catholics was vastly improved and they were acquiring positions of importance in trade, the professions and the Army remained closed to them and they were still denied all share in the government of the country.

In no part of Ireland was the Catholic population so sparse as in Antrim and Down, and according to an assessment of the population of Belfast in 1756 there were in the town 7,993 Protestants and 556 Catholics. It is true to say that the growing sympathy in Belfast for the Catholic cause was based entirely on grounds of political morality and social justice ; but it is also true that in no other part of the country was there so little ground for fearing Catholic action, and that in spite of the dreadful memories of 1641. Indeed so late as 1791 Tone himself wrote that the people of Belfast know " wonderfully little " about the Catholics.[7]

In 1784 the Belfast Volunteers invited to their ranks

> persons of every religious persuasion, firmly convinced that a general Union of ALL the inhabitants of Ireland is necessary to the freedom and prosperity of this Kingdom, as it is congenial to the Constitution.[8]

This was a significant and radical move. Nowhere in the three kingdoms had such a gesture of tolerance been made. These Presbyterian Volunteers were groping their way towards a genuine brotherhood of man, based, in their case, on complete religious freedom. Five years had yet to pass before the people of France made their momentous stand in the name of Liberty, Equality and Fraternity, which was to be hailed with rejoicing in Belfast.

It is necessary to review the causes which led to the intense sympathy felt in Ulster for the French Revolution, for, while the connection between France and other parts of Ireland through religious ties, trade, and the Irish refugees is well known, the closeness of the relationship with the North is not always appreciated.

William III, as compensation for the destruction of the Irish wool trade by the English parliament, had encouraged Huguenot families to settle in Ireland in the beginning of the century in order to develop the linen industry.* This they had done with conspicuous success in Ulster, and by now occupied positions of importance and great respect. There were also considerable trading connections between Belfast and France—for example members of the Black family were long-term residents in Bordeaux in connection with the wine business ; we have seen, too, how Captain McCracken, once a prisoner in French hands, had insisted on his children becoming proficient in the French language, and there were many other such links. But the intense interest to be felt in Ulster for the French Revolution, while it was encouraged and fed by these contacts, was due to the religious and intellectual condition of the rising middle class around Belfast.

The Plantation of Ulster in the beginning of the seventeenth century, by English and Scottish settlers under government direction, did not include the counties of Antrim and Down. Down had been planted somewhat earlier by the private enterprise of two hard-headed Scots, Montgomery and Hamilton ; and the McDonnells of Antrim, though Catholics themselves, had no scruples about importing Scottish Presbyterians to develop their lands. Consequently, by the middle of the seventeenth century there was a considerable Scottish population in the north-east corner of Ulster. This continued to

*It is said that 6,000 Huguenots came to Ireland. A large proportion settled in and near Lisburn, Co. Antrim.

CRANMORE NEAR BELFAST.

FORMERLY ORANGE GROVE, THE HOME OF JOHN TEMPLETON

be augmented by a stream of religious refugees from Scotland, Presbyterian extremists for the most part who, for one reason or another, found themselves subjected in their own country to disciplinary measures which they were anxious to avoid. Covenanters, Burghers, Antiburghers, Seceders—people who did not understand the meaning of compromise—sailed from the coasts of Cantyre and Ayr to the harbours of Antrim, the route from time immemorial of a two-way traffic between shores that are seldom out of sight. [It is said that 50,000 Scots came to Ulster in the years following 1690.[9]] Here, in the Antrim hinterland they settled, pursuing their independent courses unmolested. Through time some became integrated in the general Presbyterian community, others maintained their separateness with the tenacity of the persecuted, and all of them acted as a stimulus to an independence of mind that already existed.

In addition to this religious intensity, perhaps indeed because of it, there was widespread interest in the new philosophical thought. Locke's writings were well known, there was close contact with the Scottish philosophers, Rousseau had his admirers even in the country towns, and when Paine published *The Rights of Man* it was at once hailed in Belfast with rapture, becoming in Wolfe Tone's phrase " the Koran of Belfescu ". So, throughout the Province, but especially in the neighbourhood of Belfast, political, economic and philosophic thought had prepared the community in a remarkable degree for the great upheaval of the French Revolution, and Henry Joy, jun. [later to come down so heavily on the side of moderation] could, with sincerity, write that :

> the exultation with which they [the people of Belfast] hailed the downfall of civil and spiritual despotism in France in the year 1789, affords a decisive proof of their disinterested solicitude for the universal diffusion of liberty and peace. Their joy was expressed by affectionate congratulations to the French patriots and by annual commemorations of the destruction of the bastile, conducted with pomp and magnificance, and calculated to impress on innumerable spectators a conviction of the

> vast importance which they attached to this glorious occurance, and sensations of gratitude to the divine providence 'for dispersing the political clouds which had hitherto darkened our hemisphere.'[10]

Indeed, in Ulster, the French Revolution quickly became something more than an external occurrence; amongst the ardent reformers its ideals were regarded as a challenge, and assumed a significance unknown either in England or Scotland.

And so:

> Encouraged by the success of these glorious efforts of the French nation, the friends of Liberty in this country once more turned their undivided attention to the salutary measure of Reform, and renewed those efforts from which they had been so ingloriously compelled to desist in the year 1785. The first appearance of this revival of public spirit in Belfast shone forth on the 6th of March 1790, when it was unanimously resolved at a Meeting of the Belfast First Volunteer Company, that this company do turn out in full uniform on the 17th inst. in order to celebrate our 12th anniversary, and elect officers for the ensuing year.'[11]

To some, however, the red light of danger was apparent. Lord Charlemont, the Volunteer leader, already apprehensive of the more extreme opinion, inaugurated a Whig Club in Belfast in 1790, similar to that already founded in Dublin.

> I think [he wrote to his Belfast friend Dr. Halliday], that an institution of this kind would, by holding out a congregation to the true believers at Belfast, be a means of fixing, and even recalling many who might otherwise wander from the faith.[12]

Not that the Belfast Whig Club was by any means reactionary, for within six months of its foundation we find the members, under the chairmanship of Dr. Halliday, and with Henry Joy, jun. as secretary, passing the following resolution:

> That considering the French Revolution as one of the most important and universally interesting events which the world ever saw, and as particularly such to the inhabitants of these islands as it promises to lead the way to an orderly and gradual reform of these abuses which have maimed and disfigured the constitution we shall, as men, as Whigs—as citizens of this empire, meet on the 14th of July next, to celebrate that astonishing event, which constitutes a glorious era in the history of man and of the world.[13]

When the day of commemoration arrived the Northern Whig Club formed part of a great procession, with tableaux, organised by the Volunteers, and on this occasion " a green cockade, the national colour of Ireland, was worn by the whole body."[14] At a splendid banquet afterwards in the south wing of the White Linenhall 354 members of the Volunteer companies sat down at a single long table. Among the twenty-seven toasts appear the names of Mr. Paine, John Locke, Doctor Franklin, and Monsieur Mirabeau. In spite of the citizens' love of bonfires none were permitted on this occasion' "it having been the idea of the town that not intemperate joy but dignified, rational and deliberate rejoicing should close the scene."[15]

It was magnificent: with all allowances for the flamboyant language of such reporting, one can feel the revived enthusiasm that animated once more the old confidence and desire, and recalled the achievements of 1782.

But when the first glamour departed, difficulties set in. The Catholic issue was now dominant in Ulster, and for many there was the bewildering problem of how to do what seemed right and fair to Catholics as fellow-citizens, and maintain at the same time other cherished ideals—the 18th century version of a recurring problem.

As discussions increased opinions hardened, and the complexities of the situation were not lessened by the arrival in Belfast in October 1791, on his first recorded visit, of Theobald Wolfe Tone, then secretary of the Catholic Committee in Dublin.

Wolfe Tone and Lord Edward Fitzgerald are perhaps the best known leaders in the Irish Rebellion of 1798, Fitzgerald because of his courage and of his family background, and Tone because through his Autobiography we come into unusually intimate contact with the man and the events in which he was involved. Briefly, Tone was born in Dublin, in 1763, the eldest son of a successful coachbuilder. His father made strenuous efforts to give him a good education with the fixed intention that his first born should become a lawyer. So, at the age of seventeen, Tone rebelliously entered Trinity College, Dublin, having already given every possible indication that what he really desired was a military career. While still at College, he eloped with Matilda Witherington, " not yet sixteen, and as lovely as an angel " and after a few days of married bliss at Maynooth, the pair returned to Dublin, " were forgiven on all sides, and settled in lodgings near my wife's grandfather."[16] After various vicissitudes Tone set off to pursue his studies at the Middle Temple, leaving his wife and baby daughter with his father, who had recently sustained considerable financial losses. In spite of this sobering situation the brilliant and attractive Theobald found humdrum study in London, or elsewhere, eminently distasteful, and " as I foresaw by this time that I should never be Lord Chancellor ", he and some companions devoted a great deal of time to devising a scheme for colonizing " one of Cook's recently discovered islands in the South Seas on a military plan, for all my ideas ran on that track."[17] They embodied their scheme in a memorial to Mr. Pitt which Tone delivered with his own hands to " the Porter in Downing Street," but Mr. Pitt took " not the smallest notice of it " and, writes Tone, " in my anger I made something like a vow that if ever I had an opportunity I would make Mr. Pitt sorry, and perhaps fortune may yet enable me to fulfill that resolution."[18] To say that Tone was in fact the stuff of which the professional revolutionary is made is not to minimise the earnestness with which he later carried out his schemes, but it accounts for an early lack of a sense of responsibility.

After two years in London, this restless young man returned to Dublin, collected his wife and child, commenced once more the study of law, and was called to the Irish Bar in the fateful year of 1789. Try as he might, and there is evidence that at this time he did put his mind to his work, Tone could not settle to a barrister's routine. Instead he haunted the gallery of the Irish House of Commons, and for the first time became interested in Irish politics, with the result that he shortly produced a pamphlet entitled " A Review of the last Session of Parliament ", a defence, in effect, of the recently established Whig Clubs. When the pamphlet reached Belfast it was hailed with delight by the northern club, who " reprinted and distributed a large impression at their own expense, with an introduction highly complimentary to the author, whom at that time, they did not even know " ; and this was followed " by a very handsome letter signed by their secretary Henry Joy, jun. of Belfast."[19] At this stage Tone seriously considered standing for Parliament. Something more fateful, however, than pamphlets resulted from his frequent visits to College Green, for during one of them he met, in the gallery of the House of Commons, a young officer of the British Army named Thomas Russell. From that meeting there sprang a friendship of quite unusual sincerity and affection, and there came into Tone's life an influence that from now onwards directed the brilliance, and to some extent overcame the irresponsibility. Writing his Autobiography in Paris six years later Tone speaks of this friendship thus :

> About this time it was that I formed an acquaintance with my invaluable friend Russell, a circumstance which I look upon as one of the most fortunate of my life . . . I think the better of myself for being the object of the esteem of such a man as Russell . . . If I am ever inclined to murmur at the difficulties wherewith I have so long struggled, I think on the inestimable treasure I possess in the affection of my wife and the friendship of Russell, and I acknowledge that all my labors and sufferings are overpaid . . . When I think I have acted well, and that I am likely to succeed

in the important business wherein I am engaged, I say often to myself, My dearest love and my friend Russell will be glad of this.[20]

And then follows the incomparable description of the blissful summer on the shores of Dublin Bay :

My wife's health continuing still delicate, she was ordered by her physician to bathe in the saltwater. I hired, in consequence, a little box of a house on the sea side at Irishtown, where we spent the summer of 1790. Russell and I were inseparable, and, as our discussions were mostly political, and our sentiments agreed exactly, we extended our views, and fortified each other in the opinions, to the propagation and establishment of which we have ever since been devoted. I recall with transport the happy days we spent during that period ; the delicious dinners, in the preparation of which my wife, Russell, and myself, were all engaged ; the afternoon walks, the discussions we had as we lay stretched on the grass. Sometimes Russell's venerable father, a veteran of near seventy, with the courage of a hero, the serenity of a philosopher, and the piety of a saint, used to visit our little mansion, and that day was a *fête*. My wife doated on the old man, and he loved her like one of his children. I will not attempt, because I am unable, to express the veneration and regard I had for him, and I am sure that, next to his own sons, and scarcely below them, he loved and esteemed me.[21]

Russell's brother John and Tone's two brothers also visited the " little box " and added to the general gaiety or to the seriousness of the conversation.

These were delicious days [he continues]. The rich and great, who sit down every day to the monotony of a splendid entertainment, can form no idea of the happiness of our frugal meal, nor of the infinite pleasure we found in taking each his part in the preparation and attendance. My wife was the centre and the soul of all. I scarcely know which of us loved her best ; her courteous manners, her goodness of heart, her incomparable humor, her never failing cheerfulness, her affection for me and for our children, rendered her the object of our common admiration and delight.[22]

The "delicious" summer sped past, Mrs. Tone's health was restored, but before she and Theobald returned to Dublin, where their eldest son was shortly born, Russell got word of his appointment to "the 64th Regiment of Foot quartered in the town of Belfast." He came to say good-bye arrayed in a splendid suit of regimentals—"all clinquant, all in gold", but in spite of his lace and his finery he was set to cook part of the dinner, and eventually amidst laughter and tears the last farewells were said.

Thomas Russell, several years younger than Wolfe Tone, was born in County Cork in November 1767.[23] His father, Captain John Russell, was a distinguished soldier, having been personally commended by George II at the Battle of Dettingen, and, after further notable service, was appointed to the Royal Hospital, Kilmainham, Dublin, where he died. Thomas, like his father before him, was originally intended for the church, but at the age of 15 he went to India in the regiment of his elder brother, Captain Ambrose Russell, an officer who in his turn earned the gratitude of George III for gallantry in the war with America. After five years' service in India Thomas returned home, still intent on entering the church, but again he took a military appointment, and it was while staying with his father at Kilmainham, an ensign on half-pay, that he met Tone.

This was the gay, yet withal serious, young man who arrived in Belfast in 1790 to take up his military duties. His interest in politics would insure a welcome in this home of liberal thought, and he "found the people so much to his taste and in return rendered himself so agreeable to them . . ." that he was speedily admitted to their confidence, and became a member of several of their clubs.[24] The Whig Club received him enthusiastically as the friend of Mr. Tone, author of that admirable pamphlet, and, no doubt, the best port being produced, there was much convivial entertainment. Russell was passionately fond of music, and very soon he met Edward Bunting, now a fashionable young man, much sought after as an accomplished musician. Bunting brought him to the McCrackens, thus initiating a friendship that was to become historic; they, in turn, took him to the home of their friends the Templetons, now living at Orange Grove, where John Templeton was already occupied with his studies of the natural sciences. In the following years Russell and the McCrackens must many times have walked the few miles from Belfast to the lovely house at Malone, hidden in the trees of its extensive grounds where, in days gone by, William of Orange had halted on his march to the Boyne, and letters survive which show the wide range of interests held in common by Russell and Templeton:

> Every walk I take [wrote Templeton to Russell in prison] in the pursuit of the beauties of nature, brings to my recollection similar excursions in your company—every rare fossil that I meet with, and curious plant that I observe, causes me to find the want of my friend. Often does my imagination dwell with pleasure on the picturesque scenery of Glenave,* and the still more sublime rocks of Rathlin, neither can I go into my garden and view the little heathy bank you so often admired, without remembering the pleasure I received from your praises of my ingenuity in forming it.[25]

The following description of Russell's personal appearance is of particular interest, it is said to have been written many years later from the treasured recollections of Mary Ann McCracken:

> A model of manly beauty, he was one of those favoured individuals whom one cannot pass in the street without being guilty of the rudeness of staring in the face while passing, and turning round to look at the receding figure. Though more than six feet high, his majestic stature was scarcely observed owing to the exquisite symmetry of his form. Martial in his gait and demeanour, his appearance was not altogether that of a soldier. His dark and steady eye, compressed lip, and somewhat haughty bearing, were occasionally strongly indicative of the camp; but in

*Templeton and Russell had been on a walking tour of the Antrim Coast.

> general, the classic contour of his finely formed head, the expression of almost infantine sweetness which characterized his smile, and the benevolence that beamed in his fine countenance, seemd to mark him out as one, who was destined to be the ornament, grace and blessing of private life. His voice was deep-toned and melodious . . . His manners were those of the finished gentleman, combined with that native grace, which nothing but superiority of intellect can give. There was a reserved, and somewhat haughty, stateliness in his mein, which, to those who did not know him, had, at first, the appearance of pride ; but as it gave way before the warmth and benevolence of his disposition, it soon became evident that the defect, if it were one, was caused by the too sensitive delicacy of a noble soul ; and those who knew him, loved him the more for his reserve, and thought they saw something attractive in the very repulsiveness of his manner.[26]

So reflected Mary Ann, recapturing, no doubt, the sight of Harry and Thomas as they sauntered about the town, or set out for Orange Grove, or for long tramps into the country ; full of high spirits ; tall, well built and devastatingly handsome ; the raven black hair of the one a perfect foil for the golden locks of the other,—it not yet being fashionable to crop one's hair as evidence of one's revolutionary sympathies. But, lest Mary be accused of partiality, we turn to Mrs. McTier. Describing one of the innumerable scuffles in the streets with drunken soldiers she writes to her brother that, on hearing the to-do, " Russell went up close to them, did not speak one word, but it seems, surveyed them with such a countenance that [they] demanded the reason for the look of insolence." Words were bandied, swords were drawn and a first class fight seemed inevitable. However, the affair was adjourned till the next day, when the officers, after a little reflection, " sought out Russell and apologised to him in the fullest manner." Mrs. McTier felt obliged to add that her husband, who had been with Russell on the evening in question, had the uncomfortable feeling that Russell himself was the first, if unconscious, offender, " by a look which even at moonlight, was it seems, worse than a sentence."[27]

Mary Ann was exactly twenty years old when she and Thomas met. There is no doubt at all that she found him overwhelmingly attractive, for his " manly beauty ", as well as for the strength and goodness of his character, but there is not the slightest hint that her feelings for him were in any degree reciprocated. Russell, for his part, during these early days in Belfast, met and loved another —the beautiful Bess Goddard, but before he could take steps to secure her hand, a tragic incident occurred which blasted all those hopes.

Meanwhile, to the dashing young officer, all was gay and happy and brimful of interest. These people in Belfast were so alive, so advanced in their political thought, their talk and their clubs—whether literary or political—were so invigorating, he had never met anything quite like it.* Soon, with Henry Joy McCracken and Samuel Neilson, he was a moving spirit in a group of young enthusiasts which included Robert Simms and William Sinclair. Exasperated by the everlasting delays and deceptions of the government, and recalling the achievements of the Volunteers ten years earlier, they had become impatient with Whig Clubs and the compromises of orthodox reformers and were already perfecting their schemes for uniting Irishmen of all creeds and classes in societies pledged to more drastic action. This, Russell well knew, would appeal enormously to Tone—he must come to Belfast and meet these friends. And so it was that in October 1791 Wolfe Tone made his first journey to the North, bringing with him something of the gaiety and high spirits of " the little box " at Irishtown. After one of the many long controversies that occupied his visit he made this record in his diary :

> Joy paid my fees to the Northern Whig Club, and signed the declaration . . . Dinner at McTier's ; Waddell Cunningham, Holmes, Dr. Bruce,† etc. A furious battle, which lasted two hours, on the Catholic question ; as usual, neither party convinced. Teized with the liberality of

*Belfast at this time was frequently alluded to as the Athens of the North.

†Minister of the 1st Presbyterian congregation.

people agreeing in principle, but doubting as to the expediency. Bruce an intolerant high priest; argued sometimes strongly, sometimes unfairly; embarrassed the question by distinctions, and mixing things in their nature separate. We brought him, at last, to state his definite objections to the immediate emancipation of the Roman Catholics. His ideas are, 1st. Danger to true religion, inasmuch as the Roman Catholics would, if emancipated, establish an *inquisition*. 2nd. Danger to property by reviving the Court of Claims, and admitting any evidence to substantiate Catholic titles. 3rd. Danger, generally, of throwing the power into their hands, which would make this a Catholic government, incapable of enjoying or extending liberty. Many other wild notions which he afterwards gave up, but these three he repeated again and again as his creed. Almost all the company of his opinion, except P.P.* who made desperate battle, McTier, Getty and me; against us, Bruce, Holmes, Bunting, H. Joy . . . all protesting their liberality and good wishes to the Roman Catholics. *Damned stuff.* Bruce declared that thirty-nine out of forty Protestants would be found, whenever the question came forward, to be adverse to the liberation of Roman Catholics . . . It may be he was right, but God is above all. Sad nonsense about scavengers becoming members of Parliament, and great asperity against the new fangled doctrine of the Rights of Man. Broke up rather ill disposed towards each other. More and more convinced of the absurdity of arguing over wine. Went to the United Irish Club. Ballotted in five men, amongst whom were Maclaine and Getty; rejected one. Went to the coterie. Jordan pleasant as usual. Home at two. Bed.[28]

It was in truth a bewildering time. There were many more discussions and, at any rate, one practical achievement, for it was during Tone's visit that the plans for the Societies of United Irishmen were finally completed.[29] With another great preoccupation of liberal Belfast ringing in their ears, the founders decided that the badge of this new movement should be a harp, over the motto: "It is re-strung and shall be heard." Dr. Madden states definitely, and all his information in this connection was

*Tone's nick-name [Parish Priest] for Russell.

derived many years later from Mary Ann, that Henry Joy McCracken, Thomas Russell, Samuel Neilson and Wolfe Tone together established the first Society of United Irishmen in Belfast in 1791, and that Harry, though his name did not appear in early records, was in the confidence of the executive committee from the outset.[30] It is easy to imagine the innumerable family discussions to which brothers and sisters alike contributed, and to which the brilliant young officer from the infantry barracks was constantly welcomed. Tone, too, must have been with them many times; he records that he was taken to see "the factory for sail-duck", obviously Captain McCracken's,[31] and on another occasion they walked out to see Francis McCracken's new ship, the *Hibernia*. "*Hibernia* [he was quick to notice] has got an English crown on her shield. We all roar at him."[32]

Two days after the dinner party at Mr. McTier's, Tone returned to Dublin. He was accompanied for four miles of the way by Dr. James McDonnell, a foremost physician in the town. They had seen a great deal of each other during the last few days, for McDonnell was, if not a member of the new society, entirely in the confidence of its founders. Whether or not he agreed with all their plans it is impossible to say—perhaps he seized this opportunity to warn Tone against a too extreme programme with regard to the Catholics, perhaps on the other hand, he was completely sympathetic. So, unlike his friend Henry Joy, jun., it was never easy to know just where James McDonnell stood politically. Be that as it may, and in spite of the political stir, of the Doctor's growing practice and the already manifold responsibilities of the editor, we find these two plotting together for something far removed from controversy; for, in fact, a gathering of Irish Harpists and a Festival of Irish Music on a grand scale, to be held in Belfast in the following year.

But one word more about Russell. There had turned up in Belfast an accomplished individual from America of the name of Thomas Digges, a doctor of medicine. Already he had been working in England as American agent for the exchange of prisoners of war, and on account of his nationality and seeming intelligence he was received with open arms by all shades of liberal opinion in Belfast, no one stopping to wonder how this middle-aged gentleman of portly form contrived to pay his way. Suddenly the respectable citizens were thunderstruck by the news of his arrest, the immediate cause of legal proceedings being the inability of Samuel Neilson to retrieve a pair of silver spurs which the visitor had borrowed. Thomas Russell refused to join in the general condemnation, and was induced to go bail for Digges for a debt of £200. Nothing daunted, Digges attached himself to a party of ladies and gentlemen going to Glasgow for a holiday, and during a shopping expedition there, when the ladies were busy with silks and satins, contrived to carry off some articles for which no payment was made. This resulted in a further call from the agents of the law, and the party subsequently returned to Belfast without him. But Russell was more deeply implicated. The bond became due and, in order to meet it, the commission in the 64th Regiment of Foot had to be sold, and Thomas, now a poor man, for he had no private means, went off to Dungannon in December 1791, where, through the influence of Col. Knoxe, an acquaintance from Indian Army days, he was appointed to the lucrative post of Seneschal of the Manor Court which carried with it a seat on the magistrate's bench.[33] However, for reasons which will be unfolded later, Russell never regained financial security, he became more and more implicated in the revolutionary movement and Bess Goddard made another choice.

CHAPTER VI

THE REVIVAL OF IRISH MUSIC

1792

MEANWHILE in Belfast James McDonnell and Henry Joy, jun. continued their preparations for the Harpists' Festival, in the outcome of which the McCracken family were to be deeply involved. In December 1791 this circular was issued :

> Some of the inhabitants of Belfast, feeling themselves interested in everything which relates to the honour, as well as the prosperity of their country, propose to open a subscription which they intend to apply in attempting to revive and perpetuate the Ancient Music and Poetry of Ireland . . . In order to carry this project into execution, it must appear obvious to those acquainted with the situation of this country that it will be necessary to assemble the Harpers, those descendants of our Ancient Bards, who are at present almost exclusively possessed of all that remains of the Music, Poetry and oral traditions of Ireland. . . .[1]

No doubt the arrangements followed pretty closely the pattern of earlier gatherings at Granard in County Leitrim. The response to the appeal was gratifying, and early the following year a meeting of subscribers was held and a committee elected consisting of Henry Joy, jun., Robert Bradshaw, Robert Simms and Dr. McDonnell. Joy, Bradshaw and McDonnell were also appointed to the committee of judges which included several titled ladies.

James McDonnell was one of the outstanding characters of the town. A McDonnell of the Glens, he was born near Cushendall, County Antrim in 1762, and he and his brothers had been taught to play the harp by the famous blind harpist Arthur O'Neill. After attending the hedge-school conducted by Maurice Traynor in the caves at Red Bay, James was sent to Manson's school in Belfast and later, with his brother, studied medicine at Edinburgh.

In the thesis which he wrote for his degree he discussed methods of artificial respiration—a point not without subsequent significance in this story. After settling in practice in Belfast McDonnell devoted himself unsparingly to the development of medical science, he was instrumental in establishing the Belfast Fever Hospital [the first of its kind in Ireland], the Belfast Dispensary and the Belfast General Hospital, and he was prominently associated with the founding of the Belfast school of medicine. With John Templeton and Thomas Russell he shared a keen interest in the natural sciences, and classical and Biblical studies also claimed his attention. In addition to all this he was a great lover of music. Brilliant but unpredictable, tall and very handsome, he was to be nick-named by Tone " The Hypocrite ". While this, no doubt, alluded to his professional oath, one wonders if that strange trait was already apparent in McDonnell's character which later led him so tragically to fail his friends.

In order to achieve the purpose of the Festival the judges

> were instructed on this occasion not to be solely governed in their decisions by the degree of execution or taste of the several performers, but independent of these circumstances to consider the person entitled to additional claim, who shall produce airs not to be found in any public collection, and at the same time deserving of preference, by their intrinsic excellence. It is recommended that the Rev. Mr. Andrew Bryson of Dundalk be requested to assist as a person versed in the language and antiquities of the nation, and that Mr. Weare, Mr. Edward Bunting, and Mr. John Sharpe be requested to attend as practical musicians.[2]

It is obvious that poetry as well as music was equally in the minds of the promoters, but unfortunately they believed the harpers to be the source of both. Had the same strenuous efforts been made to collect in Belfast the few remaining representatives of the Irish bards the Irish literary revival might have been hastened by a hundred years.

A general invitation to the Harpers of Ireland was issued in April through the press, announcing the plans for the Festival and requesting performers on the Irish Harp to assemble in Belfast on July 10th "when a considerable sum will be distributed in premiums in proportion to their merits. It being the intention of the Committee that every performer shall receive some premium it is hoped that no harper will decline attending."[3] At the same time Dr. McDonnell wrote to his former teacher Arthur O'Neill begging him to be present. O'Neill was a member of the illustrious Tyrone family, and, blind as he was from childhood, had spent his life as an itinerant harper, travelling from one great house to another throughout Ireland, always to be welcomed as an honoured guest. On one such visit to Kerry, his host, Lord Kenmare, exclaimed that, as a descendant of the ancient O'Neills, Arthur should be seated at the head of the table. "My Lord", replied the blind man, "it is no matter. Where an O'Neill sits, let it be at any part of the table, should always be considered the head."[4] He was, in contrast to most of his fellow professionals, careful about his clothes and personal appearance, and the large silver buttons on his long coat bore the Hand of Ulster, the emblem of the O'Neills. He was an excellent conversationalist, had pleasing manners, and in spite of his blindness was an adept at cards and backgammon. In addition "he carried in his memory the greatest store of recollections and of traditions with regard to the harpers and composers of preceding generations."[5]

O'Neill, at sixty-three years of age, received McDonnell's letter while staying with the O'Reillys in County Cavan.

> In consequence of my rheumatism [he recorded] I felt my own incapacity, as I had not the use of the two principal fingers of my left hand, by which hand the treble on the Irish harp is generally performed. Mr. O'Reilly would take no excuse, and swore vehemently that if I did not go freely, he would tie me on a car, and have me conducted to assist in performing what was required in the advertisement before mentioned.[6]

EDWARD BUNTING

Nine other harpers assembled in Belfast—Denis Hempson—blind and almost a hundred—had travelled from Magilligan in County Derry, the sightless and somewhat disreputable Rose Mooney was the only woman,—indeed all but three of the competitors were blind, and all but the fifteen-year-old William Carr were well over middle age.

In the midst of general excitement the Festival opened on July 10th 1792. It has been suggested that the date was chosen so that the ancient music might temper the enthusiasm generated by the celebrations of the third anniversary of the fall of the Bastille, due to take place on July 14th, and for which great numbers of volunteers and their friends would be assembling in Belfast from neighbouring districts. It is just as likely that the promoters of the Festival—in most cases promoters also of the celebrations—seized the opportunity of such an influx of visitors in order to disseminate interest in their project.

The place of meeting was the lovely Assembly Room, over the Exchange, where, at one end, a platform had been erected for this strange collection of performers, most of them battered and decrepit in appearance and led by their attendants. The audience was composed of "Ladies and Gentlemen of the first fashion in Belfast and its vicinity"[7] and we may be quite sure that Mary Ann McCracken, then in her twenty-first year, was among them.

Unfortunately the weather was not auspicious : instead of midsummer sunshine Tone notes that it was "bad". He had arrived on his second visit to Belfast, ostensibly for the Bastille celebrations, but more particularly to push forward the plans of the United Irishmen, and out of courtesy, one supposes, to Dr. McDonnell, he looked in at the Festival from time to time. Musical though he was, the ancient glory of the Harpers did not impress him :

> July 11th .. All go to the Harpers at one ; poor enough ; ten performers ; seven execrable, three good, one of them, Fanning far the best. No new musical discovery ; believe all the good Irish airs are already written . . .

July 12th .. Lounge to the Harpers . . .
July 13th .. The Harpers again. Strum. Strum and be hanged . . .[8]

In spite of this acid criticism the Festival was a great success. The airs were played, the prizes were awarded, " the judges on this occasion were sufficiently competent to leave no degree of jealousy amongst the harpers respecting the distribution of the premiums " [a remark of O'Neill's which suggests less fortunate scenes elsewhere], and at the conclusion Dr. McDonnell, with a chieftain's flourish, invited all the competitors to a feast.

> We accordingly met and dined with him and if we had all been peers of the realm we could not have been better treated, as the assiduity of the doctor and his family was more than I can describe.[9]

It was, however, the results of the enterprise that made it memorable. Bunting's imagination had been stirred; Arthur O'Neill had " won and delighted him ". Attracted by Irish music since his childhood days in Armagh, he now determined, after what he called "the great meeting" in Belfast, to embark upon a systematic collection of native airs. " Animated by the countenance and assistance of several townsmen of congenial tastes and habits "[10] this self-indulgent, indolent, young man of nineteen immediately abandoned his increasing professional commitments and set off alone, from the McCracken home in Rosemary Lane, to travel to the remotest parts of Ulster, Connaught and Munster in search of the custodians of traditional music, be they country people, gentry or harpers. He began his journey by following old Denis Hempson to Magilligan, and stayed in that neighbourhood most of the summer. Then, by stages he reached Mayo, where the famous Richard Kirwan F.R.S.* received him with enthusiasm and gave him the utmost assistance. So great was Bunting's success on this journey

*Antiquarian, scientist and founder of the Irish Academy. No doubt when Kirwan visited Belfast in 1795 he was entertained by the McCracken family.

that by 1797 he was able to publish his first collection of genuine Irish Harp music, which included sixty-six native Irish airs never before printed.

It was an immediate success. Mrs. McTier asks Dr. Drennan if he has heard Bunting's Irish music :

> to me [she writes] they are sounds might make Pitt melt for the poor Irish—not a copy is now to be got. Miss Clarke perhaps can do them justice, and if when she plays The Parting of Friends you should be inspired with words as tender as the tune, you might be immortal.[11]

And in her next :

> Have you got the Irish music—it is the rage here—but unaccompanied by the voice for want of words which is much lamented.[12]

Later, when Bunting had gone on a visit to Dublin she urges her brother to meet him :

> it would be worth your while to try if you could hear him play his Irish music—sugar plumbs or sweetys is his greatest temptation, for he dispises both money and praise, and is thought a good hearted original.[13]

This was the collection which Thomas Moore plundered and modified so shamelessly for his own Irish Melodies, defending himself later by the observation that " had I not ventured in these very admissible liberties many of the songs now most known and popular would have been still sleeping with all their authentic dross about them in Mr. Bunting's first volume."[14] Bunting himself has since been accused of mutilating the harpists' airs in order to adapt them for the " piano-forte." In point of fact it was always his paramount aim to preserve as far as he could the " authentic " form of the ancient music, and this comment from the far less scrupulous Moore is a tribute to Bunting's success in this respect.

While he made no public acknowledgment in this publication of the assistance given him by the McCracken family, Bunting's notes and letters indicate that there had been the closest co-operation. It was from their home that he set out on his journeys, to it he returned and in it this unique collection was put together. Atty himself alludes to " my discovery of the structure of Irish music, etc. in your house "[15] as the crucial point in all his work. The house echoed with music—the singing of the lovely airs—the gentle notes of the harpsichord and the plaintive tones of the harp. Gay and happy, this was as much a part of Mary Ann's life as were the sterner affairs already casting their dark shadows. Here in Rosemary Lane, in the bosom of rationalist, presbyterian Belfast, the Renaissance of Irish music took place, the precursor by a century of the Irish Gaelic Revival,* which was to exert such a lasting influence on the course of the Irish nation.

Thomas Russell, too, was back in Belfast and entered enthusiastically into this family project. Within nine months of his appointment to the lucrative and socially attractive post at Dungannon he had sent in his resignation because of a disagreement with his brother magistrates regarding the preferential treatment accorded to Protestants, Russell stating publicly that

> he could not reconcile it to his conscience to sit as a magistrate on a bench where the practice prevailed of inquiring what a man's religion was before inquiring into the crime with which a prisoner was accused.[16]

Once again penniless, he lived for a time with Dr. McDonnell, who showed him much kindness and generosity, securing for him, in 1794, the position of Librarian in the Belfast Library† at a salary of £30 per annum. Music, as well as politics, drew Russell to the McCracken household, and while with Harry he would plot and plan for the United Irishmen, with the others there would be all the pleasure of arranging and playing the new found ancient airs.

But before Bunting had achieved this first triumph in 1797 the McCracken family circle had been broken.

*The Gaelic League was founded in Dublin in 1893.

†Now the Linenhall Library.

Harry and Thomas Russell were among those arrested in Belfast in the autumn of 1796—the prelude to further tragedy—and while for Mary Ann life would ultimately resume its ordered tenor, the lighthearted joyousness and gaiety were shortly to depart for ever.

CHAPTER VII

REFORM OR REVOLUTION

1791–1795

LORD CHARLEMONT and the original volunteers had faded from the picture, and small groups of earnest men, known as Societies of United Irishmen, were spreading rapidly throughout North-east Ulster and, to a lesser degree, in and around Dublin. " We are going on here with boots of seven leagues, and will soon be at liberty and equality," wrote Robert Simms from Belfast to Wolfe Tone in 1792[1] and, at the same time, Samuel Neilson reported : " You can form no conception of the rapid progress of unions here ; and I do assure you we are further forward than I ever expected we should have been in a twelve month. The universal question throughout the country is, when do we begin ? do we refuse hearth money or tythes first ? "[2] This reference to tithes emphasises the humanitarian motives of the movement. It cannot be too often noticed that, in the Northern Societies at any rate, there was, alongside of the desire for general parliamentary reform, a growing concern for the betterment of the poverty-stricken peasants and labourers of every creed—people in whose defence no body of opinion in Ireland had ever yet been organised. The movement was not at this stage highly centralised but all the members were expected to subscribe to the Test :

> I, A.B. in the presence of God do pledge myself to my country, that I will use all my abilities and influence in the attainment of an impartial and adequate representation of the Irish nation in Parliament ; and as a means of absolute and immediate necessity, in the establishment of this the chief good of Ireland, I will endeavour, as much as lies in my ability, to forward a brotherhood of affection, an identity of interest, a communion of rights and an union of power among Irishmen of all religious persuasions, without which every reform of Parliament must be partial,

not national, inadequate to the wants, delusive to the wishes, and insufficient for the freedom and happiness of the country.[3]

The only fault of these United Irishmen lay, it would seem, in their being too far ahead of their times; the principles enunciated in this declaration are to-day accepted as the foundations on which democratic associations must be built.

A great effort was made by these new reformers to resuscitate the Volunteer Movement on its original basis, and on behalf of the Societies in Dublin Dr. Drennan wrote in 1792 his famous address to the Volunteers of Ireland:

> Citizen soldiers you first took up arms to protect your country from foreign enemies and from domestic disturbance. For the same purpose it now becomes necessary that you should resume them . . . We wish for Catholic emancipation without any modification; but still we consider this necessary enfranchisement as merely the portal to the temple of national freedom. The Catholic cause is subordinate to our cause . . . for as United Irishmen we adhere to no sect but to society, to no creed but to Christianity, to no party but to the whole people. In the sincerity of our souls we desire Catholic emancipation; but were it obtained tomorrow, tomorrow we would go on, as we do to-day, in the pursuit of that reform which would still be wanting to ratify their liberties as well as our own . . . Fourteen long years have elapsed since the rise of your associations, and in 1782 did you imagine that in 1792 this nation would still remain unrepresented? How many nations in the interval have gotten the start of Ireland? How many of our countrymen have sank in the grave?

It is a stirring appeal, breathing no hint of disloyalty to the King and the Constitution, or any injury to the safety of the realm; but bitter in its opposition to

> that faction or gang which misrepresents the King to the people, and the people to the King, traduces one half of

the nation to cajole the other, and by keeping up distrust and division, wished to continue the proud arbitrators of the fortune and the fate of Ireland.[4]

The " gang " was in fact the Irish Privy Council, led by " that bouncing bully "[5] Fitzgibbon, afterwards Lord Clare. This body, appointed by the Crown, had far more administrative power than its counterpart in England, and was used by the Protestant Ascendancy to stultify such parliamentary freedom as had been achieved.

The revival of the Volunteers was considerable. The great review was held in Belfast on the 14th of July 1792, the day concluding with the inevitable dinner and no less than thirty-three toasts. A similar review was to take place in Dublin, but such activities, together with ardent declarations in favour of " a union of all Irishmen ", made Government anxious and a Proclamation was issued forbidding seditious assemblies. Belfast retaliated with stirring speeches, recruiting committees, less costly uniforms to suit less affluent purses—which were " to be seen at Mr. Cuthbert's, Tailor "—and the suggestion that, while the strong and able-bodied men of the community should " enrol themselves among their armed brethren ", those who were in an advanced state of life should " contribute to the cause in a pecuniary way, for the purpose of purchasing arms, ammunition, and accoutrements."[6] All of this was carefully noted in Dublin Castle, headquarters of the Irish government.

Unfortunately the new movement had not, as yet, thrown up a leader of national standing, and opinions, especially in Belfast, were becoming more divided. Here, in the beginning of 1792, a meeting had been called to consider the position of the Catholics.

> Gentlemen. [ran the notice which was signed by fifty prominent citizens] As men and as Irishmen we have long lamented the degraded state of slavery and oppression in which the great majority of our countrymen, the Roman Catholics, are held—nor have we lamented in silence . . .[7]

The attendance was large, so large that the meeting could not be accommodated in the Town House as arranged, but had to repair to the new New Meeting House of the 3rd Congregation, whose minister, the Rev. Sinclaire Kelburn, took the chair. [This was the congregation to which the McCracken and Joy families belonged.] Only, however, after much discussion was the following Petition passed, the words in italics being deleted :

> We therefore pray, that the legislature may be pleased to repeal, *from time to time, and as speedily as the circumstances of the whole kingdom will permit*, all penal and restrictive statutes at present in existence against the Roman Catholics of Ireland ; and that they may thus be restored to the rank and consequence of citizens, *in every particular*.[8]

Immediately afterwards a motion, proposed by Henry Joy, jun., was passed unanimously :

> that it was the duty as well as the interest of the Roman Catholic clergy and laity to make a solemn declaration of their principles, as far as they were connected with civil and religious liberty.[9]

Here is the ever recurring problem, and it is clear where Henry Joy's sympathies lay. Though he goes on to explain that the only point of difference was " whether the entire enfranchisement of the Roman Catholics, including suffrage at elections, should be *immediate or progressive*,"[10] this very point was the crux of a developing situation, the cause of an irreconcilable split within the ranks of the Belfast reformers, and it was the moderates who lost their ground. From now on Tone, Russell, Neilson and McCracken were to find in the Societies of the Belfast United Irishmen and Volunteers the soil in which to cultivate their advanced projects for complete and immediate Catholic emancipation based on Catholic-Presbyterian co-operation. Dr. Drennan could write with truth of the Northern Societies :

> You have all along been more Catholics and less Irishmen than we[11]

and again

> the Catholics are still more *religionists* than *politicians*, and the Presbyterians are more politicians than religionists. The one still cherish their creed as the first object; the creed of the other is in general Liberty and Equality.[12]

This Belfast meeting is noteworthy as being the first occasion on which any non-Catholic body in Ireland publicly stated their claim for their Catholic countrymen. The Petition was signed by upwards of 600 people, and within a fortnight was presented to the Irish House of Commons by the Hon. John O'Neill, independent member for the County of Antrim.

Discussion and argument were not confined to the spoken word. The *Belfast News-Letter* was still the only local newspaper and its editor [Henry Joy, jun.] was a man of moderate, liberal views. In this same year [1792] Samuel Neilson, now a prosperous merchant, together with twelve other prominent men of the town, including William and Robert Simms, established the *Northern Star* a competitive publication edited by Neilson, and devoted to blatantly sympathetic reporting of republican affairs in France. As a counterblast, the *News-Letter* in the following year produced an anonymous series of articles called "Thoughts on the British Constitution" written by Henry Joy, jun. and opening thus:

> At a period when Republicans are exhibited as models of perfection, I am persuaded it is consistent with the spirit of a free press, to recommend the principles of the British Constitution . . . It is the fashion of the hour, and as ridiculous as most fashions are, to deprecate the Revolution of 1688—and to despise the securities for our liberty, which that great transaction afforded.[13]

Nowhere was the controversy followed with greater attention than in the McCracken household, and not least by Mary Ann, noted even in that politically minded family for her interest in current affairs. The *News-Letter* was still very much the family print, and though Mary's opinions were steadily moving to the left of Cousin Henry's she was far too good and reasonable a Joy to discard established views without careful thought. But it was the *Star* that was read with relish. Years later it was recounted of Mary Ann that her first concern on recovering from a serious attack of fever, was that she had "missed so many Stars".[14] The production was breezy and up-to-date, it had all the exciting news, and many of their friends, notably Thomas Russell, with his *Chinese Papers* and *The Lion of Old England*, were contributors. Dr. James Porter, the Presbyterian minister of Greyabbey, wrote for its columns a serial entitled *Billy Bluff and the Squire*, a very slightly concealed "take-off" on Lord Londonderry and his henchman the Rev. Jas. Cleland, which, in conjunction with his other political activities, eventually cost the author his life.

Even within the membership of the United Irishmen differences were arising. The French excesses, epitomised by the fate of Louis XVI and his family, were becoming alarming and Mrs. McTier, that staunch and fearless supporter of progressive thought, declared :

> I am turned, quite turned, against the French, & fear that it is all farther than ever from coming to good.[15]

She and her husband, who was chairman of the 1st Belfast Society of United Irishmen, were much impressed by the clarity and wisdom of the "Thoughts on the British Constitution", and Sam

> determined at a meeting to propose a number of them should be printed and distributed throughout the country —but it would not do—*Joy* was the printer and *Bruce* the supposed author—the very reasons that, to minds of any delicacy, should have determined them to reprint a good paper. Such mean motives can hurt a good cause . . . I ventured myself to argue with some of the lads, for they are mostly such, to get the Crown added to the Harp on their buttons,—but 'they were bespoke'—'they were too small'—'they were cast' and 'it could not be engraven' and thus a good cause suffers for a *button*. You may rest upon it, others I now fear dare greater strokes,[16]

In February 1793 France declared war on England : the struggle, eventually to end at Waterloo, had begun.

No one could blame the Parliament at Westminster for being preoccupied with measures for Britain's survival, but the folly of its tactics, as far as Ireland was concerned, was lamentable. Instead of a courageous policy of parliamentary reform, which, even at that hour, would have rallied all the elements of discontent to England's side, hastily conceived deterrents served only to enflame disaffection. Security measures were rushed through the Irish House of Commons ; espionage was intensified, so that " a perfect Inquisition reigns ; "[17] leaders of the United Irishmen in Dublin were arrested to lie in prison without indictment let alone trial ; members of the rank and file, notably Defenders [a Catholic organisation] were publicly executed with every display of cruelty and humiliation ;[18] and, in order to avoid any possible disaffection of the landed interest, the ancient and all too successful remedy of bribery was once more produced. " A new cargo of pensions is said to have come over to distribute as douceurs, like lottery tickets."[19]

But much more important : in an effort to break the Catholic-Presbyterian alliance the relief measure of 1793 was passed, restoring to Catholics all the rights and liberty of citizenship, excepting admission to Parliament and appointment to the highest civil and judicial positions. While this great victory for the Catholic cause was awaiting the royal assent a crushing blow was levelled at those who had done much to achieve it. In March 1793 the Lord Lieutenant issued a Proclamation against the Volunteers in Belfast. Fourteen years after Robert Joy's first recruits had been welcomed by one Lord Lieutenant as the only bulwark against invasion, what remained of the organisation was shattered by another, and " in compliance with the proclamation, the Volunteers ceased to parade, or any longer to appear in military array." So wrote Henry Joy, jun. With this sentence of passive resignation he buried the glorious achievement of the Volunteer movement and concluded the collection of articles which he published under the title of " Belfast Politics ". One feels that he was beginning to realise with profound sadness, that the lead in the public affairs of the town he loved had already passed from him and his moderate associates.

With Samuel Neilson the reactions were very different. After admitting the expediency of complying with the order, he goes on to declare, with every suggestion of assurance, in the columns of the *Northern Star* that " the time may come, and that shortly, when *all* Ireland may be glad to see the *Saviours of their Country* once more in formidable array."[20] Reform had been driven underground, and if the Volunteers no longer " appeared in Military array " many of them were to constitute the core of the *secret* societies of United Irishmen now to be organised for the first time, and on a military basis. The formulation of those " greater strokes " already sensed by Mrs. McTier was under way.

But the invasion of Ireland was once more a fearful possibility, and this time, in order to augment the meagre protection afforded by the few troops that could be spared from the Continent, the Government had no alternative but to form regiments of Yeomanry. Whereas the Volunteers had been raised and maintained almost entirely by private effort, the Yeomanry was a paid body, costing the Government during the first three months of its existence £500,000.[21] It attracted, for the most part, reactionaries and irresponsibles and was to perpetrate some of the gravest atrocities in '98 and '99. It is said that it was the recorded cruelties of the Yeomanry that, less than a hundred years later, did much to arouse the nationalist passion of Charles Stewart Parnell.[22]

The war in Europe made itself felt in other directions. The dislocation of trade spread to Ireland, bankruptcies were frequent, and in an effort to relieve the situation grants were made by the Irish Government to unfortunate merchants. Dr. Drennan mentions the arrival in Dublin of Waddell Cunningham one of Belfast's leading traders, and his return with £30,000 for distribution :

> but [he writes] how it can make the shuttle go more briskly in either the linen or woolen branches is hard to say, while the natural vent of the goods in foreign parts is kept shut by the war, and while at the same time England is dis-

> burthening her glutted market upon us and throwing all at an underselling rate into our market when she cannot dispose of her goods abroad.[23]

Widespread unemployment resulted among the weavers in Dublin and Belfast; and in the North-east, where the manufacture of linen was so intimately bound up with the rural economy, this reacted in turn on the agricultural labourers. Moreover, armies had to be fed, and to satisfy the increased demand for meat, land previously cultivated was turned to the raising of cattle, thus adding to the hardships of the peasantry and making more than ever intolerable the iniquitous system of tithes.

In those districts of the North where the rural population was mixed, sectarian strife was an added complication. The county Armagh was specially bad in this respect. Here the protestant labourers, encouraged by the landlords, organised themselves as Peep-o'-Day Boys, while the catholics were enrolled as Defenders. Endless quarrels were fomented by both sides, cottages were burned, crops destroyed, cattle maimed, tenants evicted and many lives lost in brawls and fights ; but when culprits were brought before the courts, the magistrates, drawn entirely from the landed families, were so notoriously biassed in favour of the protestant interest that the ordinary catholic despaired of justice.

It was to this particular situation that Henry Joy McCracken addressed himself with the fullest support from Mary Ann. Religious differences, elaborate theories of parliamentary reform and constitutional action meant little to Harry, he saw only the need of human suffering, the injustice of sectarian discrimination. In this endeavour Thomas Russell, who had so lately resigned his post in Dungannon on just these grounds, was his most constant supporter. " None of our leaders " wrote James Hope " seemed to me perfectly acquainted with the main cause of social derangement, if I except Neilson, McCracken, Russell and Emmett. It was my settled opinion that the condition of the labouring class was the fundamental question at issue between the rulers and the people."[24]

If Neilson and McCracken sprang from the group of enlightened presbyterian merchants in Belfast, Hope represented the almost inarticulate aspirations of the strongly revolutionary element among the presbyterian labourers both rural and urban; he was indeed the most radical of the United Irishmen—in some respects the greatest of them all. Born in Templepatrick, in the southern part of County Antrim, in 1764, he came, like the McCrackens, of stern Covenanting stock, his father having been forced from a Highland home by religious persecution. At the age of ten "Jemmy" had received fifteen weeks of schooling, an unusual advantage for one of his class, and was hired by a nearby farmer named Bell. In his autobiography Hope speaks of his first employer thus:

> The first three years I earned my bread with William Bell of Templepatrick, who took every opportunity of improving my mind, that my years would admit. In winter he made me get forward my work and sit with him while he read in the Histories of Greece and Rome, and also Ireland, Scotland and England; besides, his reading and comments on the news of the day turned my attention early to the nature of the relations between the different classes of society, and passing events rather left impressions on my mind for future examinations, than established any particular opinions.[25]

Two successive farmers for whom he worked pushed his education still further "until I could read a little in the Bible, though very imperfectly." When about fifteen Hope was apprenticed to a linen weaver, the trade which he followed for many years in many places. His first practical connection with politics began in the Volunteers; later, with many of his Company, he joined the local Society of United Irishmen, and was elected to represent it at the central committee in Belfast. Here he met Neilson, McCracken and Russell.

Already Hope's whole interest was focussed on improving conditions for the working man in town and country; to him there was little difference between the rapaciousness of the aristocrat and of the merchant. Whilst in the rest of Ireland, he declared, the unfortunate labourer had to contend with " landlords " and " churchlords ", in the North

> manufacture and commerce, ficticious capital, ficticious credit, ficticious titles to consideration, presented the numberless interests of the few, in opposition to the one interest of the many.
>
> Such were the difficulties with which the men of Ulster had to contend, besides that perplexity arising from a pensioned clergy, puzzling its followers with speculations above human comprehension, and instigating them to hate each other for conscience sake, under the mask of religion.[26]

Anticipating by many years the work of Michael Davitt and the Land League, Hope formulated his ideas of peasant-ownership thus :

> The soil is not like the objects of commerce, which are only possessed for the purpose of barter ; it is the social capital from the cultivation of which all earthly wants are supplied . . . My concurrence shall not be given to the scheme of a delusive fixity of tenure, to enable the landlord to continue to draw the last potatoe out of the warm ashes of the poor mans fire, and leave his children to beg a cold one from those who can ill afford to give it. Is this a remedy for the miseries of a famishing people ? A fixity of tenure—a fixity for ever in famine . . .

All this evolved from his deep religious faith :

> The Most High is Lord of the soil ; the cultivator is his tenant. [It is the language of the Old Testament in which Hope has been nurtured.] The recognition of all other titles, to the exclusion of this first title has been the cause of an amount of human misery, beyond all calculation . . . the progress of christian truth, which is the perfection of good-will and God-like love, cannot be retarded.[27]

It is not surprising that between Henry Joy McCracken and Jemmy Hope there arose a bond of deep attachment and confidence : here was the leader who cared nothing for privilege and possessions and everything for the advancement of the labouring man ; here, on the other hand, was the labouring man possessed of an unusually alert and sensitive mind, able and willing to put theories into practice. There is little doubt that they learned much from each other.

There are few details regarding Harry's movements in the years prior to 1795. On his return from Scotland in 1789* he was sent to a cotton printing mill owned by Joy, Holmes and McCracken at the Falls, then a village some distance from Belfast. In 1795 this partnership was dissolved and there is more than a suggestion that Harry had not given the business the attention it required.[28] He then started a printfield at Knockaird, which cannot have lasted long.[29] It is interesting to note, in passing, that this particular branch of the cotton industry was included in the McCracken undertakings. These printfields were of necessity situated in the country ; this would account for Harry's frequent absence from the deliberations of the U.I. Societies in Belfast, and would encourage his marked interest in rural workers. With his great charm and drive, it would have been natural for him to hold high office in the movement he had done so much to create ; instead he was content to leave administration to others, notably to William and Robert Simms, Sam McTier, William Sinclaire and Samuel Neilson, and to let Neilson run the paper that was giving such admirable publicity to the cause : all he asked was to be in direct contact with the people he was bent on helping

For a time he lived in County Armagh, working in conjunction with young Charles Teeling, amongst the Defenders, urging them to break out of their religious isolation and join the United Irish movement, and binding himself in substantial sums to meet the expenses of legal aid for those of their number brought before biassed magistrates by their Protestant neighbours, often on trumped-up charges. In this he was helped by his cousin in Dublin, Counsellor Joy, and Harry's work for the Defenders attracted at one time the notice of Grattan,

*See p. 55.

when he was pleading in the Irish House of Commons for a mitigation of Catholic burdens. There is evidence to suggest that Harry was concerned in organising Defenders as far afield as the then King's County[30] [now Offaly]; later he declared that he could muster 7,000 of them in arms. He was always a vehement opponent of the tithe system, and a letter written by Mary Ann many years later can be taken as expressing the deep resentment shared by both of them against this flagrant injustice :

> All evils I think proceed from the want of real, vital and practical religion, for were all who profess to be Christians truly so in heart and practice, obedient to the commands so simple and easy to be understood . . . there would neither be slave holding in America . . . nor any of the numerous and unjust and oppressive laws with which Gt. Britain abounds, a prominent one in this country being heavily taxing the poorest sect for the support of the clergy of the richest sect from which they (the poorest) derive no advantage.[31].

Nearer home Harry worked with Jemmy Hope amongst the presbyterian tenants and farm labourers, organising them in Societies, bringing new recruits to the Belfast meetings in Peggy Barclay's tavern in Sugar-house Entry, and undertaking the unsavoury tasks of seducing militia men and carrying information between Belfast and Dublin.[32] Much of his time was spent away from home, and it is noticeable that in Mrs. McTier's letters—a veritable inventory of Belfast society from the Donegalls downwards—there are only three or four brief references to McCracken. Even among the orthodox United Irishmen he was something of a dark horse.

Meanwhile, the friendly and " respectable " pattern of Belfast life was changing. " Such are the times [wrote Mrs. McTier] . . . so strangely are causes, interests, & sentiments, fears and dangers, blended & effected by each other at present, that I wd. think it hard for the man of honor and political integrity to know how to steer, and much do I fear greater tryals yet await them." And after expressing her pity for " the Volrs. called on by the most respectable of their countrymen to continue those efforts from which nothing but good was the consequence. . . . yet spurn'd & degraded, by a base, cruel and powerful administration"; and for the military, "booed" at the theatre and distrusted by everyone; Mrs. McTier ends by remarking that, in spite of all the tribulation, "we eat, drink, chat, sometimes a little warmly, just as during the American War—but not so as either to interrupt good neighbourhood, or our Whist."[33]

It would seem, however, that Dublin Castle was determined to interrupt even the Whist. The town garrison was augmented by licentious troops who went about the streets creating trouble. In March 1793 a serious riot was started when a detachment of dragoons wrecked a public house from which a sign depicting Dumourier had, for many months, been harmlessly displayed, attacked others with pictures of Mirabeau and Franklin, and ended up with the little milliner's "who had trimmed the helmets of the volunteer light horse".[34] It was alleged, too, "that the dragoons were repeatedly observed to read a card with the names of houses which they were to assault amongst which were McCabe's, Neilson's, Hasliff's [sic], Kilbourne's and the Star office." As a result of a protest from the magistrates to the General these particular troops were withdrawn, Mrs. McTier remarking "that in any town they would have been stoned to death—but there never was a Belfast mob, happy for us at present for I do believe it was ardently sought for."[35]

But it is only too easy to create a mob, and one month later there was another street fight in which Henry Joy McCracken was involved:

> I opened this letter to tell you that this evening there was all the appearance of a Riot and good reason to believe the Military intended one against the Star Office. Haslett getting a hint of it went between 5 & 6 to Bristow [the Sovereign] who gave him a letter to Capt. Barber requesting he would be particularly careful of his men. B. told him he had heard it was whispered and that he had his picquets

ready in the Barrack in case of any disturbance. Between eight and nine two recruits, drunk, struck several people in the streets, they were beat by the Mob. The Officers and some young men of the Town met in the croud, where a Servt. of a young Officer swore he wd. defend his Master, and made several strokes at some of the croud on which he was knocked down, and his Master drew his sword & Barber laid his hand on his, when Henry Joy McCracken stepped forward and desired him not to draw it. Barber said he was Ringleader of the Mob and a Rascall. McCracken replied that he was his equal and would have satisfaction. B. said that was an improper place and he did not know him. McCracken said Mr. Bristow wd. tell him who he was, and his Name was—and he was ready to speak to him anywhere. Whether it will end here no one can tell. Thro' all the croud this Evg. I did not see a young Man that was not armed with a Stick or some good weapon.[36]

Sam McTier, who wrote this to his wife, was possibly returning with Harry from a United Irishmen's meeting, when the event occurred. Two days later he wrote her again :

We have been since my last tolerably quiet, tho' not at all free from apprehension. Yesterday morning the Sovn. sent for Hy. McCracken, to speak to him about what passed the night before between Capt. Barber; he wanted McCracken to make an apology to Barber, he refused. Col. French was present, who talked a great deal about his Soldiers being insulted in the Streets and that he would give them orders not to suffer it, and he swore by God if there was one Gun fired from any Window at any of his people he would immediately burn the Town, and he would now order three regiments more here and bring back the Dragoons.

The affair was patched up by a committee hastily convened by Henry Joy, jun. to preserve the peace of the town, and Sam McTier continued :

I think our great danger now of being involved is from a parcel of little Blackguard Boys who gather in the Streets at night, & groan the Soldiers & their cry is Smell Gunpowder.[37]

But the scuffles persisted and reports of them were widely published by the authorities in order to bring discredit on the town. Stories flew round about the vengeance vowed against Belfast, and the plans for its destruction, and " it is a common saying that the Country will never know peace 'till *Belfast* is in ashes."[38]

By similar methods the Government had stifled moderate opinion all over Ireland; the extremists went underground and survived, and at this stage the extremists were centred in Belfast. Wm. Drennan in Dublin laments constantly that " the moderate men are sound asleep ",[39] inveighs against " Neilson's system of eternal silence ", and wishes that Sam McTier " could get out of Neilson and McCracken plan and purpose." " I have a notion [he writes] we are being kept in the Secret and so are you, except Russell, Neilson and perhaps Simms." And again " I deplore deeply that there is so little open acting and so much *mole* work. It goes against my nature."[40]

The movement was still leaderless. The Dublin Societies looked askance at Lord Edward Fitzgerald, a brother of the Duke of Leinster, but, nevertheless, a young man of aggressive republican views; and Tone, who was secretary of the Catholic Committee was not really in their confidence, though he was in constant communication with Russell, Neilson and McCracken.[41]

Tension was rapidly increasing when the unexpected happened: at the close of 1794 the Viceroy Westmorland was recalled, and for political reasons at Westminster the whig Fitzwilliam was, early in the following year, appointed in his place and welcomed to Ireland with widespread rejoicing. An extensive landowner in this country Lord Fitzwilliam had previously demonstrated his liberal views on the Irish problem, and on his arrival hope revived in the bosoms of the " moderate men."

One of the first acts of the new Viceroy was to dismiss the all-powerful John Beresford, styled by some " the king of Ireland ", and member of a vastly influential family opposed at every turn to liberal measures. There were other indications of ameliorative treatment for the Catholics and, spurred by gratitude for such significant moves, Henry Grattan proposed and carried a motion in the House of Commons expressing approval of the war with France, and voting £200,000 towards the support of the Navy. A bill was then introduced, with every hope of success, for the complete emancipation of the Catholics, but when news of it reached the ears of the English cabinet there was violent disapproval, and, to the consternation and dismay of all reasonable people, Fitzwilliam, in whose heart and hands seemed to lie the longed-for solution of Ireland's distress, was recalled within three months of his appointment—one of the many fateful episodes in the story of the relations between the two islands.

Fitzwilliam himself was dismayed. He knew that for some time the idea of uniting the Irish and English parliaments had been working in Pitt's mind—was this, he wondered, part of the plan to achieve it ? " Will a rebellion " he asks " tend to further that end ? Even if it is hoped that it might indeed do so, are the means risked such as are justifiable, or such as any man would wish to risk ? "[42] Thus clearly did he see where Pitt's action would lead.

Once again, and for the last time in this phase of history, moderate opinion was dashed to the ground ; from now the extremists on either side were to have their way.

These events had been followed with the deepest concern in Belfast. When the recall of Fitzwilliam was announced a Town Meeting unanimously resolved that an address be presented to His Excellency by " three of our townsmen ", recording that :

> We, the inhabitants of Belfast, rejoiced with the millions of our countrymen on the appointment of your Excellency to the Government of this Kingdom. We gratefully admired the wisdom and benevolence of our gracious King, in selecting for that important station, at a crisis awful and alarming, a nobleman whose character, talents, and virtues, were so eminently adapted to calm the rage of party, to suppress every evil, to encourage every good, and to make a whole people satisfied, united and happy . . . We consider the day in which his Majesty entrusted the

> Irish Septre to your hand, as one of the brightest in the annals of our country; as we should that of your departure from us as a day of National mourning.[43]

On March 28th 1795 Fitzwilliam left Dublin: in Belfast " there was not a Shop or Counting-House open during the whole day—all was one scene of sullen indignation."[44] On that day Mrs. McCracken did not do her household shopping, and the looms of Mary Ann's weavers were silent, and while Harry and Thomas Russell may have gone about their " mole work " with greater intensity, Mary must have viewed the outcome with growing apprehension. Very likely it was at this stage that she said one day to Harry " If you fail you will lose your lives " to which he replied " Whether we fail or succeed we expect to be the first to fall "; " and ", added Russell who was standing by, " of what consequence are our lives or the lives of a few individuals, compared to the liberty and happiness of Ireland."[45]

To Henry Joy, jun., sitting in the *News-Letter* office the news of Fitzwilliam's recall sounded as a death knell. How could he, in face of the growing opposition of the more extreme reformers, continue to urge support for reasoned, rational development as against hasty action, when the English government had yet again proved so fickle? For upwards of ten years he had written, week in week out, upholding every measure of reform " consistent with Peace, Order and the Constitution "; he had supported the cause of Roman Catholic enfranchisement " at a time when few even among themselves entertained a hope, and before any of the present numerous friends had parted with the prejudice of education "; and now it was only too evident " that an independent Print, which neither bowed to a Court, nor flattered the people, has received its reward." Possibly the knowledge of his cousin Harry's subversive activities contributed to the agony of bitterness and to his decision to sell the *Belfast News-Letter*—the " Print " that had been so inextricably bound to his family for three generations. In a long, dignified editorial he bade farewell to his public on

May 15th, 1795, and at the same time withdrew from political activity.

A more fateful result of Fitzwilliam's recall was the intensification of the secret societies and the definite turn towards aid from France. In March 1795 Henry Joy McCracken was sworn a member of the Tenth Society of United Irishmen of Belfast, one of the newly formed extreme groups.

The French war was becoming desperate for England. Security measures in Ireland were increased, and implemented throughout the country with great brutality against the rank and file. The leaders, on the other hand, were given every opportunity to escape, the government fearing to bring them to justice, turning them thereby into martyrs or heroes. Of these Wolfe Tone was the most notorious. He was the prime agent in the Catholic-Dissenter combination, which, in the view of Castle administrators, must be immediately broken, they being of the opinion that without Presbyterian stiffening the Catholics could be bribed and cajoled into docility. There was, of course, nothing to fear from the other Protestant element.

So by devious methods Tone became aware that he could depart peacefully or face the certainty of Newgate Jail if he remained. He decided to go, believing that, with his able lieutenants still at large, he could further his aims for Ireland more judiciously from beyond her shores. And it was from Belfast that he and his family embarked.

It was anything but a secret departure. After saying good-bye to Dublin the little party, consisting of himself, his wife, three children and his sister, boarded the coach for Belfast where they remained for almost a month, and "were every day engaged by one or other—parties and excursions being planned for our amusement."[46] It was the month of May, and this time there is no mention of bad weather, there seems indeed to have been perpetual sunshine. William and Robert Simms arranged a magnificent picnic to the Deer Park. A large tent was pitched and the entire families of the Neilsons, the Simms, the McCrackens, the Tones and, doubtless, others disported themselves on the gentle slopes of the Cave Hill for the whole day, dining and spending the time "deliciously". There was another glorious picnic to Ram's Island in Lough Neagh—adults and children, food and everything else being transported the 20 odd miles from Belfast on horseback or in carriages—"nothing" wrote Tone "can be imagined more delightful."

But there was another excursion, more momentous and more serious. This time the women and children were left at home, and Tone, Thomas Russell, Samuel Neilson, the two Simms, Harry McCracken "and one or two more" climbed to the summit of the Cave Hill. There on the ancient site of MacArt's Fort, surveying the vast panorama that stretches in every direction—the Mourne Mountains, the Lagan Valley, the Derry mountains, Slemish in Antrim, the lovely blue Belfast Lough at their feet, the sea beyond, and farther off still the Scottish shores—there they "took a solemn obligation . . . never to desist in our efforts, until we had subverted the authority of England over our country, and asserted her independence."[47] For good or ill Wolfe Tone was leaving his imprint on the North.

So the weeks passed in friendly coming and going—Dr. McDonnell calling one day to present a "small medicine chest with written directions" for use on the voyage—till at length there was the final gathering for farewell. It was held, we may assume, in the McCrackens' house. Great preparations had been made for the sumptuous supper, the dining room and drawing-room were thronged with guests, there were games for the children and singing and music for the grown-ups. Mr. Bunting "had thrown the enchantment of music over the whole evening, by his unrivalled performance on the harp," and Harry had excelled himself in his zest for arranging a party. Conversation and good fellowship prevailed, till—at a pause—the haunting, exquisite notes of "The parting of Friends" rang out—the air which, when it appeared two years later in Bunting's Collection, was hailed as the most lovely of all. It was too much for poor Matilda Tone—she dissolved into tears, and in those days tears were exceedingly infectious,—Atty should really have had more sense! But Thomas Russell was at hand and he it was who saved the situation. Years afterwards Mary Ann remembered how with his charming, gentle, understanding manner "he consoled the lovely mourner, and her almost equally afflicted husband", bidding them to think of their sure return under happier conditions: and so, with smiling good-byes, the party ended.[48] Next day, June 13th 1795, Theobald Wolfe Tone and his family—escorted to the quay, we may be sure, by many friends—embarked on an American ship, crowded with 300 passengers, and, sailing down Belfast Lough, began their six weeks' voyage to Wilmington, North Carolina, U.S.A. The fugitive departure had been transformed into a triumphant farewell.

McART'S FORT, CAVEHILL, *c.* 1830

CHAPTER VIII

KILMAINHAM

PART I

1795–1797

WOLFE TONE had gone, but the associates he left behind in Belfast zealously pursued the policy they had formulated together. Dr. Drennan notes frequent visits to Dublin of Neilson, Simms and Tennent on business about which they do " not chuse to be very explicit ",[1] but remarks that Simms and Tennent are " too prudent men to be engaged in anything amiss ".[2] Probably these visits were connected with the return to Dublin from Paris of Lord Edward Fitzgerald, now accepted by the extreme section of the Dublin Societies, and shortly to become the most romantic leader the United Irishmen were to have.

Already uncertainty and rumours of invasion were undermining morale in Belfast. " Mr. Holmes and Ewing go to Bath this winter. . . . they are just old and rich enough to be panic struck. Lady H. has just called to take leave, and I would not be surprised at some others stealing away ".[3] And in despair for her country Mrs. McTier continues :

> Are there no wise benevolent, and truly patriotic beings . . . that guided by virtue only, and having no mean nor selfish passion actuating them, dare step forward, and with the most pure intentions dare to stem (even for a time) those horrors which seem to await our Country . . . No one can pretend to say, if arms are once resorted to—where the evil may stop or who or what principle may be safe.[4]

If only her wish could have been fulfilled !

Meanwhile the Irish Government was not unaware of what was happening ; the Chief Secretary had his well paid army of spies. " I do believe that the Inquisition in its worst days was not worse than the laceration of character wh. is exercised at present" writes Dr. Drennan,[5] and in a long passage he elaborates his statement that " In the professions of Law and Divinity, there is not a man who is not offered his bounty and drink money ".[6] Apart from this rather high-class but no less effective form of bribery, it is recorded in the *Account of Secret Service money applied in detecting treasonable conspiracies* " that the figure spent by the Irish Government between August 1797 and September 1801 on the maintenance of ordinary espionage was £38,419 8. 0. "[7] a noticeable sum in those days.

It was well known in Dublin Castle that by 1796 Wolfe Tone had arrived in France from America, and that he and emissaries from Ireland were urging invasion. Lord Camden was now Viceroy, and Castlereagh, his able young nephew once the hope of the Northern whigs, had been recalled from his seat in the English Parliament to assist, and subsequently to succeed, Chief Secretary Pelham. For Castlereagh constitutional reform was one thing, eminently desirable in its place, but treasonable dealings with Britain's enemies in time of war were quite another. With his opportunities for a wider outlook he now viewed the Irish problem in the light of European events, and against the background of England's most grave peril. He judged, and rightly, that the Presbyterian element in the North was the real centre of genuine republican sympathy, and once and for all the North must be rendered ineffective. So, in September 1796, accompanied by Lord Downshire, Lord Westmeath, and an imposing military entourage, Castlereagh himself arrived in Belfast carrying warrants for the arrest of Neilson, Russell, Teeling and five other prominent United men.

This would-be terrifying display of authority was somewhat of a fiasco. Lord Westmeath conducted a personal search for Neilson in Counsellor Sampson's house, ransacking every room, including that of Mrs. Sampson just recently confined, Neilson, meanwhile, being engaged in his usual business at the Exchange. He and Russell gave themselves up voluntarily, Neilson observing " that a speedy trial was all that he wanted, and that he hoped however for the sake of the public sentiment and for peace, that he might not be, as many men of late had been, kept in gaol for a year without any trial at all ".[8] Poor Neilson, within a fortnight Habeas Corpus was suspended, neither he nor Russell had any trial at all and endured imprisonment for sixteen months and six years respectively.

Though the Belfast wits were quick to exploit the humorous aspects of Lord Westmeath's performance[9] this was a gravely portentous occurrence, and when the ten coaches accompanied by a strong escort of dragoons drove out of the town and, late on the following day, clattered through the streets of Dublin conveying the prisoners to Newgate Jail,* rumours were rife of invasion, plots and more arrests.

Mary Ann, at home in Rosemary Lane, sat down to write reassuringly to her brother John's wife, then at Moneymore, a small town near Dungannon :

> My Dear Mrs. John
>
> I recd yours last night & am sorry to hear of the illness of your head & eyes but beg you will wave all ceremony with me & never write to me when it is attended with the slightest pain or injury to yourself. As yet we have met with no misfortune, tho' numbers of people have been taken up here this family has escaped, & as you may always allow a great deal for exaggeration you should not suffer yourself to be alarmed by every idle rumour, you will be sorry to hear that your favourite Mr. Teeling is among the prisoners confined in the Donegall Arms, but I believe there is nothing against him—Your daughter Ann still continues improving & increasing in everybodys esteem and affection—I am glad to observe that energy appears to be the predominent feature in her character which I think is the firmest foundation to build on, and she has got a double tooth seemingly without either pain or sickness & will soon get another. You forget to say anything about your young son. I hope he is thriving well & that he may be as fine a child as Ann. John thinks he

*Some of them were shortly moved to Kilmainham.

will be handsomer and has a better mouth, however beauty is but a trifle, but at the same time a very agreeable trifle—

Wm. & Mrs. McCracken went [to] Ball[y]walter from Dunover where they had been for this fortnight past so I cant tell when she may want her little articles but think it probable alarming times may cause her to want them sooner than she should do, tho' we had a letter from Wm today in which he says she still continues very well—My Father seems to be recovering but very slowly the rest of the family are well & in tolerable spirits, they all join in affectionate regards with yours sincerely

M.A.McC.[10]

This is the earliest of Mary Ann's letters to come down to us. Its opening may sound a little stiff and formal, perhaps this was the first occasion on which the young wife had left the hospitable roof of her in-laws. Obviously a small daughter remained behind, and if the seemingly unflattering remarks about the baby's appearance were intended to console a young mother disappointed in the looks of her first-born, they also show that Mary's great admiration for Mary Wollstonecraft had already begun,—the emphasis on sturdiness and energy as opposed to insipid feminine charms might come straight from *The Vindication of the Rights of Women* published only four years earlier. The Joy background and David Manson's training had prepared an adventurous mind to assimilate new ideas. While Mary McCracken was by no means the only young woman in the town familiar with the writings of Rousseau, Godwin, Mrs. Barbauld, and the rest, her uniqueness lay in the fact that, to a far greater extent than any of her contemporaries, she translated these ideas, critically and selectively, from the realm of theory to the needs of her own surroundings. The process had already started, and it was to direct her thoughts and actions for the rest of her life. That others could be merely critical the following comment shows: Miss Jane Greg, a contemporary of Mary Ann's, on a visit to Bath at this time, writes to her friend Mrs. McTier an account of meeting Hannah More and her sisters, and, after mentioning the schools and other good works initiated by these illustrious ladies, witheringly adds that she found their "minds crippled in an astonishing degree".[11] But Jane Greg, critical and intelligent though she was, continued to live her life of luxury and idleness, whereas Mary McCracken was already practicising what even Mary Wollstonecraft could only hopefully suggest when she wrote that:

> Women might certainly study the art of healing and be physicians, as well as nurses . . . They might also study politics, and settle the benevolence on the broadest basis . . . Business of various kinds, they might likewise pursue, if they were educated in a more orderly manner.[12]

But for all her calmness and progressiveness Mary Ann must have been tortured with forebodings as she composed herself to write that letter. Harry was from home; Thomas Russell his bosom friend, Samuel Neilson his close associate and young Charles Teeling his fellow-worker among the Defenders in Armagh, had all been "taken-up"; how long could he himself escape? For some time he eluded his pursuers. The Sovereign himself, as chief magistrate, joined in the urgent search, writing as follows to Lord Downshire:

> I much fear that McCracken had some notice from Dublin or [from] here of the intended proceedings against him—Atkinson the high Constable, who lives opposite to McC's Father's house assured me he was not there. Mr. Skeffington, Mr. Brown and I agreed not to go to the house untill we were certain he had returned to it as that might defeat the whole business. I watched in Atkinson's house for five hours, and Atkinson watched the greatest part of the night. Mr. Skeffington and Mr. Brown patrolled the streets in hope of seeing him but he never appeared . . . As McCracken is frequently sent out on a mission to the country, perhaps he may return soon. I will have a watch upon him day and night and your Lordship may be assured he will certainly be apprehended unless he has already flew from justice.[13]

Two days later, on Oct. 10th 1796 how or where we know not, Henry Joy McCracken was arrested, taken to

Dublin, and lodged in Kilmainham Jail. From now onwards every stage in the bitter tragedy was shared by Mary Ann, every step taken on Harry's behalf was directed by her. The first thing to be done was to go up to Dublin to see him, difficult though it might be to gain admission. Immediately preparations were commenced for a journey which, in those days, could not be lightly undertaken. Neither Margaret nor Mary had travelled so far before, and it was agreed that John and Atty Bunting should accompany them, probably combining business with their duties as escorts; indeed, in spite of the anxiety that occasioned the visit, the sisters went armed with a large consignment of their muslins which they hoped to sell. It was November when they set off, making the journey by coach to Newry, and thence by the 'Flying Coach' to Dublin, twenty six hours' continuous travelling.[14]

Cousin Henry Joy, the Counsellor, had for some time been residing in the capital " in a very genteel well-furnished house ", in Temple Street.[15] After studying law for six years in London and Paris, and " not at all conceited though his friends had formed high expectations for him "[16]—he was building up an eminently respectable law connection in Dublin. His sisters Harriet and Grizzey lived with him, " two warm-hearted Belfast girls " Dr. Drennan found them, " much more for the French than their cousin Henry "[17] [Joy, jun.], but their brother was cautious and viewed these political doings of his relations with grave concern. Nevertheless, he made every effort to be as friendly as his legal mind would allow, and the earliest letters of this period of captivity were exchanged between the Harrys at Temple Street and Kilmainham Jail.

Dear Harry, (writes the Counsellor)

I arrived here late last night from Belfast where I left all your family well. Your sisters intend coming up in the course of this week to see you. Is there anything you wish for that I can supply you with. Let me know if there is. Inform me how you are that I may be able to assure your

MARY ANN McCRACKEN AND HER NIECE MARIA, *c.* 1801

friends that you are tolerably recovered from your indisposition.

Yours,
H. Joy.

Dublin
7th Nov.

Scrawled at the bottom is Harry's reply.

Dear Henry,
I am at present in excellent health but closely and indeed rigourously confined—denied the use of pen, ink, or paper or the consolation of any living creature, the keeper and turnkeys excepted, who find me everything I wish for. I much fear the girls will be denied admission.

Yours truly,
H.J.McC.[18]

2 o'clock Monday.

Probably Margaret and Mary Ann stayed with their cousins, and from the "genteel" house in Temple Street made their way out to the little village of Kilmainham, passing the recently completed Four Courts, the Phoenix Park, Swift's Hospital and the grounds of the Royal Hospital, from where, on a fateful day six years earlier Thomas Russell had sallied forth to attend a sitting of the House of Commons in College Green, and to meet, by accident, Theobald Wolfe Tone.

It is easy to reconstruct the scene. Kilmainham Jail stands now as it stood in November 1796, massive, gaunt and terribly forbidding. It was then a new building, considered modern and healthy and vastly preferable to Newgate in the heart of the city, where Russell was confined and where he was to remain for almost three years. As Mary Ann approached its formidable exterior, she could not foresee the succession of Irishmen for whom, as political prisoners, that great sinister door would open, creaking heavily on its hinges; nor could she know that a hundred and fifty years from that dreary autumn the one-time bastion of autocratic authority would be falling into disrepair, unused and unheeded. On the day that she and Margaret presented themselves at the gateway the place was bustling with activity. Whether it was due to the intervention of the Counsellor, the natural humanity of the guard, or the persistence of Mary Ann, we do not know, but, in spite of Harry's fears, the barriers went down before her, and, following the jailor along dark resounding passages, the sisters reached his cell.

To her dying day Mary would not forget that first experience of captivity. There was Harry in the bare, dark cell, the chill and dankness of it already penetrating his very bones, his golden hair and beaming smile now shining against the general gloom. No record has been left us of that meeting, but into its fleeting minutes family news, political information, plans and hopes must have been crowded; already there was the constant uncertainty as to when or where a trial would take place.

Margaret and Mary stayed in Dublin for several weeks. We do not know if they saw Harry again or if they were able to visit Thomas Russell at Newgate. No doubt John and Atty found pleasure in showing the girls the great sights of Dublin—then in the hey-day of its brilliance and wealth, and there was a large circle of Northern connections and sympathisers to entertain the visitors. Dr. Drennan called to see them, and expected to meet them at dinner at the house of Oliver Bond,[19] and without doubt they would meet Mr. Dixon and his family, "a rich Catholic tanner who lives near the Prison and has uniformly been most civil and hospitable to the Northern Friends".[20] But Mary Ann was in no mood to enjoy the distractions of sociability. Her mother sensed the worry, and sought to cheer her anxious daughter:

Dear Mary [she wrote on November 16th, 1796]

I wrote your sister the 14th but as I got a Frank I thought you would be glad to hear from us as often as possible. I was sorry to find by John's letter to his wife that you dont like Dublin tho' I was sure it would be the case, but I hoped your seeing Harry and that perhaps you might get some of your Muslins sold would partly reconcile you to it—there was five taken up yesterday and sent to Carrick on a bad woman's Oath—Joseph Cuthbert, Tom Storry . . . and O'Donnell Clarke and Tom Stewart and a sadler. This day there was a poor man in fever stole out of his house and went through this street calling out a Republick for Ireland and he was a Republican, he had a hankf tied about his head and as pale as Death. In a few minutes he had after him a great multitude of soldiers—when I looked out our window I saw a little Officer put his hand to his sword and [order] him to hold his tongue. They carried him to the Guard house when to their great mortification they found the man deranged of a fever. John does not mention anything about Mr. Bunting, indeed his letters are so short they are not satisfactory. Our friends here are all very attentive to me and I could do pretty well about your business if I had money to give the weavers and indeed they behave very well. I hope you will try to see as many places as you can while you are in Dublin, and tho' the times are not so pleasant as we could wish them I hope they will mend and I have found, what I thought to be distressing, turn out for good and we should always trust in Providence that can bring good out of evil. I saw Miss Templeton to-day, they are all much the way you left them. The Miss Tombs drank tea with us tonight. Poor Ellen Holmes is very ill they think its the measles. Pray let us hear from you, I thought when you left this I was to hear from you very often—All the family joins me in affectionate complements to our friends at Kilmainham and to you and John and Peggy and Mr. Bunting and am

Dear Mary your affectionate mother Ann McCracken.[21]

Far from reproaching her children for their political activities it is obvious that Mrs. McCracken gave them full support and sympathy, and knew about their friends and associates. She herself had been an ardent admirer of Thos. Paine until he turned his attacks to religion, and this letter bears evidence as well to her courage as to her strong, unshakable religious faith—the same that guided her father and was to be the enduring consolation of her daughter. With one son in prison, and the town seething with unrest, it would seem, indeed, an understatement to describe the times as " not so pleasant as we could wish." Already a prison ship was anchored in Belfast Lough and in that same week Mrs. McTier was writing that " a whole society of fifty-two United Irishmen were taken by 2 officers on Saturday night—10 from Coleraine were that day sent on board the tender marched thro' the streets handcuffed two and two together."[22]

It is interesting to note the reactions of the McCracken family to the city of Dublin. In one of his letters from Kilmainham commenting on the endless monotony of prison life Harry expresses the same disapproval :

> However, we contrive to pass the time as pleasantly as you can imagine considering that we think as little of the North as possible, for the comparison is nothing in favour of the Capital, except Mr. Dixen and family, who will always in every place be remembered with veneration by us, they are a set of Gasconaders, in every respect unlike Northerners.[23]

And Harry's knowledge of Dublin was not confined to his present situation, for he had been a frequent envoy to United circles in and around the capital. The Northerners went into this struggle with no sense of inferiority, nor with a country-cousin's awed adulation of the great metropolis and its inhabitants. Rather they looked upon themselves as the heralds and leaders of a new gospel, as indeed they were.

So began months of endless anxiety for the McCracken family. Harry was already suffering severely from rheumatism, though Dr. Stokes' " directions " were of great service.* Counsellor Joy continued his friendly help, sending in January, with a kind note of inquiry, a " pot of raspberries "—he was a keen gardener. Conditions improved, perhaps in part owing to the Counsellor's influence, and also to that quality in Harry which everywhere endeared him to his fellows. The jailor made arrangements for him to join a circulating library, and a ball alley was provided for exercise. The State prisoners were allowed to meet each other at intervals and were no longer confined in single cells.

*Dr. Whitley Stokes, Fellow of Trinity College and a United Irishman.

John arrived on a visit in March. Letters were received and sent as opportunity offered, though seldom committed to the mail, and even those entrusted to some reliable carrier had to be written with circumspection. But Harry was no great letter-writer, and besides, with all this frustration and uncertainty, what was there to write about?

> I have nothing to say, only to give my wishes of welfare to all friends. Saml., Chas., and Jas. send their love to you. I shall be more attentive in writing you next opportunity.[24]

And again:

> Being very bad at putting compliments into words and making use of terms of affection, tho' not quite destitute of regard for both friends and acquaintances, I request you will supply my neglect.

To which is added this postscript:

> N.B. My father and mother must not be understood in the above because it should always be understood that they are certainly the first in my affection.[25]

Meanwhile Napoleon Bonaparte was leading the French armies victoriously through Europe, and in the ports on the other side of the English Channel the fleets of France and her allies awaited their opportunity for invasion. The situation for England was becoming desperate: there were signs of disaffection at home; in April 1797 a section of the British navy mutinied at the Nore. Every precaution must be taken against trouble in Ireland; in March there was another round up of Northern insurgents when William McCracken was arrested and, with a batch of twenty or so Ulstermen, arrived in due course at Kilmainham. Mary Ann describes these happenings thus:

> April 13th 1797
>
> Dear Harry,
>
> I recd yours by J. Haffey, and have still to regret your

being so much hurried that your letters are neither so long or particular as we could desire. On Friday night last there was a search made in John Alexanders by Col. Barber, the high Constable etc. and a society of United Irishmen consisting of twenty-one members who were in the house at the time taken up, James Burnside and another weaver of Johns and one of ours were among them, and they are all confined in the Artillery barracks, fortunately for Alexander and his son they were not at home at the time and have kept out of the way since. Two boxes were broke open one of which belonged to Mr. McCabe and it is said there were some letters from Mr. Russell to him in it, and in the other there were five guineas which they also carried off with them, it is supposed Newell* the painter was the informer and that idea seems to be confirmed by what happened last night. John's family were knocked up about twelve o'clock and as soon as the door was opened the whole party rushed upstairs to J. Gordon's room (who has left John some time ago) they were conducted by a little man dressed as a cavalry officer with a handerchief tied across his mouth who everyone of the family instantly recognised to be Newell, having seen him there frequently with J. Gordon. He went directly to a hole in the floor under the bed which Gordon had showed him before, but fortunately there was nothing in it but a little hay. John invited them to search the rest of the house which they refused and would only examine the yard, and they looked above the cowhouse where had formerly been some guns, but found nothing. Jackson, who was tried along with Hart, and J. Haffey are both taken up, also Butcher another of Cuthbert's foremen, Kane and Templeton of the Star Office, together with many more whose names I dont know. Your old friend Owen Burn who had sworn against B. Coile was the man that was hanged at Omagh ten hours after he had committed a robbery. It is supposed that the prisoners here will be taken to Carrick tomorrow to be tried and I am happy to hear that all the United Irishmen in Derry have been acquitted.

Remember us as usual and believe me to be

Yours affectionately

Mary Ann McCracken.

*A notorious spy.

> A person called on Frank a few minutes ago to tell him that Wm was taken up, he was in a tavern with two others when that same little villain Newell came in disguised as he was last night and pointed him out, and familiarised as we now are to such incidents it would scarcely affect us were it not for the present situation of his wife. She does not yet know it and I do not know how she may bear it.[26]

The letters that passed between the brothers at Kilmainham and the family in Rosemary Lane are of special interest because of the scarcity of other similar records, and also because of the intimate picture they give of the various people concerned. Unfortunately the series is not complete for, while Mary Ann treasured for many years all that had been written to or by Harry, letters to William were obviously retained by his family. Likewise, none of Margaret's letters remain, for she seems to have written chiefly to William. Mary eventually gave her collection to Dr. Madden to assist him in writing his history of the United Irishmen. They now repose, with the rest of the Madden papers, in the Library of Trinity College, Dublin, and it is from them that these extracts are taken.

There is something peculiarly tender about original family letters, written with an assurance of understanding, perhaps with less care for style and content than others, and for that reason with more spontaneity and abandon. In this case, as one handles the very paper on which messages of rare poignancy, courage, integrity and affection were written, as one sees how the words were formed—sometimes so hurriedly to catch a chance messenger—and the pages folded, one is conscious of sharing in a human experience of unusual intensity. Each of the writers is portrayed as in a miniature. Firstly, William: kind and affectionate, always ready to give others the benefit of the doubt, and deeply in love with his young wife Rose Ann, whose health at the moment of his arrest was causing some anxiety. In the first letter written to his sisters after arriving at Kilmainham he begins:

> I wrote Rose Ann since I came here desiring her to take as much exercise as the weather would permit. I now beg of you to urge her to do it as I fear she may neglect it and I am fully persuaded it is necessary for her from being accustomed to long walks with me. Only two or three days before I was prised I heard Eliza Templeton ask if she would be able to walk to Orange Grove, as I know it is quite within her ability take her there and oblige me.[27]

And, a day or two later:

> I am greatly obliged to the Templetons, it is just acting in character for them to do acts of kindness.[28]

His letters are long and kindly and beautifully written, and always with an effort to be reassuring and cheerful:

> We grow daily better acquainted with the gaol and can bear the confinement with greater ease, indeed we are getting now and then a little more of the necessaries. The day before yesterday we got an additional stool to sit on which with the one we had before will allow six out of nine sitting at once, before we could only allow three to sit at a time and yesterday we got a very great comfort a wooden bowl to wash in. My watch makes an excellent substitute for a looking glass to shave myself at. We can now get stripping ourselves when we go to bed and I really think one is more refreshed than when obliged to lay down with their cloths on tho the sleep should continue equal in length of time. However there is still one thing that takes from the comfort that when the light of the morning comes we find we have more company than we either bargain or wish for, but this I suppose is inseparable from the beds and bedding of gaols and yet I believe we have been worse treated than any other prisoners on the same charge. The prisoners of the other yard blame us for not complaining enough, but they forget the great difference there is in situations, they can make themselves be heard at any time by the house and we are in so retired a place that we only see the girl twice a day (at breakfast and dinner) and perhaps the jailor or assistant once in two days. But as poor Richard says—its nothing when ones used to it. I never thought I could bear close confinement so well as I do, indeed I never felt anything for myself except the first time you come to see me in the Artillery

Barracks [in Belfast] when I must confess I was a good deal agitated. I dont believe even that should be placed to my account for I only felt so when you were present and some short time afterwards. If you had hapined to call the next day when Coulston was out you might have been as long as you pleased with me.

I am Dear Sisters
Your most affy
Wm McCracken.[29]

That William was making the best of a pretty bad job is evident from his next letter, this time to Mary :

I do not doubt but Father and any of the family might get to see me as John done yesterday, but everything about this place would appear to them so disagreeable that I would rather they should not unless we get removed to some other part of the jail that might appear more comfortable. Tho' the appearance might not be favourable yet we can make ourselves very snug. I mean this day to remove my bed to another cell where there is more room, we have choice of them and there is seven in this ward. We have ourselves divided into three in a cell so that we just occupy three at night and keep another, the largest, as a common hall . . . Give my love to all the family and to all friends. Tell them its only the separation from them that makes this place feelingly disagreeable.[30]

Not even galling prison routine could alter his gentle disposition : he writes to Margaret

I spent most of the forenoon with Henry yesterday and when Mrs. Rn. [wife of the jailor Richardson] came to take me away she let him come with me so that we were together all the day, indeed I think that even these people might be brought to do a kind action ; I dont know if it would be a good way to make this woman a present of half a piece of muslin, it might get us indulgences of this kind, which I need not assure you is a great treat, if you think with me send it to me and assist Rose Ann to chuse me a light waistcoat, I can get it made here. I dont believe I wrote her this day but will tomorrow.

I am dear Margt
most affecty
Wm. McCracken.

We have heard there are to be a great number of Orangemen in Belfast the 12th. God send they may do no harm. I feel greatly for you all till I hear from you afterwards.*[31]

Two days later he wrote to Mary Ann, telling her among other things of a visit from Counsellor Joy, who brought with him the cousins George and James Joy and little Robert Holmes :

The Counsellor only got up to see me, but I took the oppy of the door being opened to let the Counsellor out to run out to the hall just to shake hands with them . . . I'm sure it is a great blessing to Henry and I to hear in every letter that our Father and Mother continue in good health and spirits, it is only what may hapen to you that are at home that can have any . . . You have a queer idea of monoply when you blame me with it respecting Rose, from what you say of her you must acknowledge that I did not pay her more attention than she deserved, you can't say that I did not wish her to be perfectly acquainted with you, I was convinced you would like each other when you were. Write to me how John was when you last heard from him. I had long and disagreeable dreams about him last night, among other things I thought J. Ramsey's house was on fire and like to communicate with his but for Harry and I that got it extinguished.[33]

Obviously Rose Ann and her in-laws were getting on successfully together, a fact which brought happiness to Kilmainham.

As the months went by it was Rose Ann's turn to be anxious for her husband's health. There was the constant fear of fever in the prison, and William had not been well. On the back of one of Mary's letters to Harry this little note is written in Rose Ann's clear hand :

As William will not answer my letters I am now going to try what success I have with you, but there is great excuse to be made for you as your rheumatism is not quite gone, if you are not very ill with it when you receive

*First public procession of Orangemen in Belfast, 7,000 marched. Genl. Lake was present, going on to another demonstration in Lurgan where 12,000 are said to have paraded.[32]

this you will much oblige me by writing a few lines by return of post, as I fear that William is not well, if he is I think him very unkind, he never was so long before without writing me but the time he was ill, if you are not able to write yourself Mrs. Richardson will take the trouble of writing me a few lines. If I was sure that you and he were both well I would not be so uneasy as I am at present. We shall have the pleasure of seeing you as we intend leaving this for Dublin next week. Your friends here are all well. Miss Mary will tell you all the news. . . .[34]

The purpose of the visit to Dublin will later be told. When Rose Ann saw her William she could not leave him, and remained with him in the prison till his release.

We spend our time [she wrote from Kilmainham] much in the old way, we walk a little, read some and in the evening play cards. We contrive to make the day pass tolerably well considering all things. Remember me in the most affectionate manner to all the family my dear Miss Mary, and believe me to be yours affectionately[35]

R. A. McCracken.

An odd little touch of formality !

There is but one letter from John and it is written to Harry. He was, on the other hand, the most frequent visitor to Kilmainham, no doubt his visits coincided with journeys to Dublin on business. This letter opens with what must be a fairly authentic account of an instance of all too frequent brutality :

Belfast. 26th July, 1797.

Dear Harry,

I am sorry to hear that your health has been worse than usual, and that some late occurrances have rendered your present situation rather more unpleasant than even confinement in gaol ought to make it.* However, I hope you will come to a right understanding again, and not afford a subject for rejoicing to your enemies. For this some time past I have been loitering my time at Moneymore, where an opportunity of writing to you was not to be found, and I had nothing to tell you of except the barbarities committed on the innocent country people by the yeomen and Orange-

*These will be mentioned later.

men. The practice among them is to hang a man up by the heels with a rope full of twist, by which means the sufferer whirls round like a bird roasting at the fire, during which he is lashed with belts, etc., to make him tell where he has concealed arms. Last week, at a place near Dungannon, a young man being used in this manner called to his father for assistance, who being inflamed at the sight struck one of the party a desperate blow with his turf spade; but, alas! his life paid the forfeit of his rashness; his entrails were torn out and exposed on a thorn bush.

This is one barbarity of the many which are daily practised about the county Tyrone and Armagh; however, the county Antrim is not so bad, but I believe is not much better. . . .

Then follows a long and rather detached description of a ferocious clash not far from Moneymore between Orangemen and yeomanry on the one side, and the Kerry militia on the other. Such brutalities were all too common between the various factions and give a gruesome picture of the terror that prevailed. Civil war is always brutal, and men on every side were driven by fear and mistrust to acts of fearful cruelty, though in this respect the North suffered less than some other parts of the country. John's letter concludes thus:

As I am making a settlement of my books I wish you would send me the Book and Accounts I gave you the last time but one that I was in Dublin, do not forget it the first opportunity, give my respects to Lieutenant Burnside and the remainder of your companions and believe me to be Dear Harry

Your affc. Brother
J. McC. Jun.[36]

Is this a rather ironical reference to poor James Burnside, one of the most trusted of the McCrackens' weavers whose devotion to Harry's cause had recently landed him in Kilmainham? John could not bear the seriousness of these political ventures, their toll in all that he cared for was too high; so he pushed them from him and turned with relief to his ledgers and his accounts.

There are, as has been said, no letters from Margaret—Harry's belong to the next chapter.

CHAPTER IX

KILMAINHAM

Part II

It is however with Mary Ann herself that we are chiefly concerned, and in this correspondence she suddenly bursts upon us in the full blaze of maturity. Hitherto it has been necessary to sketch in somewhat lightly, against the known background, the almost unknown figure of the young woman. Now she confidently steps out of obscurity, mistress of herself and of every situation.

And here is the first of her letters to Kilmainham, or, more correctly, the first that has been preserved :

March 16th '97.

Dear Harry

Since I wrote last I could find but another opportunity, and not liking the mode of conveyance did not take advantage of it, you are not therefore to suppose, that the silence of your friends is owing Either to indifference or neglect but merely to want of opportunities. We were very uneasy about you for some time but are happy to find by the accounts that you are getting better. John is just arrived and delights us all by the agreeable intelligence he brings us of your mended health. There cannot be more extraordinary Revolutions in Politics than what have taken place of late in the minds of many people here—a Ci-Devant Major of the Belfast Volunteers and a Cousin of our own told Frank last night that a friend had shewed him the United Irishman's test, that he approved highly of it, and would not have the least objection to take it, as he had done more violent things often before. Whether this is the effect of fear or conviction I shall not pretend to determine, but it is very evident that since the people have appeared to be the strongest party their cause has gained many friends, some of them I suppose from conviction . . . A certain article which was the only cause of uneasiness to you at the time you were taken up, was concealed in the house till the late strict search which has been made about town, and not daring to keep it any longer, we gave it in charge to a man in whom we had confidence, who buried it in the Country, so that its being found can't injure any person. The black men have been visiting some houses in town last night and, taking arms out of them, and it is generally thought, that ere long we will be out of the King's peace, the General here says that he will put us under martial law directly. There were six prisoners brot to Town this evening, for refusing to swear allegiance and came undismay'd singing Erin go Brath. It would equally please and surprise Mr. Russel to hear that a certain Botanical friend of ours* whose steady and inflexible mind is invulnerable to any other weapon but reason, and only to be moved by conviction has at last turned his attention from the vegetable kingdom to the human species and after pondering the matter for some months, is at last determined to become what he ought to have been long ago, Frank proposed him at the last meeting of the society, and I hope his sisters will soon follow so good an example. I am glad John is come home for more reasons than one, John Gordon did not behave as well as possible while he was away endeavouring to frighten Mrs. McCracken, by telling her, that he would make John suffer when the revolution would commence and always praising McIlveen at John's expense, but what was still worse, he beat the servant maid one night when Mrs. McC. was in our house, and hurt her so much that she had to be bled and was very ill for several days. I mention this as I understand he is high in confidence.

I have a great curiosity to visit some female societies in this Town (though I should like them better were they promiscuous, as there can be no other reason for having them separate but keeping the women in the dark and certainly it is equally ungenerous and uncandid to make tools of them without confiding in them.) I wish to know if they have any rational ideas of liberty and equality for themselves or whether they are contented with their present abject and dependent situation, degraded by custom and education beneath the rank in society in which they were originally placed ; for if we suppose woman was created for a companion for man she must of course be his equal in understanding, as without equality of mind there can be no friendship and without friendship there can be no happiness

*John Templeton.

in society. If indeed we were to reason from analogy we would rather be inclined to suppose that woman were destined for superior understandings, their bodies being more delicately framed and less fit for labour than that of man does it not naturally follow that they were more peculiarly intended for study and retirement, as to any necessary connection between strength of mind and strength of body, a little examination will soon overturn that idea, I have only to place the McCombs, Val Joice and our worthy Sovereign opposite to Mr. O'Connor Mr. Tone and our dear departed Friend Dr. Bell (three little men possessing much genius) to show the futility of such an arguments. But to return, is it not almost time for the clouds of error and prejudice to disperse and that the female part of the Creation as well as the male should throw off the fetters with which they have been so long mentally bound and conscious of the dignity and importance of their nature rise to the situation for which they were designed, as great events at least display if they do not create great abilities I hope the present Era will produce some women of sufficient talents to inspire the rest with a genuine love of Liberty and just sense of her value without which their efforts will be impotent and unavailing, their enthusiasm momentary as a glittering bubble which bursts, while it rises, and as every discarded affection leaves a damp and melancholy void in the mind where it has been once entertained, so those who are flaming for liberty today with out understanding it (for where it is understood it must be desired as without Liberty we can neither possess virtue or happiness) may perhaps tomorrow endeavour to damp the ardour and cool the courage of others when they begin to reflect on the danger which they incur and the little advantage which they derive from it. I do not hold out the motive of interest as an inducement for man to be just, as I think the reign of prejudice is nearly at an end, and that the truth and justice of our cause alone is sufficient to support it, as there can be no argument produced in favour of the slavery of woman that has not been used in favour of general slavery and which have been successfully combatted by many able writers. I therefore hope it is reserved for the Irish nation to strike out something new and to shew an example of candour generosity and justice superior to any that have gone before them—as it is about two o'clock in the morning I have only time to bid you good-night—

Believe me
Yours affectionately
Mary.

This spontaneous flow of thought illustrates not only her own constructive mind, but her unquestioning confidence in the sympathy she would evoke from Harry. There she sat, the house all quiet, the quill pen travelling frantically over the paper, the writer pausing neither to draw breath nor to put in stops, till, as the candle flickered in its socket, she realised with a start the lateness of the hour. When in the cool light of the later morning she re-read her letter nothing was deleted and three postscripts were added; the second containing one of her rare but glowing compliments to Harry:

> Do not forget to remember us affecty [to Messrs.] Neilson, Barkly and Teeling—
>
> As much of what I have written would [appear] to be mere bombast or fanciful speculations to those who are under the influence of common prejudices it is not to such I write, but to one whom I suppose to be capable of forming an opinion from his own experience without consulting the stupid multitude of common thinkers—
>
> Do not neglect the use of your french dictionary and grammar—John Templeton keeps his always either in his hand or in his pocket.[1]

No need now for speculation: what more illuminating picture of a remarkable young woman could have been left us? This is Mary Ann McCracken, aged twenty-six years. Here is her interest in politics, in the affairs of the town—here are her friendships and her severe criticisms—here her passion for education, and her intense ardour for equality of opportunity for women, which singled her out from her more notable contemporaries, and which, while she was never merely a feminist, places her in the vanguard of the modern movement for the emancipation of women. In one respect at any rate her great wish for the Irish nation was fulfilled, for of all universities that of Dublin was the first to confer its degrees on women.

In order to appraise her rightly one must always have in mind the background against which these years were set. The general dislocation of trade was being acutely felt in Belfast, the town was riddled with spies, in the very month in which this letter was written General Lake had issued his proclamation calling for the surrender of arms, and Mary herself describes the beginnings of those house-to-house searches when no dwelling was safe from the invasion of the military, or of marauders arriving with blackened faces to take from the terrified inhabitants anything they could get. Though the comment in the *Northern Star* that, with so many citizens of distinguished integrity and honour being taken up, " it looks as if the felons alone were to remain outside of the gaols "[2] may have been an exaggeration, many were certainly held on the flimsiest pretexts and without hope of trial. People continued to fly from the town, others to seek refuge in Belfast from the country districts and, in the general consternation resulting from Hoche's attempted landing at Bantry Bay, recruiting for the regiments of yeomanry was accelerated by the Government. At the same time the pretence of normal life went on. Coteries met, dances were held, and General Lake and his officers were welcomed at both.[3] " Slimming " was the general rage, and one bright young thing going to a Ball " with one thin petticoat " caught such a cold that she had to keep to her room " with a blister which discharged so well as to give great hopes from its effects."[4]

Incidentally, the foregoing letter raises one important question : was Mary Ann herself a United Irishwoman ? Societies for women had certainly been formed[5] most likely with the object of collecting funds and providing comforts, and also of restraining the tongues and quickening the ears of members. Rose Ann, probably before her marriage, was a sworn member, and was engaged from time to time in carrying secret messages[6]; here we have Mary Ann hoping that the Templeton girls would follow the good example of their brother ; and it was out of keeping with her character for her to expect others to undertake responsibilities which she would not shoulder herself. Still, it is clear from the letter that the " female societies " were as yet unknown to her, and there is no indication in this correspondence or anywhere else that she ever joined one of them, in fact one is strongly inclined to assume that she did not.

Meanwhile she had much else to occupy her mind. In the first place she and Margaret continued their muslin business in spite of increasing difficulties, for, in addition to the general dislocation, their weavers were being arrested, and there was the practical difficulty of securing enough cash for wages. In England the financial situation had become so strained by the enormous cost of the war that the Bank of England was only saved from bankruptcy by the passing, in a single night, of a bill suspending payments in cash and making bank notes legal tender for any amount. Similar action was taken in Dublin, with the result that in Belfast, as elsewhere, cash was very hard to come by. Old Mrs. Drennan, for example, anxious for change " produced two ten guinea notes and in a great hurry sent them to the Bank for guineas but to her great dismay none would be paid."[7] Still, fashion demanded muslin, plain and embroidered, for the high-waisted dresses and the gentlemen's cravats. " Very, very white Muslin and Charity Sermons are the rage here " writes Mrs. McTier from Dublin, and Dr. Drennan " bought six cravats of *very* white muslin at Mrs. Hinck's yesterday for which I paid two guineas."[8]

The difficulties of the situation spurred the sisters to fresh efforts, for, with characteristic consideration for their workers, they determined to keep their business going.

> I was very much pleased [wrote William to Margaret] to find by your letter that you could keep your people together in such times as these. I know it is more for their good than any profit you can have that makes you continue the business.[9]

Immediately after his arrest he had sent them instructions regarding the work to be carried on in his own factory:

> I forgot when writing to Frank that I wished him to buy a bale of Surat cotton for the outspinners to be carded on the small machine, keeping her in good order by taking cards off the others as she may want them. John will take the woof so made and will have a saving of 3% a lb. from the price he pays Boomer and will leave me a trifling profit which, however small, will help to pay the rent, there are three pieces of fustian ready for finishing desire for to get them done and Orr will give the price he is getting the same quality for, the Amt with the ballce [which] will be got from Sedgewick will pay my workers demands and leave something for Rose Ann, which I think she will want.[10]

Obviously Margaret and Mary were well acquainted with the workings of William's mill and his up-to-date machinery. When one considers the experience and practical ability involved in such transactions one is struck by the contrast between the McCracken sisters and, for example, Mrs. Gaskell's *Cranford* ladies, or poor Fanny Burney enduring her dull existence at the Court of George III. Others besides the McCracken sisters were engaged in trade. Rose Ann, writing to Mary from Kilmainham, refers to some transactions over calico:

> I do not recollect saying that any person was in my debt for Calico, if I did I was wrong, 13 or 14s would be too little, I could get that for them when brown. As I am quit[e] out of the way of knowing the price of almost anything your brother John will tell you what you should ask.[11]

Indeed in every respect there was a robustness and independence about Belfast women at the close of the eighteenth century that was quite unknown to their Victorian granddaughters.

Spinning and weaving were fast evolving from a cottage craft to an industrial undertaking. Whereas, in the case of linen, the flax was frequently grown in the neighbourhood where it was spun into yarn and woven into cloth by members of the same family working in their own time, and according to the routine of rural life; with cotton, not only had the raw material to be imported, but the new machinery, installed in factories, was swiftly ousting the hand spinner and weaver, so that the workers must needs go to the machines. Thus it was that factory workers became employees in a sense never applicable to the traditional workers in flax. Margaret and Mary Ann were intimately connected with this evolution.

To Mary Ann the increasing possibilities of mechanical substitutes for human labour were fascinatingly attractive—as far as that went she had been born at the right moment. The swift development of machinery at the close of the 18th century must have held for adventurously minded people of that day something of the same magical spell as does the prospect of automation and atomic power in ours, and the choice to use it for good or ill confronted them also. Though no one worked harder than Mary herself, she could not tolerate the endless drudgery which so generally provided the only means by which the poor could earn enough to keep body and soul together. How could they ever improve their situation, she would ask, if there was no time or energy left for leisure or education? The new machinery would give them both. No one would have appreciated more than Mary the domestic labour-saving devices of the twentieth century—dreary housework had no appeal for her, and in one of her letters to Kilmainham she suggests to Harry that he should utilise his time by developing his taste for mechanics:

> There are two subjects that have always made me wish for knowledge in that useful science. Would it not be possible to contrive some useful machinery to supply the use of horses and servants, at least it would be worth the labour of many years to try some experiments to that purpose.[12]

It may have been a half fanciful suggestion, conceived perhaps during that long journey to Dublin, when the recollection of David Manson's Flying Chariot flashed on her mind. Always a lover of animals, she longed that something might be done to mitigate the thrashing and straining that travelling by stage coach involved ; and—as for household drudgery !—there was everything to be said for the invention of some kind of a " mechanical Jane."

But the weavers themselves were her paramount concern. Uncle Robert had introduced the spinning and weaving of cotton in order to give employment, and it was, as had been said, largely with that end in view that his nieces carried on their business. From those early days when, with her mother, Mary had called in at the Poorhouse on the way to their garden, she had from one source or another been closely acquainted with the ever recurring nightmare of unemployment, and the struggles of the poor to earn their bread. Work was the first essential if people were to secure for themselves food and shelter, and subsequently the leisure for education and freedom. Whether she knew it or not, she was grappling in her thinking with the problem which was then beginning to isolate the North-east corner from the rest of Ireland, namely the impact of modern industrialism on an agricultural economy. The disabilities endured by the labouring classes were intolerable to her. It is noticeable that while her more famous contemporary in philanthropy Hannah More accepted in fact, as well as in speech, the current phrase " the lower orders " the term was never used by Mary McCracken. But then, Mary Ann was never merely the philanthropist ; she did not want, primarily, to do good to people, but rather to insure that they would have the means to achieve good for themselves. Though she did not call it by a name, what she and Harry cared about, and Thomas Russell too, was the dignity of human personality, the assurance of basic human rights. They were the advance party of the nineteenth century social revolutionaries, blazing a trail along quite new paths. Tragically, the only tools they could find to clear the undergrowth, and blast away the obstacles that confronted them, were the pikes and other paraphernalia of a political struggle.

There it was—and so these letters are full of concern

for weavers and other humble people caught up in the conflagration, though at the same time any who failed in their duty, whatever it might be, did not escape the condemnation of this exacting young woman.

As well as the muslin there was the Irish music. As we have seen, it was in the McCracken home and during this period of turmoil that Bunting's work progressed; from there he came and went on his trips to London, Dublin and the distant parts of Ireland, and it was now in this very year that his first collection was published. In August 1797 he had gone to London, and, in spite of having "promised positively" to write, no news had been received. Mary, always anxious about Atty when he went off on his own, confessed to Harry that

> We dont know how to make inquiry, as writing to strangers in London about him wd. be placing him in such an awkward situation and hurt his feelings very much.

Before the letter was despatched to Kilmainham, however, word had come from the traveller and the news that

> the Irish Music is complete all but the Title Page, and he has the prospect of making a great deal of money by them, this will [please him] as much as it does us.[13]

A month or two afterwards Atty, having returned from London, set off with John for a few days at Magilligan—probably to tell old Denis Hempson the great news that the first collection of the harpers' airs had been launched. "I wish much" wrote Harry from his prison cell "that I could have been with them."

In addition to these various interests there were the obligations and pleasures of family and friends. Continual anxiety meant a heavy strain on the health of the parents, and there are references in the letters at different times to the illness of Captain McCracken, now well advanced in years.

Francis it would appear was in constant danger, and from time to time left home for greater safety.

> Is Frank out of the way ? [asks Harry.] I have heard so and it has vexed me a good deal but perhaps it is best so.[14]

Later there is this in a letter from William :

> In all the letters I have received I have never got a sentence or word of information how Frank comes on, tho' the very first letter I wrote when I came here was to him. If I thought he was out of the way I would be very anxious to get out on bail, that I might fill his place in some manner the best I could. As yet I have always desired that Counsellor Joy should not urge it and when ever I see you (if that's to happen) I will convince you I was right.[15]

The children of Henry and Robert Joy were, in the main, constitutionalists—but such differences of opinion did not interfere with cousinly affection. Ellen, who as a child had helped her father to " correct the press " was now Mrs. Tomb, mother of a grown-up family, and between her eldest daughter Barbara and Mary Ann there was a life-long friendship. The only one in the connection who seems to have found it somewhat difficult to maintain the friendly intimacy was Henry Joy, jun.—political differences cut very deep with him.

Outside the circle of relations there were other friends, but none so near and close as the Templetons of Orange Grove. The name occurs constantly in the letters to and from Kilmainham, for the friendship between the families went back to childhood days in High Street, and more recently there had been the happy gatherings of young people in the country house at Malone. To Mary the family was especially dear, and Eliza Templeton the friend to whom, through all her life, she flew for consolation and support. The companionship of the brother John was also a source of infinite pleasure. Mary shared with Thomas Russell an amateur's enthusiasm for the natural sciences, and the two of them would listen to John Templeton's dissertations on botany, zoology or geology with deep enjoyment. Together they watched him lay out his lovely gardens with rare trees, shrubs and flowers : Orange Grove must have been the scene of many of Mary's happiest moments. No wonder she records with delight when John Templeton joined a society of United Irishmen. There is a revealing reference to the family in one of Harry's letters : Mary had been staying at Orange Grove, presumably because of the death of an aged aunt who had made the place her home, " I suppose " writes Harry to Margaret, " Mary is returned from Orange Grove as I am sure the Templetons have more sense than to require much condolence."

But overshadowing all her other interests and responsibilities was Mary's care and anxiety for Harry himself. Instinctively she knew how his active nature would rebel against the restriction of prison life. If the more gentle and placid William could adapt himself in some measure to the strange conditions of captivity, Harry's spirit was outraged at every turn. He, who depended so much on contact with his fellow-men, whose energy and enthusiasm was fed by the devotion and loyalty unconsciously demanded and so generously given, how could he endure the bitter loneliness and the cruel frustration of a jail ?

At the outset he made a valiant effort to accept the inevitable :

Kilmainham.
19th Jany 1797.

Dear Sisters

I take the opportunity of writting to you by our very good friend Mrs. Neilson, who can tell you our situation better than it is possible for me to describe, indeed there can be verry little variety of incident in a Jail, one day must be an almost perfect picture of an age where we are shut out from the World. The only variety that may arise here must be in our own ideas, and that of each other, or our visitors, however, we contrive to pass the time as pleasantly as possible . . . The other day I wrote Frank by Jas. Haffey . . . since then I have been informed that the two men who swore against T. Richardson and I have been sent on board a Tender. I suppose, or rather I was confidently informed, that Govt despaired of their evidence being worth anything as they had already perjured themselves by diserting and no County Antrim Jury would listen to them. When I wrote

> Frank I was just wakened out of a good sleep to write, as Haffey was just setting off, and had hardly time to open my eyes untill he must go, so I suppose very little sense could be made of it, as I can scarcely recollect one word of it. . . .[16]

With excessive enthusiasm he threw himself into such pastimes as were available :

> The fatigue of Ball playing has made me incapable of writting you very correctly.[17]

> We are all well and get the use of a yard and play ball from morn till night.[18]

How well Mary knew the force of his " restless activity."

The deep affection between these two was based on the pursuit of an identical ideal by complementary methods ; each had for the other that degree of diversity that impels attraction. To Harry had been given all the genius of a leader—in this respect he was entirely his father's son. He loved his fellowmen, all of them, and was loved by them ; but his passion to redress the wrongs of the down-trodden and unfortunate left little time to enjoy the friendship of his equals. With none of his grandfather Joy's " reasonableness " he was, as each situation arose, instinctively aware of what he must do, and, without counting any cost or listening to any reason, he swept on to action.

Mary, on the other hand, followed the same ideal primarily by way of the intellect—though mercifully no labels can wholly delineate the facets of human personality ; indeed she herself records that " deeply contemplative character " which Harry later developed, and when in her own case, and it so often happened, her emotions were stirred she was driven forward by the impulse of two impelling powers. She was, as far as any human being could be, completely in Harry's confidence with regard to his political activities. She knew all the people of consequence in the movement, she was aware of his tireless work for the Defenders in Armagh, and had accepted the prospect of armed rebellion as inevitable.

She was perfectly familiar with guns and pikes and the hiding places of arms, with the wretched business of espionage and the lowest levels of intrigue. Nothing daunted her, as Harry knew well, and her ardent spirit and sympathetic insight radiating through every letter, must have been balm to his tortured soul, as he fretted himself ill in Kilmainham.

26. 3. 97.

Dear Harry (she wrote)

The intelligence contained in yr. letter to John fills us with a variety of contradictory sensations, hopes and fears, pleasure and anxiety alternatively take possession of our minds and render us most restlessly impatient, not that we wd. feel the slightest degree of uneasyness if Law and Justice were synonimous terms, or if even our present laws, bad as they are, were to be administered with candour and impartiality, but our oppressors are so atrociously wicked that there is no enormity of wh. they do not seem capable, & may perhaps have recourse to private if public means should fail However they can go no farther than they are permitted and who can tell how short their reign may be, as all things are under the direction of a Being infinitely wise & powerful who can bring good out of evil & who orders all things for the best (however they may appear to our finite comprehension). Let us not be terrified or dismayed, but repose with unlimited confidence where we can never be deceived. If the compleat Union of Ireland should demand the blood of some of her best Patriots to cement, if they will not sink . . . their duty, but meet their fate equally unappalled, whether it be on the scaffold or in the field convinced that in the end the cause of Union* and of truth must prevail and that happiness flowing from Liberty and Peace will ultimately bless the united efforts of their country.

Every act of coercion on the part of government like the effect of pressure on the arch serves but to bind the . . . more firmly together & render them an example of wisdom & moderation worthy the imitation of all future generations. Do you think we may look for the same degree of patience & forbearance from them in prosperity wh. they

*It should be noted that this word is frequently used before 1800 to denote the union of all Irishmen in Ireland.

have shown in adversity? I fear not, the unexampled inhumanity and repeated irritation they have experienced will I fear instigate them to revenge & render it difficult to restrain them from returning with interest the evils they have so far endured.

Your friends here think you ought to employ Counsellor Joy both on account of his relationship & of his attention to you (I am sorry John was so very difficient as never to call on him when last in Dublin) things are now come to such a crisis that it cannot injure the Counsellor to undertake your cause, but would rather be of use to him, which is an additional reason why you should retain him.

The Bundle of clothes that were sent you contain a new pair of blankets an old under one a pillow and quilt lined with diaper, 2 pillow cases one bolster case one pair pantalons & a pair of red slippers—You would do well to have your bed & the other furniture packed up & sent to some friends to be forwarded . . . as you will require to get every accommodation of that sort in Carrick—do not forget the French dictionary, syntax and grammar, all which are very necessary at present as almost everybody in Belfast are learning French. Remember us as usual & believe me to be yours affectionately

Mary.

On the back of this letter is noted in her own handwriting:

Belfast—1797 M. A. McCracken to H. J. McCracken in Kilmainham in expectation of his being sent to Carrickfergus & full of moralising and praise of the Irish man perhaps . . . deserved.[19]

Some weeks later Mary writes again, following up her letter about Col. Barber's raid [see p. 125].

April 18th 1797.

Dear Harry,

I recd yours of the 8th by J. Haffey yesterday, but have still to regret your being so much pressed in point of time, that your letters are never as long or particular as we could desire, however you are not more deficient in that respect than some of your fellow prisoners are, who might as well as you understand economy better than to send a sheet of paper with a doz. lines written, when you must have time enough to spare. Col Barber has been very busy all day searching for the cannons at the flour mills, Armstrong's and Cotton Valley, and I am sorry to tell you he has had much success as to find the spunges, carriages and boxes. Lamont the Miller is also taken prisoner, and threatened with being sent on board the Tender if he does not discover where the cannons are. A strong guard is placed on the flour mills (where the spunges were found) and another at Armstrong's, it is supposed that information had been given by one Wilson (apprentice to Spotswood the baker) as they went directly to the place. It is not a trifling degree of pleasure you will feel on hearing that all the prisoners at Armagh of the right sort have been acquitted, that the Judges are behaving extremely well and have taken up the High Sheriff and Obins a magistrate who snapped a pistol at a man for refusing to take a national note. Sparrow, another magistrate who behaved equally well, you may remember, at the wake of the man who was butchered at Market hill, I am happy to find is also lodged securely in a house that is not his own*—a gentleman who has just come through the County Monaghan says that he literally travelled through fire, as the whole country seemed in a blaze, with the bonfires on account of the universal acquittals for sedition etc. Skeffington† received an annoymous letter today which has alarmed him a good deal. I am told that it was elegantly written and that it informed him if he intended to pack a jury his own life should pay the forfeit of the blood that would be shed. What effect this may have will soon be known, it was generally thought that none of the Belfast people would be called on the juries as an hundred and fifty of Lord Hertford's tenants were summoned, and only a few good people from this town by way of a cloak. James Joy has really resigned his commission in the Yeomen in consequence of their having refused to obey him as their officer, one of them came to parade with a piece ot orange ribbon in his breast for which our friend turned him out of the ranks, having forbid it before, on this about twenty of them turned out, and declared if he was not allowed to fall into the ranks neither would they, they surrounded James &

*A reference to imprisonment.

†Magistrate in Belfast.

damned him if he had any croppy* blood in his veins, what business had he among them, and one declared if he thought there was one drop of croppy blood in his own arm he would cut it off. There has certainly a most astonishing change taken place among our relations, within a short time past they are all grown quite moderate, and it is but a few days ago that the girls were praising Mr. Erskine's pamphlet and said that it was the first thing which began to convince them. But their brother† is come down and he is convinced also that the present administration are deserving of the utmost contempt, and that a reform must and will be had, is not that a change for you. I am sorry to hear from your letter to John by J. Hughes, whom we have not yet seen, that you are still kept such close prisoners, especially as there is no prospect of your being brought to trial. However all is for the best and repining is useless. I suppose you have heard that the nine men who were so long in the Artillery barrack are at last sent on board the Tender, it would be well if the whole fleet were manned with such as them, it would stand us in stead. The hand-cuffs were not taken off untill they were just going into the boat, and they are now quite glad of the change, their situation is so much better than it was—remember me to Messrs Neilson, Teeling, Barkley and believe me to be

Yours affectly

Mary.[20]

The next letter is six weeks later.

Belfast. 2nd June 1797.

Dear Harry,

Your almost continual neglect of availing yourself of any opportunity that occurs of writing to your friends in Belfast is enough to make us suppose you have by this time entirely forgot them or that if you do think of them sometimes it must be with indifference. Three letters came to hand to-day from Wm by R.S. and not a line from you. I am glad to hear you are so well and in such good spirits which I hope will continue as I fear your enlargement is not so near at hand as we hoped some time ago. There appears to be a general (tho not universal) depression of the public spirit & what is still worse Belfast has greatly

*Rebel.

†Counsellor Joy.

lost the confidence of the country, from being prudent and cautious on a matter of great importance which some violent and impatient men have been induced to consider a disertion of their cause. Some however think this a mere pretence to excuse their own visible timidity or that it is owing to the diabolical suggestions of some Traitors, but be it from what cause it may it is certainly very vexatious. However Frank thinks it will be but temporary and that a little time will show their error. Those who endeavour to serve the public ought always to have some better motive than love of Fame (the only incentive of ancient heros) which is so precarious that the same man the public would exalt to the skies today, they would perhaps tomorrow transfer to the dust. Though not in the least inclined to superstition yet the lingering situation of affairs frequently reminds me of an old prophecy which Dr. McD told us of in winter, which said that the disturbances in this country were to begin between the scythe and the sickle, the hay harvest is already begun here. It is a great pity the people did not always keep in mind that they should never do evil that good may come of it and that what is morally wrong can never be politically right. Have you not observed that since the assassinations began the cause of the people (which had before been rapidly gaining ground) has gradually declined and after the general swearing it has been still worse and tho' this does not appear to be the direct cause yet perhaps it may be in part ascribed to it [for] when we once deviate from the straight [path] of rectitude it is difficult to return and . . . virtue is the only sure support of public . . . Frank has some notion of going to Dublin [in the next] few days but is not yet quite determined it does not depend altogether on himself. John is at Moneymore with his family, he has [been] only a fortnight in Belfast since he was in Dublin. This goes by George Joy who is going from home partly, I believe, from a desire of changing the scene for the recovery of his spirits after his daughter's death, he is to be accompanied by his brother James and little Robert Holmes. Your old friend George Dunbar is returned from London and gives a great acc^{t} of English loyalty. A packet of letters was dropped yesterday by a gentleman on his road to Dublin which unfortunately came into Whinnery's hands, however there were none from any of this family in it. . . .[21]

The letters from Harry are still too infrequent to satisfy the anxious Mary Ann. To her it was ever a relief to give vent to her emotions by letter writing ; to Harry the pen brought no such outlet, his letters are poor and his spelling careless. Sometimes he may have wondered if she realised at all the dreadful numbing monotony of prison life, where, as he had told her, " there can be verry little variety of incident in a Jail." She realised it better than he knew, and her craving for news represented her constant desire to know that the temptations of captivity were being withstood.

The feeling against Belfast to which Mary refers may have been due to the wish among leaders elsewhere for immediate insurrection, and she was probably right in her conjecture that the conflicting opinions were being played off against each other by the Castle spies. Dr. McDonnell's old prophecy regarding the time of year at which the rising would take place was to prove accurate, but twelve months had yet to elapse before the storm broke. Mr. Whinnery was the post master in Belfast, and fatal it was for any subversive correspondence to fall into his loyal hands. The reference to the assassinations is important. As in every rising, numbers of the most violent characters had banded themselves together, swearing that in their fight against the established order, they would not stop short of assassination especially where informers were concerned. Though in no way countenanced by the responsible societies of United Irishmen such violence undoubtedly did the cause much harm. It would seem fair to claim that in the North outrages of this nature were considerably less frequent, due no doubt to the definitely humanitarian principles that actuated the northern rebels.

As well as the family news that is scattered through every letter, the sympathy felt for Harry by the Templeton family is faithfully passed on by Mary ; indeed one feels that the very frequent messages from Eliza were sent not only to cheer the prisoner but to further the interests of Mary's much loved friend. Unfortunately, they failed to arouse any particular response, and Harry's letters are full of this kind of acknowledgement:

> Remember me affectionately to the Templeton's and tell Eliza that I have a thousand thanks to give her for her kindness but at present am not able.[22]

Poor Eliza! On one occasion she went so far as to add a sentence to one of Mary's letters, but in the next Mary has to say

> We wrote several times to you last week which I suppose you have by this time recd. Eliza Templeton wrote a few lines in one of them, but as she did not put her name in full perhaps you would not know who it came from.

One imagines that with very little trouble Harry could have had Eliza for his wife. In spite of rebuffs the messages continue, to be answered again by Harry: "Tell Eliza I am a lazy, good for nothing fellow that has hardly a word to ask how all their family are."

The idleness of prison life Mary Ann regarded with horror. William might be able to find employment "writing Calendars for the Terms and for the Sessions and . . . for the Grand Jury almost every day since you left, and was yesterday employed by a Justice that I met in the parlour to write a bail bond", and one can readily imagine him transcribing the formulae in his clear, even hand; but nothing like that would attract Harry, who preferred to throw himself about in the ball alley if he was not lying miserably despondent with rheumatism. Mary tried her best to encourage his not very great interest in reading, and in the next letter, dated 10.8.1797, which accompanied some recently published books, she launches out into one of her dissertations as naturally as in the old days when she and Harry, and so often Thomas Russell, would discuss just such subjects by the warmth of the winter fire or on the long walk to Orange Grove.

> We send you Mrs. Wollstonecraft's travels thro' Norway Sweden, etc. On reading it I think it seems rather a descrip-

tion of her own feelings which appear uncommonly exquisite, than of the country she passes thro', but as every production of such a one possessing such talent is interesting I hope you will find it a more pleasing amusement than drinking. We have also added Mr. Godwin's new publication which I suppose you have not yet seen. It is less excentric, that is to say more consistent with common sense, than his Political Justice. How does it happen that people do not act according to their reasoning as he notwithstanding all he says against matrimony is now married to Mrs. Wollstonecraft who had once an equal contempt for the ceremony, but she was cured by experience for Mr. Emily* [sic] the gentleman to whom her letters are addressed was much attached to her and wished to marry her, but as she was greatly involved in debt she refused to submit to what she called a monkish ceremony as it would oblige him to pay what she contracted to serve her friends. This I think was a false principle of honesty as it was more fit that she should be in debt to her husband than to anybody else. The event proved she was wrong for though she considered the contract as binding as any ceremony could make it the gentleman did not and when she returned from her travels with her infant daughter whom she had taken with her altho' it was his business which she was about which his situation prevented him from doing himself, yet she got him publically living with an actress. The effect this had on a woman of her feeling is easier imagined than described, she refused even to see or speak to him more . . .

Then, knowing full well the steadying effect of responsibility, Mary concludes with this admonition:

Mrs. McCracken gives Wm entirely into your charge and expects you to guard him like the apple of your eye and keep him and whatever might injure him at a distance from each other, as from what we hear we are not a little afraid you all make a good deal too free with yourselves. Could you not find more amusement in reading than drinking, now that you subscribe to a circulating library. If you wish for a novel next to Caleb Williams for originality get Emma, it is written by Mary Hayes Mrs. Godwin's particular friend.[23]

*Imlay.

Harry himself refers to Fénelon's Telemachus, which he was laboriously reading in French—hoping for assistance from a French prisoner recently arrested for spying—and to Godwin's *Caleb Williams*:

> If you wish for a true picture of the inside of a Jail read the 2nd Chap. 2nd Vol. of Caleb Williams; from being confined with such a variety of characters and all sorts of crimes charged on them, it makes a sort of amusement viewing the different turns of mind. In the appartments allotted to us six northerns, we have got two very respectable men from the Rock on treasonable charges . . .[24]

Without doubt Harry's interest lay in people:

> Yesterday [he wrote to Margaret] two men were executed in front of the Jail for Robbing the mail in June last, they died with the greatest fortitude. It gives one a sort of carelessness about death to see such sights, one of them John Bynge wrought in Belfast with a Charles Davis when I was taken up, he knew me very well, and lamented greatly that he was to die for a crime he was ashamed of and not for the good of his country; the morning of his execution he said to the prisoners you will live to see your country free while I die for my folly. Going past our window for execution he turned round and saluted us three times with the greatest composure.—You see that if there was anything worth while writing about you would have it when such a trifle occupies so much paper. Mary still blames me for leaving so much paper waste, but what can one fill it with? . . . Being very bad at remembering who I ought to compliment, that's too cold a word, but no matter you know what I mean, therefore give my love to a Thousand people and believe me to be Yours affect[ly]
>
> Hy J. McCracken.[25]

When in April 1797 the great batch of Northern prisoners arrived the dreadful monotony was momentarily dispelled:

> Dear Mary,
>
> On Saturday arrived here 19 prisoners from the North all in very good health and spirits. When they arrived we

were all locked up in our several rooms, whilst I was looking out into the condemned yard Jas. Burnside with several others steped into the yard and told me who were the prisoners, presently my door was opened by the Jailor who brought in Mr. Kilbourne [*sic*] and Dr. Crawford. At their backs stood a very long ugly officer and two *great gentlemen*. The Jailor ordered me out as those two prisoners were to have that room, where they have remained ever since having everything very comfortable, but very closely kept. However we send them under the door paper etc. and get in sometimes to chat a little with them. The other prisoners were divided into two Lots, one lot has got possession of the ward where the Stag was (he has gone to Down) Wm. H. Speers, Dr. Nixon, J. Greer, W. Kane, W. Templeton, A. Clarke, J. Haffey and J. Kennedy are of that lot with whom we have a constant communication as they are not locked up, they are very merry altho' as yet they have very bad beds. I expect in a day or two that Wm. Speer and Nixon will be put over to us. J. Burnside, H. McManus, R. Neilson, D. Toolan, H. Kirkwood, J. Barrett and T. Jackson alias Dry, compose the other Lot and are confined in that part of the Jail that you have to go through the Kitchen to. Burnside behaves remarkably well, so does Toolan, they keep up their spirits very well, indeed they are capital fellows except Kirkwood who has been crying all morning. I fixed a string out of J. Shanaghan's room where I now stay, to their ward by which I send wine and whatever they want across to them, J. Burnside being their agent. Hardly were they arrived when J. Richardson came here from Newgate, as he is namesake to our vagabond he was instantly sent among us. I have been interrupted to let Mr. K. and Dr. C. have our room untill theirs should be cleaned. I have had a good deal of chat with Mr. K. he has been very poorly this morning but is now a great deal better—and got into good spirits. Let all the friends of the lads know their situation, it is as comfortable as can be expected in everything except beds which will be better every day as both the Sheriff and Inspector Archer are gentlem and men of humanity—They have began the system of terror here, this day came in a Taylor charged with being a United Irishman, he is now in the same ward with Burnside. They have extended as far as Bantry Bay where they are taking people up, in short every part of the country is equally alike ill-affected. Remember me affectionately to all friends—so much of my time has been [engaged] by our new admitted felons that it has prevented me from writting as long a letter as I would wish, or being as particular as you would like. We are just informed that J. Cuthbert, Story and the Gordons are coming here, if so we will have a great garrison. When you write let me know how R's children are.

H. J. McCracken.[26]

K. Bastile 24. Ap. '97.

Richardson desires to be affectionately rem^{ed} to all the family.

A list of relatively unknown names to us, but clearly the old spirit is reviving through contact with his beloved men. It is easy to picture the bustling throng in the prison yard. Harry, locked in his cell, but eagerly surveying the scene from a grating ; James Burnside, reconciled even to captivity if it brought him nearer to his master, slipping over as the opportunity occurred to give the names of the new arrivals. Sinclaire Kelburn was the minister of the McCracken's congregation—never a United Irishman, but still remembered for his Volunteer sermons when he entered the pulpit of the Third Presbyterian Church clad in his uniform and grasping his musket—how glad Harry would be to see that friend and hear his news. Alexander Crawford was a physician in Lisburn ; apparently the two professional gentlemen were treated with due respect. The others were all working men well known to Harry, most of them weavers, one of them a printer in the office of the *Star*, and James Haffey, so often a trusted messenger, would carry no more letters between Kilmainham and Belfast. It was unusual for prisoners of this type to be sent to Kilmainham, more often the great numbers of labouring men, taken up either in town or country, were herded on to the prison ships in Belfast Lough to endure, through the spring and hot summer, conditions of fearful overcrowding. Mrs. McTier writes to her brother :

Men are brought in dayly to be put on Board the Tender—

> one was taken from his house yesterday where Mr. Magee was getting some work done—the only reason a piece of an Ash Tree in his loft. On the Quay a decent man who was seeing others shipped off was ask'd what has that man now going done—nothing reply'd the other but lived in peace & union with his neighbor. I have the honor of being his Father—a Day of dreadful retribution is at hand.[27]

Perhaps the most welcome of the newcomers was Thomas Richardson, Harry's close collaborator in Armagh. They had been arrested together but till now Richardson had lain in Newgate. What a time of excitement ensued, what surreptitious visits to other cells, what messages, what schemes for future contacts! Harry was in his element; everything was being planned; Mary, who knew all the families, was to take messages to the anxious relatives—again and again Harry is thoughtful about this—and one wonders if the unhappy Kirkwood was the object of that famous jest when Harry, dressed as a clergyman, visited a possible renegade to warn him of the eternal damnation awaiting deserters and informers. There is no difficulty now in finding news for a letter.

The first mention of William's arrival comes in Harry's next:

> Speer told me this morning that Wm has been in excellent spirits ever since he received a letter from Rose Ann—you know the situation of their apartments with respect to ours & that we have to confine our conversation, however we have a little chat through the separation door once or twice a day. Mr. Kilburn is in most excellent spirits, he has written a letter to my father this day which he showed me . . . You know already from Wm that I am no longer a State prisoner but detained as a common felon, this will naturally produce a change in the part of the Jail I will be confined in. Mr. Stubbs (the sheriff) has taken such an interest in whatever concerns any of us that he has ordered the Men's Infirmary (which you have been in) to be fitted up for us. The apartment is superior to any other in the Jail, the floor excepted, when there no friend will be refused admission, and as I can communicate with all the

Jail it will be a more open and free intercourse with the World for the rest, than any they have enjoyed since the appointment of our present Keeper, who's wife this day told me every convenience her house could afford was at my service . . . Mr. Richardson wishes much to have Matilda taught musick, consult Bunting about the propriety of it, and what the expense of an instrument. He and Charles desire to be remembered to you and Margt. Let me know how you all are, tell Rose Ann I rejoice at her recovery . . .[28]

If those at home were anxious for the welfare of the prisoners, the prisoners themselves were at the mercy of every rumour regarding the fate of Belfast, and while Mary is still reproaching Harry for the lack of letters [many were delayed or lost] he writes in June '97 :

Dear Mary

I feel that I very justly deserve your reproaches for not paying the attention that I ought in writting often to you, but believe me it is not that I am callous about my friends, rather impute it to the reverse, as every day we hear such reports from the North that often I have supposed it would be useless writting as the next post I expected would bring an account of your being burned out, then with the certainty of all letters to you, or from you being opened by that scoundrel Whinnery has made it unpleasant . . .

He had been moved again, this time to the former women's infirmary :

without being permitted the use of a yard, and receive no other support than Jail allowance, except what we furnish ourselves . . . we contrive to live very comfortably, cooking day about, some of us are very good at it and others very middling . . . Jas. Burnside keeps in excellent spirits, enquire for Thos. Dry's wife let her know that he is very well, I am afraid that she is in great distress—Danl Toolan requests to be remembered to my father, let his wife know he is well, in short all the prisoners here are well, since I came to this part of the house Willm got permission to come to see me for a few minutes never in his life did he look better. I have always when I sit down to write a seriousness about me that prevents me from writting half as much as I intended at first, we have had a long conference with Mr. Stubbs about our situation it will be altered for the better tomorrow . . .[29]

In his next letter Harry mentions another complication:

> It is expensive to live here, plundered by Turnkeys, etc. and still more so when confined with others who cannot support themselves nor yet be left to themselves. You may easy see that I wish for some money, but not much. I received the two guinea notes and two that John paid for me which is all that I have got to support myself and some others since the 10th May.
>
> I hate money, it makes me melancholy to think about it, and has entirely prevented me writting this time . . .[30]

In those days prison authorities provided little more than the cell, empty save for unsavoury bedding; there was a meagre allowance of food, but for this, and for the extras that they themselves must needs provide, the prisoners were entirely at the mercy of the turnkeys. Actually the Inspector General, and the Jailor Richardson and his wife—the latter no doubt placated by presents of muslin—treated the prisoners with consideration, but the lesser officials were, almost as a matter of course, dishonest. It is characteristic of Harry that he could not leave his unfortunate comrades, with no friends of their own outside to help them, to fend for themselves, and he knew that he would not appeal in vain to Mary. On the other hand William, with all his gentleness, never mentions the needs of these humble prisoners, in fact never mentions them at all: it was no wonder that Harry was so loved. All this business of privilege and wealth worried him: "I hate money, it makes me melancholy. . . ." In him the ardour for equality was particularly strong, at times tending to make him bitter. With no bitterness, but with a prodigal disregard for this world's riches, Mary Ann lavished, now and always, what money she had in the service of others.

There was still the constant uncertainty as to when or

where the prisoners would be tried, would they be transferred to Carrickfergus their county town, would the the normal course of justice be allowed to take its way? Rumour throve in such an atmosphere. Mary Ann mentions the raising of one false hope, and there must have been many: someone reading a letter from Dublin " intentionally obscure " leapt to the conclusion that the prisoners were to be released. Instantly

> the good news spread through the Town and smiles of pleasure and exultation brightened every countenance. I ran in to congratulate Mrs. Richardson who had already heard the joyful tidings and was weeping with delight, but short was our triumph, her tears soon flowed from another course and all our joy ended in disappointment. Within about half an hour Mr. Hunter returned with a dejected look and voice to tell us that he was not now so sanguine . . .[31]

Little wonder that in Kilmainham nerves became frayed and tempers shortened. Harry's rheumatism was very severe " and the unsociableness of the State prisoners makes it painful to write about their situation or even to think about it." This is the first mention of a deep-cutting quarrel between Harry and Samuel Neilson, noteworthy now only for the light it throws on the characters of the participants. At the outset of their confinement in '96 the original group of prisoners had agreed among themselves not to seek individual release. Though this decision might conceivably have remained binding on the prisoners themselves, it was naturally impossible to prevent their relatives from using what influence they could command, and apparently steps had been taken to secure the liberation of Samuel Neilson, Henry Haslitt and Charles Teeling. William's suspicions had already been roused:

> I dont like to say anything without having knowledge of the subject . . . I think all is intended for the best, but and till I have reason I will not think otherwise. I have too good an opinion of the men to allow me, tho' I must confess there are prisoners that might have been consulted, that were not . . .[32]

Harry, for his part, was furious, and went straight to the offenders telling them exactly what he thought, with the result, as he wrote to Mary,

> that some of the prisoners here have been very angry with me because I took notice of an impropriety (to give it the softest term) in their conduct. They have written to the North about it, now if you will ask Mrs. N. in what manner I used Saml. ill I will be obliged to you, for the others may have motives *besides the justness of the thing* . . . and hurt their friends to raise themselves, yet will I rather suffer than coppy what I despise so much . . .

And in a postscript there is this pregnant sentence :

> The first day I can free myself to sit down I will write to Margt. Her opinion and mine are nearly the same now respecting the selfishness of mankind, although formerly very different. You will say we see the worst side of man in Jail ; true, but I did not think he had so bad a side.[33]

Mary replied at once :

> Belfast. 10.8.1797.
>
> Dear Harry
>
> Tho' yours of the 3d gave me extreme pleasure in many respects, yet the melancholy reflection of the disappointment you feel in your opinion of mankind (which is perhaps the most painful conviction that can force itself on our experience and is always produced by the most distressing of circumstances, the changeableness of those we thought our friends) has considerably lessened it. That[1] one in whom selfishness was always visible should act consistently is not surprising, nor is it so that he whose[2] boyish vivacity tho' pleasing had such a mixture of levity as to prepare one for improprieties in his conduct, should tire of his situation and grow captious and fretful, but that the[3] man who always appeared to have the affection of a brother and the esteem of a friend for you and who piqued himself so much on his candour and love of truth, should act so disingenuously towards you, equally pains and astonishes me. I have not yet spoken to Mrs. Neilson on the subject as I am not certain that you are serious in desiring it and I do not wish

Presumably 1 = Henry Haslitt ; 2 = Charles Teeling ; 3 = Saml. Neilson.

to give unnecessary uneasiness to anybody especially one to whom we were so much indebted for kindness and attention at a time when we required it, and I am pretty certain that from her husband there were no complaints as she made a point of showing us all her letters since we came from Dublin, a mark of confidence I did not much relish, as it demanded a return and that did not altogether accord with my ideas, besides I thought it imposed a degree of slavery upon herself, as she appeared ashamed to withdraw it, tho' the two or three last times we did not share ours in return, not that we kept them back so much from reserve as because we did not happen to have them about us when we saw her until they were out of date, and when they did not mention her husband I thought they wd. not be very interesting to her and still less so when he was mentioned with disapprobation. Frank will give you a shawl of our manufacturing for a present to the Jailor's wife either as a reward for past kindness or to procure it in future.

* * * *

It gives us all infinite satisfaction to hear our friend Russell is well and in good spirits. I was much afraid he had no companions to his taste and of course that his spirits would flag, he still continues to be the first of men in the esteem of his young friends the Tombs, especially Isabella, who had heard a few days ago that he was soon to get out and begged [her] sister Babs wd. make Ellen teach her a tune she had observed he seemed to like, it was ' Away with you, kiltie ' that she might be fit to play it when she wd. see him again, which she can now do . . . . . On looking over what I have written I think we are rather festidious, and that we ought to make great allowances for the actions of those who are still in a painful situation and who may perhaps be under considerable embarrassment about their family affairs, but nobody could have more consideration for the weakness of others than you used to have without your usual philosophy has forsaken you. However we shall expect a full & circumstantial account of everything as you know Frank's [torn][34]

Mary's handling of this incident emphasises her restraint and uncompromising fairness. How well she understood

Harry and sympathised with his disappointment, but in such a delicate situation temper must not override prudence, and consideration for others.

Frank's visit was of little avail, his strange partiality for Henry Haslitt infuriated Harry still more :

> . . . When Frank was here he could know very little about the situation of *our* minds, or the causes of *our* actions, as he gave us very little of his company, he sat down three times in our room, once he stayed better than 10 minutes the other times, taken together, might amount to about 5 minutes, by that you may judge how much he heard from me. Perhaps as he spent most of his time in Jail with others he may have formed his opinion from them—indeed he appeared very much distressed when here, & I am sure he was so, to see the conduct of the people here, little wonder when one of his greatest favourites struck me on the head with a saucepan of scalding water without any provocation & battered my poor pate untill the pan was crushed compleatly, & would have continued longer his employment if he had not been prevented, then to show his courage when on equal terms he slunk off,—but he is Rich and honourable, out of twenty two none but two have escaped his kindness that way. I should have given you a full account of what was the origin of all disputes here, but have been for some days past ill with Rheumatism. This day I am much better & will if I continue so answer all your letters received yesterday by Mr. D.[35]

Meanwhile William wrote to Margaret :

> . . . The information that Mary wishes for of our internal arguments it is impossible for me to inform you of, after the many different times I have said that everything that hapened here should rest & abide with ourselves, & nothing but seeing the innocent charged with faults committed by others will induce me to speak & I hope that will never happen, if it does I will endeavour to lay the saddle on the right horse as far as comes within my knowledge. Both Frank and Mary give me a great deal too much credit on Account of temper. I dont believe anyone felt more than I did nor was more inclined to resent certain actions, but I considered our situations & the harm it might do the whole & I must confess, tho I have the good

fortune to meet the approbation of you all, I will say Job himself could not hold out much longer. I know I am perfectly unequal to the task (its a bad simile but I'm much vexed.) . . .[36]

Mary wrote at once :

Belfast. 11 Sept. '97.

Dear Harry

I did not receive yours of the first instant till Thurs. last & had by that time given up all hopes of it as I supposed it had been detained at the post office on account of some unguarded expression & was therefore very glad to find I was mistaken as it came by a private hand. We were much more shocked than surprised at the brutal behaviour of one who was always reckoned a Tyrant & who has been so universally disliked that I have frequently wondered at Frank's attachment to him, however we took care not to mention it to my Father or Mother as we knew how much it would vex them, and there is already too much made public of the interior transactions of the prison and that I believe with exaggeration—I have not yet come to an explanation with Mrs. Neilson as I thought the only proper method of so doing was by enclosing all yours and Wms letters in which you had mentioned the affair, as I considered it but fair to be as candid on the one side as I expected her to be on the other, besides I thought it would be the only way to convince her in what style you spoke of it, as I imagine you have been greatly misrepresented, but this I did not think myself at liberty to do without Wms leave and yours, if you both approve of it you may let me know when you write next . . .[37]

The necessary consent was given but before anything further transpired there came the shattering news of William Orr's trial and sentence—the last bulwark of freedom was gone, justice could no longer be expected.

Sept. 27, 1797

We are informed [wrote Mary to Harry] that Bills of Indictment were found at Carrick Assizes against all the State Prisoners who are present confined in Dublin, and all those who have been liberated on bail except Wm Davidson, but are not sorry to hear that the Trials cannot come on before Feby, as that of Mr. Orr's trial has clearly proved that there is neither justice nor mercy to be expected, even the greatest Aristocrats here join in lamenting his fate, but his greatness of mind renders him rather an object of envy and admiration than of compassion. I am told that his wife is gone with a letter from Lady Londonderry to her brother* on his behalf, if this be true I think it shows her to be equal in firmness and energy of character to her husband. If you have not already heard it you will be surprised when I tell you that old Archd Thompson of Cushendall was foreman of the Jury, and it is thought will loose his senses if Mr. Orr's sentence is put in execution, as he appears already quite distracted at the idea of a person being condemned to die thro' his ignorance, as it seems he did not at all understand the business of a juryman. However he held out from the forenoon till six o'clock in the morning tho' it is said he was beat and threatened with being wrecked and not left a sixpence in the world on his refusal to bring in the verdict guilty, neither would they let him taste of the supper or drink which was sent to the rest, and of which they partook to such a beastly degree. Was it therefore to be much wondered at if an infirm old man should not have sufficient resolution to hold out against such treatment? It will not much surprise you I suppose to hear that two Attorneys have turned Informers at Downpatrick, one of them cousin to Charles Brett, a doctor also has acted the same worthy part which is extraordinary from the liberal education they in general receive, but if we live long enough I suppose we will not be surprised at anything.[38]

The close of this letter contains the suggestion, already quoted [p. 132], that Harry should devote some of his time to improving his "taste for mechanics", Mary Ann judging that the tragic news would be another cause for angry brooding. Already she had decided that further writing about the Neilson quarrel was useless, she and Margaret would go to Dublin, and, as William had been ill, Rose Ann would accompany them: "We intend going up either the latter end of next week or the beginning of the week following, we would

*Lord Camden the Viceroy.

therefore wish you both to apply immediately for leave to see us, that there may be neither delay nor demur when we arrive."[39]

It must have been a difficult visit and it took place exactly one year after the first momentous journey. In spite of her natural inclination to take Harry's part Mary felt that on this occasion he was being petty and unfair. She was the first to admit that of all the prisoners Samuel Neilson had suffered the most grievously. Not only was he the father of five young children, but all the considerable fortune from his self-made business had gone into the *Northern Star* of which he was the chief proprietor and editor. This treasured venture he had had to leave to the care of others, and in May 1797, after a courageous existence of five years, during which the cause of liberty had been fearlessly if too vehemently proclaimed, the premises were raided by the military and all the valuable machinery and type completely wrecked. Little wonder that worry and long imprisonment had seriously undermined Neilson's health. With unbending integrity, which not even her brother's misery could shake, Mary must have reiterated all these points to Harry, indeed he himself realised how much Neilson had endured : " I am very sorry [he writes at this time] to hear of any accident happening to Mrs. Neilson, she has suffered very much, it is now nearly 12 months since Sam was taken, during which she has had little else than trouble & disappointment."[40]

We know nothing of the actual meeting with Harry nor of the long discussions that must have taken place. We do not know where the sisters stayed ; but, in the quiet of some room in Dublin, Margaret and Mary Ann pondered the whole sad business and came to a decision. Perhaps she could not trust herself to be sufficiently firm when confronted with his countenance, clouded with unhappiness and cruel suspicion ; perhaps she doubted her own ability to marshal her arguments convincingly from memory in his presence ; perhaps she wished to give him an example ; perhaps she may even have been indulging her own need for the solace afforded by her pen—whatever it was, Mary sat down and in this most loving letter sent her entreaty :

Dear Harry,

Well knowing the candour and generosity of your heart, I am certain an explanation is as much wished for by you as by the person to whose peace of mind it is so very essential, and as you can never find him alone would it not be better to come to the point by writing than to wait for an opportunity which may not occur, and thus defer it until it is perhaps too late. Besides it would agitate and affect him less, and that in his present state of health should certainly be considered. Another reason why a written explanation should be proposed is, that it would be more decisive, and less liable to misrepresentation, as the words of a conversation may be forgotten, and others substituted in their place apparently similar, but not bearing exactly the same meaning, and that without the least ill-will or intention. As a simple relation of facts is all that is necessary to restore harmony and affection, you whose motives, words, and actions will all bear the strictest investigation, need not shrink from the task. Ought men of superior sense and probity, who have long enjoyed mutual esteem and confidence, and who never for an instant suspected each other's integrity, to suffer themselves to be disunited, and their affections estranged by the misrepresentations of fools or knaves, when it is so easy to come to a right understanding, by merely declaring the truth? If anything contrary to that was requisite, I would not urge you, for much as I regard his peace of mind, and much as I value his life, if both depended on it, I would be the last person in the world to wish you either to utter or to sign a falsehood —if that were necessary to restore him. Is it not the duty of every person to promote the happiness of others as much as lies in their power? and in the present case it is not merely the happiness of one or two individuals that is concerned, but in this case the links that connect men, and render the happiness of many in some measure dependent on that of each individual, is rather more extended than usual, and it is the ardent wish of all your mutual friends to see you again united and on the same footing of esteem and affection, if possible, as formerly. Is it not injurious to the cause of union when two men, who from the first went hand in hand endeavouring to promote it, are thus at variance? Would not such an example of disunion betwixt themselves, and that without any serious breach of friendship, afford a triumph to your enemies, and occasion vexation to your friends? Will they not point at each of you as you pass: 'See there goes a promoter of Union, he could not agree with his bosom friend?' And certainly the situation of your families is deserving of some consideration; both have suffered much of late from a variety of causes, and ought you needlessly to add to their unhappiness? Not that your sufferings should induce you to do anything in itself wrong to alleviate them; but would you not feel most unhappy yourself to think you had at least embittered the last moments, perhaps shortened the days of a friend, when it was in your power to comfort and console him? You are above that little narrow pride so inconsistent with real dignity, of hesitating to make the first advance, or I am much mistaken in your mind. Sense and integrity are pearls of too great price to be cast aside for every failing, and, if you both examine yourselves, you will perhaps find that there are very few for whom you have so much esteem and affection as you have for each other. Consider, my dear Harry, how much is at stake; for while the envenomed dart rankles in his bosom the wound can never heal, and it is in your power and yours alone to extract it; I therefore entreat you will seriously reflect on the subject, and remember that an entire reconciliation between you is not only the earnest wish of all your friends, but must be that also of every friend to your cause.

Your ever affectionate Sister,
Mary Ann McCracken.

She was just turned twenty-seven; she had taken on her shoulders all the family responsibility; Francis had failed, John was no use in such a situation, her parents were bowed down with age and anxiety. On the outside of the letter is this note in Mary's own writing:

> written in Dublin in 1797 Oct. the reconciliation afterwards took place.[41]

That is all we know—her love and wisdom had prevailed.

The sisters returned immediately to Belfast, and Rose

Ann was left to care for William. On her arrival home Mary wrote this note hastily to Harry :

> Belfast. 3 Nov. 1797.
>
> I wrote this morning to Mrs. Wm intending to send it by post but was rather late, and understanding that Phoebe Burnside wished for a letter to Kilmainham where her and her daughter Peggy set out for this morning on foot,* I sent Tom Ramsey after her on a horse with it, as I thought in her present situation any appearance of neglect must give her double pain. I know you all too well to think it necessary to request you may use your interest to have her well treated. As there was nothing of any consequence in the letter I need not repeat it except that we arrived safe without being much fatigued, and found all our friends well & in good spirits . . .

Obviously the long awaited trials were now definitely expected, for Mary continues :

> I need not tell you what Jurors are summoned as there are many going or gone up who can give you much more information on that subject than I could possibly do, but my Mother charges me to tell you that she had it from good authority that Conway Carleton who is one of the number, said on All Hallows eve to Christn Hudson that if he was to be on your Jury you should never come home as you had, he said, twisted off his rapper about two years ago, and requested the other would remember you also in the same kind of manner if it came to his turn which he promised also, but I dont suppose it is necessary to warn you of these two men as you know them already. As John's affairs are not yet settled and he does not know when they may, it will not be in his power to go up before the trials come on, but as there are many Belfast people going up at present who will both be able and willing to serve you I hope you will be at no loss. Counsellor Joy set out this morning on horseback, but does not expect to be in Dublin before Sunday, of course we did not write or send anything by him.[42]

As if to bring uncertainty to its climax, along with the seeming imminence of the trials came also vague rumours

*A journey of 150 miles.

of release, and in the unaccountable ways of autocracy it was rumour that proved true. Harry suddenly mentions five men being liberated, as no bill was found against them.

> It is impossible [he writes to Margaret in the middle of November] to say or to account for any proceeding of Government, as they appear the most capricious of mortals on the face of the earth, without either principles or wisdom, it is possible they might be ashamed of confining men 14 months for nothing.[43]

A few days later Rose Ann sends Mary continued good news:

> Kilmainham. 25.11.1797.
>
> My dear Mary
>
> I am happy to have it in my power to inform you that Mr. Torney along with 13 more prisoners were liberated yesterday and cannot imagine how you heard the news so soon, we had it from young McGuicken* who was their agent he was in high spirits at his success in being part a means of getting them their liberty. I have some hopes of Williams getting out on bail from a conversation Counsellor Joy had with the Atty General one day last week, in consequence of which William wrote a memorial to the Lord Lieut. which the Counsellor is to present, and the Atty General said if it was referred to him he would take the bail and then Wm and I would have nothing to do but set off for the North, the only thing that could make that unpleasant is the Idea of leaving Henry behind us. I think if there was proper application made he would get out, many people have got out on bail on their being represented to be in a bad state of health, it could be said with more truth that he is in a bad state of health than of any that have yet got out on that plea . . .[44]

Harry himself is hopeful, and writes to Mary three days later:

> I received Margt's letter yesterday with a note for 5 guineas which came in very good time as Mr. Archer is to bring a physician tomorrow to visit me, who I expect will certify

*The Belfast attorney.

that if I am kept here all winter it will be almost certain death for me. Mr. A. is sure that I will get out and has promised to interest himself in the matter. He will go with the certificate himself to Cook & represent in very strong terms my situation ; it was very fortunate that you left the muslin with me, as I have written a note to Mr. A. with it saying you had sent it to him, this is a little trick to flatter his vanity and make him more active for the present. I have promised to get him a book, which I beg you will endeavour to procure for me, it is 'Political Lectures' printed by J. Story about the time I was taken, if you get it send it by the post office, directed to Rev. Foster Archer, Inspector General, under cover to Mr. Taylor, secty to Mr. Cooke, Dublin Castle, as by that means it will save postage and come quick . . .[45]

The excitement can more easily be imagined than described ; hurried letters reached Mary Ann, for money was needed to pay what was owing to the jailor's wife, as well as the doctor for his certificate, and other expenses.

Kilmainham. 4 o'clock. 6 Dec. 97.

Dear Mary, [this from William]

We received two letters and the money. Mr. Archer is just come here and informs us that bail is ordered to be taken of both Harry and me, from this we will require more money than I expected. I suppose we may need 15 guineas more, but cant yet have any proper idea of what fees, etc. may be necessary, but I expect none of them will be as heavy as the first we have paid that is the physician's. Please God we will be with you soon, and I hope Henry will soon be well when he gets with the family . . .

And then, in exultation, he writes on December 9th to his parents :

Dear Father & Mother,

I have at last the pleasure to write you from outside the Walls. Henry & I were admitted to bail yesterday which I suppose you are already acquainted with as Counsellor Joy said he would write as I could not get time, after the business was over I had to return to Rose Ann. She and I will set off immediately for home as soon as we hear from you, but Henry will not leave this for some few days after us. He must call & see all the people that were so friendly with him whilst he was living on Jail allowance. I think he is better already, at least he is in better spirits and consequently looks a great deal better. I think we may leave this on Wednesday Morning in the Newry fly and get the mail from that, in that case you will see us Thursday night. We left the prisoners all pretty well except S. Neilson who I think is worse again. Henry was to see the friends in N . . . . te* and I will try and see them this day. I think there is some hopes of T. Richardson and James Greer getting out, but we will know more of that against Monday. Rose and I would have set off immediately but that the finances were quite reduced, we will be sorry to leave Henry behind us but he thinks it absolutely necessary to call on the friends I mentioned, and we are too impatient to see you all to wait for that. I can have no sort of news, but that of our being out which is everything to us for a few days & then we will be with you.

I remain dear Father & Mother
Yours most affectly
Wm McCracken.[46]

So end the Kilmainham letters and the fourteen months of misery and anxiety that they represent.

*Newgate.

CHAPTER X

ANTRIM

1798

No description remains of the return of the brothers to Belfast or of what went on in the house in Rosemary Lane during the weeks that followed their release, but at any rate Harry was nursed back to health amidst the comfort and cleanliness that Margaret and Mary Ann would provide. By the end of February 1798 he was well again and back " in the business of the Society ", travelling to Dublin, ostensibly to sell his mother's cambrics,[1] but really to help the weaver prisoners not yet released, and to act as liaison between the North and the Leinster directory of the United Irishmen, now under the acknowledged leadership of Lord Edward Fitzgerald and the directing force in the whole movement. In May he writes to Mary:

Dublin. 8 May 1798.

Dear Mary,

I should have answered yours of the 4th May sooner, but you know how much I dislike writting when I have nothing particular to say that it is useless to make any apology. Burnside sets out this night for home on horseback so that it will be after you receive this that he will be able to get home. I have been obliged to borrow money to send him off. Barrett is recovering very slowly but he is entirely out of danger. When you work for our good friend T.R.* measure Wm's wrist and make some allowance larger. R.* is very well but when I told him Bunting was ill he appeared very uneasy for him and advised when I would go home (which will be in a day or two) for he and I to take a trip to the Giant's Causeway. All our friends here are well. I never seen Harriet Joy look better, nor Grace in better spirits. I have been with Jas. McAnnally respecting my Mothers cambricks, there is 50 ps on hand which he thinks he will not be able to dispose of at the Invoice price,

*Thomas Russell.

particularly the coarser lots wh. remain entire, and thinks if there is a demand at home for them it would be better to send them down, they are in very good order as I examined them. The trunk you order I will have left there & if my mother orders these home they can come in it, there is three ps of coarse lawns in bad order which will come with them or if, the cambricks stay, be sold for what ever they will bring. I have been often with S. Neilson, he appears what he did before he went to Jail, where I have been & all the attention that I cd. expect paid me—Tell Frank that he did not keep his word to me with respect to sending money, people cannot live here on air, nor travel home without some little support, let him consider the case of two unfortunate beings in a strange place without a penny, eighty miles to travel & one of them sick—If I had the names of the people on board the tender, with the names of the Capt. on board & the regulating officer on shore it is possible I may be of use to them—let it be sent to B. Coil who knows what use to make of it. I should now tell you why I have not left this, it is some friends have insisted on my staying—Give my love to all the family & believe me to be yours affty

Hy. J. McCracken.[2]

The old friendly authoritative spirit had revived : he was on good terms with the officials in the jail, with the Joy cousins and, as always, intimately concerned about the welfare of his subordinates. Probably the last sentence refers to a political commitment, as the next letter written four days later suggests :

Dublin 12th May 1798

Dear Mary

It gives me great uneasiness not hearing from home these 4 days as my father is so ill. You all think I have acted wrong in staying here so long, it would at least appear so, but perhaps when I explain what has kept me you will acquit me of a charge of want of affection which I feel at present my conduct *appears* to deserve. I have been with Maguire, he says he can't sell fancy goods. Coil seems to wish for them most, in future it may answer a good end to recollect their wishes in making up Boxes for them. My Mother's Cambks they in Maguir's hands he has promised to endeavour to push off, he has been offered money for them this week, as they are in very bad order I advised him to make the best of them he could & get them immediately turned into money—The people expect to have the soldiers living at free quarters in the City, they have already seized on Sweetman's house in the Country, every day searching for pikes & shafts thro all parts of the town, and carrying off all the timber that might be converted into that use, there is this day a proclamation offering a thousand pounds for Lord Edwd Fitzgerald, and another from the Lord Mayor ordering a return to be made of all the strangers that sleep in the City that the disaffected fugitives may be found, there are most horrid accounts from the county Kildare you must certainly have heard some of them, but I suppose the worst you have heard is nothing in comparison to the real state of that unfortunate Cy. . . . Give my love to all the family & believe me to be

Yours affectionately,
Hy J. McCracken.

I have said nothing about going home, however that does not make it the more distant. You know, it is one of Godwin's principles, make no promises.[3]

The insurrectionary movement was working itself quickly to a crisis, and in the face of approaching action all animosity between Harry and Samuel Neilson had disappeared. Neilson had not been released until February 1798 and then had remained in Dublin, working in the inner circles of the Societies there, and becoming, after the arrest of most of the Leinster directory in Oliver Bond's house in March, the close confidant of Lord Edward. Still depending on French aid, plans were developed for a general rising in the early summer. Senior officers were appointed to command the insurgents in the different counties, in the North Robert Simms and the Rev. Steele Dickson were to be in charge of Antrim and Down respectively, with the rank of General. Considerable sums of money had been sent to France from Belfast to expedite the invasion, and it was reported that in Dublin " Saml. Neilson was riding about night and day organising the people."[4]

The Castle authorities were completely aware of what was happening—it was never lack of information that accounted for their apparent dilatoriness in nipping the rebellion in the bud, and on March 30th the country was declared to be in a state of " actual rebellion."

Then, at the crucial moment, came the great blow; the French withdrew their offer of assistance. By now the " United " men all over the country were in a ferment, desperately driven by the ills they were pledged to remedy, and goaded to still greater fury by the free quartering of troops, the floggings, pitch-caps and other fearful accompaniments of the search for arms. Further restraint would have been difficult had the leaders wished it, but the controlling group in Dublin decided on immediate rebellion—French or no French. It is difficult to say how much their long confinement had isolated Neilson and McCracken from Northern opinion. From what is known to-day it seems obvious that they should have realised that, in the first place, a decision to act without foreign aid would in some quarters in the North be strenuously resisted, and secondly, that over the past months a radical change of outlook had taken place in a section of the Presbyterian community.

As we have seen, it was the American example that stimulated among Northerners the first great movement for liberty, and in due course the French achievement was hailed with rapturous applause. But, as we have also seen, some of the wiser heads realised before long that the French pace was too quick and too uncertain. Moderation is always difficult, and though Henry Joy jun. had been wise enough to advocate it, he possessed none of the qualities of leadership, otherwise he and his friend Dr. Halliday might have altered the course of Irish history. However, as French imperialism grew, stretching its rapacious arm from Europe to America, industrialists in Belfast became uneasy, peaceful relations with the U.S.A. being vital to their trade. Furthermore, the progress of the insurrectionary movement within Ireland revealed that the educated wing of the Catholic population had no sympathy with radical views. The sops thrown to them by the Government in its determination to separate Presbyterian and Catholic opinion, namely—the recent enfranchisement, and the endowment of Maynooth as a seminary for training the priesthood, had been to a great extent successful, and when Tone's dynamic personality was withdrawn from the Catholic Committee, aristocratic and clerical influence gained ground, and this sectarian element disgusted the Presbyterians. " A wonderful change " wrote Bishop Percy of Dromore " has taken place among the republicans in the North, especially in and near Belfast. They now abhor the French as much as they formerly were partial to them, and are grown quite loyal. . . . It is owing to the scurvy treatment which the French have shown to the United States of America, so beloved and admired by our Northern Republicans."[5] About the same time Secretary Cooke wrote: " The quiet of the North is to me unaccountable; but I feel that the Popish tinge in the rebellion, and the treatment of France to Switzerland and America, has really done much, and, in addition to the army, the force of Orange yeomanry is really formidable."[6]

There is no indication in any of the Kilmainham letters that Mary Ann was aware of this subtle change, and we do not know how far Harry became aware of it in his few months of liberty. As always, the McCrackens were more concerned with the common people, and the rank and file in Ulster never wavered in their purpose—Jemmy Hope and his like could be relied on to the end, though indeed Hope himself had sensed that in some quarters the movement for reform was " merely between commercial and aristocratical interests, to determine which should have the people as its prey ",[7] and that any firm cohesive purpose was lacking. Many of the men who held positions of responsibility within the Societies he mistrusted more for their sins of omission than of commission:

> I do not rank them with the common herd of traitors, they were rather men who unthinkingly staked more than was

really in them—they were like paper money, current for the time, keeping business afloat without any intrinsic value.[8]

And again:

> The seeds of corruption, it was evident to me, were sown in our society, but I was unable to convince my acquaintances, my observation was only useful to myself, and prepared me for the worst, which realised my dreariest forebodings, without however sinking my spirits in the least, or making me regret any step I had taken.[9]

The Government was well informed of any cleavage in opinion and of how, in the last resort, the various rebel commanders would act:

> At present [writes Mrs. McTier] all here is detestable Plot and low cunning—suspicion & ineffectual secrecy where both sides gain much true information yet both are betrayed—Not a word or look on any subject above the weather or the card table, that is not noticed, & I believe there are few in any Town who have not some sort of spy on them- -It will be long before this devoted Country recovers even the stupid contentment it enjoy'd 7 years ago.[10]

In the North, the General for Down, the Rev. Steele Dickson, was arrested, and in Dublin five days before the insurrection was due to begin, Lord Edward Fitzgerald was captured. Nevertheless, plans for the Rising were pushed forward. The signal for action was to be given on the night of May 23rd, 1798, when, if preparations were complete, the mail coaches leaving for the country were to be overturned in the outskirts of Dublin. Throughout the four Provinces of Ireland eager and excited men were waiting, breathless, for the signal, and when news flew to the North that the Newry coach had been burned at Santry thousands flocked to their posts, armed for the most part with pikes, to engage at last in conflict for liberty and justice. But—the General for Antrim hesitated, almost certainly on this question of action without French aid, and then resigned: the General for Down was already safely housed in the Tender.

To even the most unsympathetic the poignancy of the situation must be apparent. That the North—cradle in Ireland of ideals of freedom and justice far in advance of general acceptance—the home of men willing before any others to lay down their lives to attain them—the Province that had provided the pattern of military preparedness—that the North should at the critical moment present a spectacle of paralysed chaos, is almost unbelievable. Yet so true was it that subsequent historians of the Rebellion can, in their lengthy and lurid chapters, relate its progress in the South, in the Midlands and in the East, and leave almost, and in some cases altogether, unmentioned anything that did happen in the North.

In the general dismay and consternation Henry Joy McCracken was acclaimed the leader. With amazing vigour and resourcefulness he planned a campaign and rallied the men of Antrim, Down, Armagh and Tyrone.[11] The countryside was infested with military, but he sent messengers here, there and everywhere, though there was no time for consultation, no time to discover how many of the insurgent officers remained at their posts.

The town of Antrim commanded a key position; from it communication could be maintained between the counties of Antrim and Down in the east and Tyrone and Donegal in the north-west, and the way to the south kept open. So, determining to strike there himself, Harry ordered the various colonels in the counties to attack the military posts in their neighbourhoods, issuing to one this stirring proclamation:

> Tomorrow we march on Antrim—drive the garrison of Randalstown before you, and hasten to form a junction with the Commander-in-Chief.
>
> Henry J. McCracken.[12]
>
> The First Year of Liberty
> 6th June 1798.

He planned that the attacking forces should converge on the town from four directions, he himself marching at the head of one contingent, composed, by a strange coincidence, of men from Killead, the home of his own

Joy ancestors. They swung along in the early morning freshness of a June day, singing the " Marsellois Hymn ", and this—" The Swinish Multitude ", to the tune of " The Lass of Richmond Hill " :

Give me the man whose dauntless soul
Oppression's threats defies,
And bids, though tyrant thunders roll,
The sun of freedom rise ;
Who laughs at all the conjured storms,
State sorcery 'wakes around,
At power in all its varying forms—
At titles empty sound.

Give me the soul whose 'lustrious zeal,
Diffusing heaven-born lights,
Instructs a people how to feel,
And how to gain their rights ;
Who nobly scorning vain applause,
Or lucre's fraudful plan,
Purely enlist for freedom's cause—
The dearest cause of man.

Hail ye friends united here,
In virtue's sacred ties !
May you, like virtue's self, keep clear
Of pensioners and spies,
May you by Bastiles ne'er appalled,
See nature's right renewed,
Nor longer unavenged be called
The swinish multitude.[13]

On they marched, musketeers in the front, pikemen in the centre, the rearguard bringing up the one and only cannon, a " brass piece " that had belonged to the Volunteers, now unearthed from its hiding and mounted on " a common car." Jemmy Hope was leading a detachment, so was Rose Ann's brother, James McGlathery, and William McCracken was somewhere in the little army, 500 strong. Not all the combatants were arrayed in smart uniforms, but when they reached the burying-ground at the eastern approach to the town of Antrim,

Harry established his Headquarters there and the green banner was unfurled.

The town was not strongly guarded. Within an hour or so the insurgents had gained control, and for one fleeting moment victory seemed theirs.* But Harry's plans had been betrayed to General Nugent, and the reinforcements that so soon arrived from nearby camps were overwhelming. After fierce fighting the rebels scattered, and Harry, with the faithful Jemmy Hope and a band of followers, took refuge in Donegore Hill, still hoping to retrieve their fortune.[14] But it was not possible. Other engagements had been attempted in some districts according to his orders, elsewhere his commands had been ignored or betrayed, and with the defeat of the Down rebels, led by Henry Munro, at Ballynahinch on June 12th the rising in Ulster was ended. Had it not been for the treachery within the insurgent ranks, Harry, by his superb courage and personal bravery, might indeed have countered that fateful resignation of Robert Simms. He had rallied the rank and file and had defied the powerful garrison of the North; "when all our leaders deserted us" wrote Jemmy Hope "Henry Joy McCracken stood alone faithful to the last."

Everything, as he well knew, had been risked in that attack on Antrim, now but one fate awaited him if he fell into the hands of the Government forces; still, his insistent desire was to break through and join the rebels in Wexford.

What happened next has been told by Mary Ann. When, about 1840 Dr. Madden embarked on his memoir of Henry Joy McCracken, it was of course from Mary that he sought help, and, though the narrative that she wrote for him will ever be treasured as her personal record of the close of her brother's life, it lacks the vitality of her spontaneous writings, and quite naturally minimises her own part in the bitter ordeal.[15] I have decided, therefore, not to quote it in full, but drawing

*Lord O'Neill, who as the Hon. John O'Neill had received old Francis Joy's vote at the Antrim election of 1790, was mortally wounded while directing the Yeoman Garrison.

on it for information have endeavoured to do greater justice to her own remarkable courage, endurance and resourcefulness.

When news of the defeat at Antrim reached the McCrackens no one needed to tell them that the position was perilous in the extreme, not only for Harry and William but for the whole family. The rebels and their associates were now at the mercy of a government determined to stamp out rebellion with all the ruthlessness that generally characterises such a performance. In his proclamation to the insurgents of Down, dated June 12th, General Nugent gave warning that if his instructions for the surrender of arms and prisoners were not immediately complied with he would " proceed to set fire to and totally destroy the towns of Killinchy, Killyleagh, Ballynahinch, Saintfield, and every cottage and farm house in the vicinity of those places, carry off the stock and cattle, and put everyone to the sword who may be found in arms."[16] He exhorted the inhabitants to comply, as this would be the only opportunity they would have " of rescuing themselves and their properties from the indescriminate vengence of an army necessarily let loose upon them." In Belfast, curfew was still rigorously enforced, at nightfall each house must display the names of all persons within, all exits from the town were carefully guarded, and General Nugent had announced that no one could leave the town " unless they go for the purpose of residing at their houses in the country, and it will be necessary for them to have *passes* for their protection, as the officers have directions to take up all persons who do not reside at their own houses, or cannot give a satisfactory account of themselves."[17] No house was immune from the demands of the military for free quarters. Mrs. McTier, after relating how such orders were presented to herself and to her aged mother, declared that her " doors have been locked almost ever since, and all packed up for flight if absolutely necessary."[18] The Poorhouse had been requisitioned and was full of soldiers. Flogging in the street was so common that the yell of the suffering victims " ceased to excite even astonishment."[19] Two hundred lashes was the usual order, and the following incident, related by Jemmy Hope almost in parenthesis, was an hourly occurrence:

> When I got to Hughes' in Bridge Street they were preparing to flog men in High Street . . . One of Hughes' clerks came up and said they were flogging Kelso, and in a little while the servant girl ran into the room in haste, and said that Kelso was taken down, and was telling all that he knew.[20]

For a week no word of the brothers reached Rosemary Lane; the family was sick with apprehension and Mary Ann and Rose Ann determined, in spite of the continued vigilance of the military, to set out in search of Harry and William, an exceedingly perilous undertaking. Presumably they went on foot. It was by all accounts an unusually hot and lovely summer, they were dressed most likely in the long cotton frocks of the period with straw bonnets, and they must have carried provisions and money both for themselves and the fugitives, all the time anxiously evading the soldiers. The first evening found them at Whitehouse, a small village four or five miles distant from Belfast on the shores of the Lough. Here, at a gardener's lodge, they found Rose Ann's brother, and the three were taken to a more remote cottage nearer the Cave Hill where they got a bed for the night. As news had reached them by this time that William was safely hiding in the house of a relative of Rose Ann's, Mary begged her sister-in-law to return home, but she insisted on continuing in the search for Harry. On the second day they proceeded alone, going from place to place in the desolate hills seeking information, traversing country quite unknown to either of them with unusual courage and determination. Then in the back room of a lonely cottage they found eight fugitives discussing what they should do. One of them was very slightly known to Mary. She at once entered into their deliberations, recommending " them strongly to separate and return to their homes. . . . they replied that there was something in view, but in the event of its not taking place, they would follow my advice." Three of these men—one was a schoolmaster—escorted the two women farther into the hills to where they thought Harry might be found. On they went, across fields, drains and ditches, reaching the heather-covered moors. Then, after what Mary Ann calls " a brisk walk " for a further two hours or so, they arrived at the bleak, deserted eminence of the black Bowhill. There on the brow, his gaze scanning the vast stretch of country below him, sat Harry with Jemmy Hope and five other companions.

Fatigue and weariness vanished at the sight of the astonished welcome on his face. Mary Ann records that Harry seemed " surprised and rejoiced " at seeing them ; so he well might be. Where on earth had she come from, how had she found him ? She had never failed him yet, and here she was, at the bitterest moment of his life, miraculously beside him, utterly unexpected and so amazingly reassuring. They sat there for a long time, well into the mid-summer night, " talking over their adventures and escapes ", and then Harry took the girls to a cottage where " we were received in darkness, the woman not daring to light a candle or make the fire blaze." Here he left them, it was too dangerous for anyone to offer shelter to the fugitive, but he promised to return at seven in the morning. They rested their weary limbs, huddled on a chair and a stool.

> We thought the night very long, [Mary recalls] but when seven o'clock came and no Harry appeared, we became very uneasy, but still more so when one Leith, a thoughtless fellow, accompanied by the school master, arrived, and had not met with him, not having taken shelter in the same place. He came at last, having waited for the others, till after nine o'clock. We then set out on our way home, and he accompanied us a little way, wishing to see McG.* whom we sent out to him. Even then they had hopes of another movement.[21]

*Rose Ann's brother.

After a shorter and easier journey Mary Ann and her sister-in-law reached Rosemary Lane, exhausted, but as triumphant as such ominous circumstances would permit, for contact with Harry had been established. Immediately she sent him money and clothes by various messengers, and eleven days after the Battle of Antrim he wrote thus :

Monday, 18th June 1798.

Dear Mary

Yesterday I received a letter from you enclosing two guineas and this day a Bundle of cloathes (by the Bearer) part of the cloaths I sent back as not having occassion for them, the things you mention as being sent to some part of the shore I never received, but the ½ guinea and trifles sent by G. Gray came safe and the flannel waistcoat you sent has no sleeves however it came in very good time as I had much need of a change having never had that luxury [since] I left home before. I will endeavour to arrange matters so that anything I want will come regularly to me, at present I cannot as my lodging is the open air, which with great abundance of exercise keeps me in good health & high spirits, altho my companions are not so numerous now as they were lately. *These are the times that try men's souls.* You will no doubt hear a great number of stories respecting the situation of this country, its present unfortunate state is entirely owing to *treachery*, the rich always betray the poor. In Antrim little or nothing was lost by the people until after the brave men who fought the Battle had retreated, few of whom fell, not more than 1 for 10 of their enemies, but after the villians who were entrusted with the direction of the lower part of the County gave up, hostages and all, without any cause, private emolument excepted, murder then began and cruelties have continued ever since. It is unfortunate that a few wicked men could thus destroy a county after having been purchased with blood, for it was a fact which I am sure you never knew that on friday the 8th June all the county was in the hands of the people, Antrim, Belfast and Carrickfergus excepted. When I see you I will tell you a variety of little anecdotes that have occurred since I left home—let me hear all the news and when opportunity serves send me newspapers. Remember me to all the family and friends who I doubt are few and believe me to be

yours truly

Hy J. McC.[22]

It is the last of his letters, and it is addressed to both sisters. Nothing had shaken his confidence in the common people.

Shortly afterwards Mary made another journey to see him, this time to David Bodle's cottage on the Cave Hill. She had procured a forged pass and had arranged with the captain of a foreign vessel to take Harry on board at a secluded spot on the shores of Belfast Lough—for yet another refugee America was the longed-for haven! Alas, no record remains of the rapid and perilous planning, or of those who assisted her in this bold scheme for Harry's escape—perhaps some of her father's seafaring friends came to her aid. Everything must be done with the utmost secrecy—soldiers and spies combed the town and its environs, every movement was watched. At last the moment for flight arrived; his mother had sent him, as a parting momento, her own copy of Young's *Night Thoughts*, the final farewell messages had been delivered, when, on his way to the place appointed for embarkation, Harry was recognised by a party of Carrickfergus yeomen and, with his two companions, arrested. Even then there was an opportunity of escape, but he would not take it, refusing to involve the others in additional danger.

So, on a Sunday afternoon, July 8th, 1798 one month after the Battle of Antrim and Mary's 28th birthday, news reached the McCracken household that Harry was a prisoner in Carrickfergus Gaol. "Immediately" she records "my father and I set off for Carrickfergus." The completely new situation required instant action, and again it is Mary who rises to the occasion and assumes responsibility. Frank and William were both in hiding, John would not or could not be helpful, Margaret dreaded spectacular adventures, and Atty Bunting, though so much one of the household, shared none of these responsibilities. So, with as much haste as was compatible with the comfort of the old, infirm sea-captain, they set off in a chaise to drive on that summer's afternoon by the shore of the Lough to Carrickfergus. That evening she wrote to Margaret :

Dear Sister,

We went directly to the Jail on our arrival here & were told by the Jailor that he had strict orders not to let any person see Harry yet notwithstanding which he ventured to let us speak to him for a few minutes. He is very well & requested we would not let ourselves be vexed on his account let his fate be what it might, the only thing he thinks his friends can do for him is to get his trial delayed which he wishes very much, or perhaps they could get leave for him to leave the country. My father thinks we should return home as the Colonel to whom Miss Bradshaw applied, Mr. McNevin not being at home, said that it was impossible any person could see Harry or his companions there were such strict orders from Genl. Nugent, if therefore any of his friends think of coming to see him they must apply to Genl Nugent for an order.

Col. Anstruther also said that they did not know when they would be tried but that they should have timely notice of it.

We intend leaving this at 7 o'c in the morning if nothing happens to prevent us

farewell

M. A. McC.[23]

Next morning father and daughter made one more effort to see Harry, but all they could do was to speak to him through a window. He asked that John would come to see him, and sent to his mother the ring that Thos. Richardson had made for him, bearing a green shamrock and inscribed with the words : " To the sacred memory of Mr. Wm. Orr who died for his country at the altar of British tyranny, 1797." The gift was an eloquent tribute to the sympathy that existed between Harry and his mother. He wished her to bear in her heart not only the memory of himself, but of the cause so soon to demand his life.

A week of suspense went slowly by, and then in the late afternoon of July 16th word arrived that Harry had been brought to Belfast. Again, there was no time for indecision. Mary and Margaret together, "immediately set out to try if we could see him." It was but a stone's throw from the house in Rosemary Lane to the centre of the town, where, in Castle Place they found him, a rebel prisoner in his own town, standing exposed to the public gaze in the heat of the summer sun, surrounded by a guard of a dozen soldiers. They could only watch with him, there was no opportunity to speak one word, but at least they would remain to share his lot. It must have been a fearful ordeal. Then orders came, and Harry was marched off, down Corn Market to the Artillery Barracks in Ann Street,

> We hastened, [says Mary] to Colonel Derham who lodged in Castle Place; we knocked at the door, and just as it was opened, the colonel, who had been out, came up; and when we earnestly requested he would give an order for admission to see our brother, who was to be tried the next day, he replied that, 'If our father and mother, sisters and brother, and all the friends we had in the world, were in similar circumstances, he would give no such order.' He had by this time entered his hall-door which he shut against us with great violence.

They returned home in despair; then someone discovered that a number of officers were dining that evening at the Exchange—so

> . . . we hurried there and sent a message to Colonel Barber,* who instantly sent out a young officer to accompany us to my brother; and when we apologized to this gentleman for giving him so much trouble, he said 'He did not consider it any trouble, and would be glad to serve us.' I did not learn his name. When we reached the place of confinement, he very kindly stood at a distance from the door of the cell, that we might have an opportunity of conversing at our ease with our brother.[24]

*He who had first met Harry in the street fight five years earlier p. 100.

After nearly half a century how gratefully she recalls that act of courtesy.

The court martial had been fixed for the following day, July 17th, at noon. Harry did not know who was to witness against him, but whether the evidence were true or false would make little difference. For some reason that is now quite obscure he was anxious for his cousins Mary Holmes and Mary Tomb to be there to give evidence that they had persuaded him to leave Belfast before the battle of Antrim. Word was sent to Mrs. Holmes, and very early next morning [the day of the trial], Mary Ann set out by carriage for Lisburn ten miles distant, where Miss Tomb was staying with friends. All the way back, Mary, racked as she was with anxiety for Harry, had to calm her greatly agitated cousin, a young woman of about her own age. They went straight to the Exchange, where the trial had already commenced, Mary's eager glance sweeping the crowded room for Harry.

> The moment I set my eyes on him I was struck with the extraordinary serenity and composure of his look. This was no time to think about such things, but yet I could not help gazing on him, it seemed to me that I had never seen him look so well, so full of healthful bloom, so free from the slightest trace of care or trouble, as at that moment, when he was perfectly aware of his approaching fate.[25]

Mary Ann and her father were the only members of the family present. She was given a seat near the table where Colonel Montgomery was presiding, and there she stayed, calm and collected, almost to the end. The Crown Attorney, John Pollock, opened the case for the prosecution, and he hoped, with a promise of banishment, to gain from Harry incriminating information about other insurgents.

> Immediately preceding the examination of the witnesses, my father, who was just recovered from a severe and tedious fit of illness, and who appeared to be sinking beneath the weight of old age and affliction, was called aside by Pollock, who told him that he had such evidence against his son as would certainly hang him ; that his life

> was in his hands, and that he would save it if my father would persuade him to give such information as Pollock knew it was in his power to do namely, who the person was who had been appointed to command the people at Antrim, in whose place he [McCracken] had acted. My father replied that he knew nothing and could do nothing in the matter; he would rather his son died than do a dishonourable action. The tyrant, however, not content with the trial of his virtue, would torture him still farther by calling Harry to the conference, and repeated the same offer to himself, who well knowing his father's sentiments, answered, that 'he would do anything which his father knew it was right for him to do.' Pollock repeated the offer, on which my father said, 'Harry, my dear, I know nothing of the business, but you know best what you ought to do.' Harry then said 'Farewell, father,' and returned to the table to abide the issue of the trial.[26]*

Poor Mary Ann, her heart breaking with this cruel torturing, knew now what the end must be. After that last farewell she took her father home, but was back in a moment, listening to perjured evidence and half-true statements. It was very warm, and at one stage Harry complained of thirst. Rushing home to get him an orange or some wine she met Mrs. Thompson, wife of a calico print cutter who had worked for Harry and had very recently been flogged in the street for refusing to give evidence against him. This woman, as devoted as her husband, begged to be allowed to swear that she had seen Harry in Belfast on the day of the battle. Rebuked by Mary, she insisted on going to the Exchange to make her proposal to Harry and his attorney, Mr. Stewart. But they would not accept it. The case dragged on, Stewart doing his best to gain a compromise on the sentence. Mrs. Holmes withstood a barrage of cross-questioning from Pollock, but Mary Tomb wept so bitterly that she " could hardly answer a single question." Then Mary herself was called. Outwardly calm,

*The man whom Harry thus defended with his life was Robert Simms. He was arrested very shortly and confined in Fort George, Inverness-shire, till 1802.

> I stated [she said] what appeared to me to be unlike truth in the evidence that had been given by the witnesses for the prosecution, expressing the hope that they would not consider such evidence sufficient to take away life; the testimony of one witness impeaching the character and credit of the approver, on whose statements the charge was mainly dependent for support.[27]

One wonders what impression the scene made on Colonel Montgomery—the tall, handsome young man, tanned by his outdoor living, facing death with a look of "extraordinary serenity and composure", and supported by his sister, so fragile in appearance but calm also in the midst of this fearful ordeal. Harry had whispered to her that she must be prepared for his conviction, but she knew that already, and was by now planning the next move, the last remaining effort that must be made to save his life. Before the trial was completed she slipped out of the room, sped home for a hasty consultation with her mother, and in an instant Mrs. McCracken was on her way to seek an interview with General Nugent, to beg as a favour what Harry had scorned to accept as a bribe—banishment. It was of no avail, the General would not see her. Mary hurried back to the court room to find that the trial had ended and that Harry had been taken away. She followed him down Bridge Street, across High Street, down Corn Market

> . . . to the Artillery barracks, where [she records] I saw Major Fox just going in, and asked his permission to see my brother; he desired me to wait a little, but I followed him, and when he came to the door of my brother's cell remained behind him at a few paces' distance; the door of the cell was opened, and I heard him say 'You are ordered for immediate execution.' My poor brother seemed to be astonished at the announcement; indeed he well might be, at the shortness of the time allotted to him; but seeing me falling to the ground, he sprang forward and caught me, I did not, however, lose consciousness for a single instant, but felt a strange sort of composure and self-possession; and in this frame of mind I continued during the whole day. I knew it was incumbent on me to avoid disturbing the last

> moments of my brother's life, and I endeavoured to contribute to render them worthy of his whole career. We conversed as calmly as we had ever done. He said 'I wish you to write to Russell, inform him of my death, and tell him that I have done my duty' . . 'Is there anything else you wish me to do?' I asked. 'No', he replied, hesitatingly; but from his look I judged there was something occupying his thoughts which he did not wish to mention. What was then stirring in his mind flashed on mine like lightning, and vanished at the moment; but subsequent circumstances recalled it, and the source of his anxiety became a source of comfort to me, and the means of fulfilling a duty to his memory.[28]

He then asked particularly to see the Rev. Sinclaire Kelburn, the family minister, as it would gratify his parents, but the Rev. Steele Dickson, now detained in the barracks, arrived first. When Mr. Kelburn reached the cell, knowing that he was looking on the prisoner for the last time, he burst into tears, exclaiming "Oh! Harry, you did not know how much I loved you." With a valiant effort to recover his composure he made some joking remark to Major Fox about his old "fowling-piece"—a jest at the Government's confiscation of arms—and Harry, appreciating the intention, "looked at Dr. Dickson and smiled." Trivial incidents, maybe, but they represent a wealth of love and courage. There was a short prayer. Then Mr. Kelburn made the suggestion that Mary should return home with him, "which I refused."

Sometime during that crowded day she and Harry found opportunity to talk

> . . . with tranquility on the subject of death. We had been brought up in the firm conviction of an all-wise and overruling Providence, and of the duty of entire resignation to the Divine Will. I remarked that his death was as much a dispensation of Providence as if it had happened in the common course of nature, to which he assented.[29]

Knowing that the interview must soon be terminated, Mary had one last request:

> I asked for a pair of scissors that I might take off some of his hair. A young officer who was on guard [his name was George] went out of the room and brought a pair of scissors, but hesitated to trust them into my hand, when I asked him indignantly if he thought I meant to hurt my brother. He then gave them into my hand, and I cut off some of Harry's hair, which curled round his neck, and folded it up in paper, and put it in my bosom. Fox at that moment entered the room, and desired me to give it to him, as ' too much use ' he said, ' had already been made of such things.' I refused, saying I would only part with it in death ; when my dear brother said, 'Oh ! Mary, give it to him, of what value is it ? ' I felt that its possession could be a mere gratification to me, and, not wishing to discompose him by the contest, I gave it up.[30]

"About 5 p.m. he was ordered to the place of execution." The gallows was erected in front of the Market House where he had had his classes for boys and girls and which stood on ground presented to the town by his great-great-grandfather the Sovereign George Martin.

> I took his arm, [writes Mary] and we walked together to the place of execution, where I was told it was the General's orders that I should leave him, which I peremptorily refused. Harry begged I would go. Clasping my hands around him, (I did not weep till then) I said I could bear anything but leaving him. Three times he kissed me and entreated I would go ; and, looking round to recognise some friend to put me in charge of he beckoned to a Mr Boyd, and said ' He will take charge of you.' . . . and fearing any further refusal would disturb the last moments of my dearest brother, I suffered myself to be led away.[31]

On that summer afternoon the street was thronged with their townsfolk from every walk of life : executions were a public occasion, and those who wished to watch the spectacle in greater comfort hired windows overlooking the scene. To shield herself somewhat from the staring crowds Mary had drawn the veil of her bonnet over her face ; it was afterwards said that a soldier had lifted the veil with the point of his sword and cut it off.[32]

But very many amongst the throng were there, not

from idle curiosity, but from a desire to follow to the end the man whom they venerated as master, leader and friend. It was well known that Harry possessed to a remarkable degree the quality that commands devotion, and every precaution had been taken by the military against a demonstration in his favour, including a strong guard of dragoons.

It was a fearful scene. Three weeks previously James Dickey the attorney from Crumlin had been hanged, and his head cut off and placed on a spike on the Market House. Four days later the same sentence had been passed on John Storey the Belfast printer, who had been a fellow prisoner with Harry at Kilmainham. Both these men had fought at Antrim. In the beginning of July Hugh Grimes and Henry Byres, leaders at Ballynahinch had suffered likewise.[33] There they were—four heads with their sightless eyeballs staring down on the little procession making its way to yet another hanging. In the glare and heat of that exceptionally warm summer flies buzzed around the festering flesh, and the Town authorities issued a warning against the consumption of uncooked fruit.[34]

When Mary Ann left him, Harry stood, tall and majestic, looking after her till she was out of sight. Later she heard from others of the calmness and composure with which he faced death and of the last minute intervention by Major Fox to save his life, moved this time perhaps more by admiration for his heroism than by the desire for information. Why, his uncomprehending mind may have wondered, must such incredible fortitude, such poise, such self-control, be so uselessly squandered, the fellow must be given one more chance to get away. Harry answered him with a smile.

There are good grounds for supposing that when all was over it was Mrs. Burnside who received the body of Henry Joy McCracken from the hangman and performed the last ministrations, a poignant tribute to the abiding devotion and loyalty of his weaver friends.[35]

All the while Mary had still one fragile hope—could life be restored to the strangled body by artificial means?

There was some cause for her hope. Had not James McDonnell, their intimate friend, made, from his student days, a special study of artificial respiration, and did not the General Hospital, so recently opened in the town as a result of his ceaseless effort, include as one of its declared functions the resuscitation of drowned sailors? It may be that Mary bribed the executioner to do his work with special care, she must have known that for some reason General Nugent was prepared to spare Harry's body the further ignominy of decapitation, and would order that it be given to his family for immediate burial. At any rate she sent an urgent summons to Dr. McDonnell, and to Mr. McCluney " our apothecary ", to come at once to the house, she herself remaining by the body, while so many crowded in to pay their last tribute of love and respect. But Dr. McDonnell did not come; instead he sent his brother, " a skilful surgeon." Why this strange man failed to respond to the call of his friends will, presumably, never be known; Mary mentions no excuse, nor does she hint reproach. She joined the other members of the family and awaited the result with " indescribable anxiety." The surgeon's labours were of no avail, time was passing quickly and the body must be buried by nightfall. As the little funeral cortège set out for the Parish Burying-ground Mary realised with horror that none of the family, nor any relative, would accompany it, " so I set out to follow them to the grave." A kind hearted sympathiser drew her arm within his to escort her, and her brother John, hating and detesting the whole business as he did, could not endure to see her go alone. He ran after her, stayed by her side, and, when at the sound of the first shovel-full of earth falling on the coffin she collapsed, it was he who brought her home. The day that had begun at 6 a.m. with the hurried drive to Lisburn was now ended.

It seems incredible that next day Mary was able to write, as Harry had requested, to Thomas Russell—that she could muster the strength of mind and body to address herself immediately to this sad task. But it was the only thing still to be done for " her dearest brother ";

and to sit down quietly and relate the whole story, incident by incident, to someone so dear to her and to him was, of itself, a comfort and solace to her aching heart, though she was sending also her own farewell. No one, not even her mother or William or Margaret, understood so completely as did Thomas the idealism and the faith that lay behind Harry's actions. This is the letter—addressed to Newgate prison—the only one from Mary Ann to be found among Russell's papers, and it begins without any formal opening:

Belfast, 18th July 1798.

In obedience to the last request of a much-loved brother, I write to you who were his dearest and most valued friend, to inform you of the interesting but affecting particulars of his death, which took place yesterday in pursuance to a sentence of Court Martial by which he was found guilty of being a leader of the Rebel army in the battle that was fought at Antrim on the 7th of June last, though the witnesses who swore against him contradicted each other in some material points and one of them declared the other, who was the same man that swore away poor Storey's life, to be a man of infamous character, and not deserving of the smallest credit. I should have informed you as perhaps you do not see the public papers, that he was taken on the 7th instant along with 2 or 3 others by two of the Carrick yeomen, a mile or so from that town, and depending on a pass that had been procured for him in a feigned name he did not think of making his escape till it was too late, he and his companions being unarmed and having no means of defence whatever. I am thus particular because he has been accused of cowardice in suffering himself to be taken at all tho' he had no possible means of resistance. He was committed to Carrickfergus Jail where he was closely confined in a cell until Monday morning last, when he was brought up to Belfast and lodged in the Donegall Arms which is now a prison, from which he was removed in the afternoon to the Artillery Barracks, his trial came on yesterday at 12 o'clock at which I was present that I might bear testimony to his conduct which was cool collected and composed during the whole day, he took notes of the trial and remarked on the contradictions of the witnesses, but at the same time was certain of being convicted, as the trials here are mere matters of form, not one having been yet acquitted. I was also present when he received his sentence and was ordered for immediate execution, at which he neither changed countenance nor colour, but still retained his usual cheerful composure, for though he wished to live to serve his friends and his Country yet he was resigned to die, on being asked if he wished for a Clergyman he said he would be glad to see Mr. Kilburn who was accordingly sent for, and in the meantime as Dr. Dickson was confined in the same prison he requested to have his company which was also granted, with whom he conversed with firmness and ease, he said he was now vexed at having been angry at those by whom he had been cruelly treated, one of them in particular and from whom he would never have expected such conduct, not content with perverting Henry's words in excuse for his own base desertion, he even attempted to blacken his character by accusing him of crimes which he never either committed himself nor suffered others to do on whom he had any influence.

Mr. K. when he arrived was so overpowered by his feelings that it was a considerable time before his tears and sobs would permit him to utter a short prayer, after which as the time was short I began to take off a little of Harry's hair to preserve it for a few of his friends, when Major Fox entered to order him out and told me I might save myself the trouble as the General had ordered him to take it from me, against this I remonstrated but in vain, he would take it from me by force if I did not give it up which at Harry's request I did, who reminded me of what was true that it was but a trifle.—I accompanied him to the place of execution, where I wished to remain to the last, but even that small consolation was denied me. I was forcibly torn from him as they said by the General's orders and should have made more vigorous resistance, but Harry requested me to go and I feared disturbing his mind in his last moments by such an unequal contest—I have been told since that when I left him Major Fox came up to ask him for the last time, an offer of pardon having been made before trial some time if he would give any information, at which he smiled and told Fox he wondered what reason he had for supposing him such a villain but as they were now to part forever he would shake hands with him—I was also informed that when he ascended the scaffold he attempted to address the people but the noise the horses made was so great that he could not be heard. A few minutes put him beyond the power of oppression, but robbed his friends of a treasure never in this world to be recovered—never did I see him look so well so interesting or seemingly in such perfect health as that day and the evening before, notwithstanding the hardships he had of late undergone being mostly exposed to the open air and sleeping frequently on the cold wet ground and enduring difficulties of every kind—it is some small consolation that even his enemies were forced to admire his conduct both from what they say and from the evidence by which he was convicted, he acted like . . .[torn] . . . the last and smiled when the rope was put about his neck. I was allowed . . . [torn] . . . of embracing his lifeless corpse on condition of interring it before dark and the numbers in that short time who crowded in to weep over it, showed how much he was beloved. It was as impolitic as cruel to murder one who was the idol of the poor, he who was so patient of injuries, so benevolent of heart, hundreds now pant for revenge whom he had the power and benevolence to restrain, but this could neither restore him to life nor would it gratify him if he was sensible of it.

At the same time that he desired me to write he bid me to vindicate his friend Mr. Richardson's character from the unjust suspicion which had been cast upon it by his fellow prisoners and for which the testimony of a dying man who had been his most intimate friend will surely be sufficient.

I have been thus minute because it is probable we may never meet again, as Frank intends leaving this unhappy Country in a few days and the rest of the family mean to follow him as soon as he can prepare a place of refuge in some distant land where we may in peace cherish the remembrance of him whose loss we must ever lament, whose memory will be always dear to us and whose virtues we will still admire and revere. At the same time we should endeavour to be resigned to the will of that Being who overrules and directs all things, and who would not suffer us to be afflicted but for some useful purpose. That the cause for which so many of our friends have fought and have died may yet be successful, and that you may be preserved to enjoy the fruits of it, is the earnest wish of one who remains with the truest regard your sincere friend

Mary Ann McCracken.[36]

Little did she know in what circumstances she would again meet Thomas Russell.

It was some forty years later that Mary Ann wrote the account of her brother's execution for Dr. Madden. As she pondered on the tragic events, and the fatal disunity that led to the Northern impotence, her unfailing sense of justice once more asserted itself. How *could* Robert Simms—one of the original secret committee who had formulated in 1791 the whole idea of the Societies of United Irishmen, a proprietor of the *Northern Star*, the constant advocate of armed revolt, and a prisoner for some months in Newgate, how could he, at the critical moment, have so greatly failed the Cause? There must be some reason, some explanation. So, she adds this paragraph:

In justice to the Northern directory, I must remind you that Harry brought the message from Dublin respecting the plan and time of action. He could not be mistaken, but they might have misunderstood him so far, as to have thought that the first signal was only one for preparation and that it was to be followed by another, giving a certain knowledge of the rising in Dublin having taken place; and this not being the case they were not warranted in acting; and by being over cautious the opportunity was lost, which never returned; at all events, I do not think they were influenced by personal cowardice. The general, who was one of the directory, was, and still continues, a man of most exemplary character, both moral and religious, and a man of such a serious, thoughtful mind, so truly conscientious and well disposed, that he could not be supposed likely to enter into either a dishonest or an impracticable scheme; and his example, moreover, had great influence in inducing others to join the union.

As for Harry: after all these years

Notwithstanding the grief that overcame every feeling for a time, and still lingers in my breast, connecting every

> passing event with the remembrance of former circumstances which recall some act or thought of his, I never once wished that my beloved brother had taken any other part than that which he did take.[37]

Along with the record, written in her own clear handwriting, she sent to Dr. Madden a little packet of folded paper, about two inches square. Inside was a curl of hair, fine and silky, and exquisitely golden. He wrote on the outside " A lock of Henry Joy McCracken's hair, sent me by his sister ", and pasted it carefully into his great portfolio of letters and papers : there it can be seen to-day, still bright. As Mary Ann had watched beside that dear body, awaiting the arrival of Dr. McDonnell and the apothecary, and well beyond the imperious interference of Major Fox, it is not difficult to imagine that she had satisfied that " mere gratification to herself ", and now, as a mark of her great esteem for Dr. Madden she sent him a little bit of the treasured memento.

CHAPTER XI

THOMAS RUSSELL

1798–1803

FOR the McCrackens there seemed now no respite but in flight. Francis, fearing that the extent of his implication in the United movement would certainly be discovered, left the country within a fortnight, determined to find a "refuge" for all the family in America.* Many others departed likewise, among them William Thompson, the the calico printer, whose letter of farewell was kept by Mary as one of her greatest treasures.

> Miss Mary [he wrote in a beautiful copy-book hand]
> Excuse the Manner I take, to return my thanks for the goodness & care, you took in my late little Mischances, for to you I may say I owe my Health ; I would have returned my Warmest Thanks Verbally; only a Crissis like this; When you have lost a Brother, Mankind a true Friend ; & Myself the only man on Earth I ever had a True or sincere Regard for, or Perhaps ever will ; as I shall quit this Country in a few hours, never to return, any Trinket sent to me, that ever Belong'd to him, I would look upon it As the Instrumental Part, of my Religeon, & learn from its Philanthropick owner to Live & Die—
> Yours for Ever Oblig'd Umble Servt
> Will Thompson.[1]

No need to point out that William was an Englishman—probably he was one of the workers that Harry had brought back with him from Scotland not yet ten years ago, who had found in the high-spirited young employer, not only a considerate master, but the leader who understood as no one else did the aspirations of the poor. The "little mischances" were the 200 cruel lashes borne unflinchingly for that same loved leader, the wounds from which Mary had dressed and tended so skilfully as to save his life. It was his wife who would so willingly have perjured herself at Harry's trial.

*He returned shortly, and the plan for emigration did not materialise.

To add to their anxieties, William McCracken, on emerging from his hiding place, was " taken up." Again it was Mary Ann who acted. Within so short a time of the execution of one brother she sought and gained an interview with General Lake to plead for another, and as a result William was released on bail.[2]

For Mary there was but one gleam of brightness. Before leaving for his self-imposed exile Frank visited the prisoners still confined in Belfast to say farewell, and carried back to his sister a message from the Rev. Steele Dickson, asking her to come to him on " urgent business."[3] Not till then did she learn of the existence of Harry's little daughter, and that his inability to make provision for her had been his only sorrow in his last moments. The child was about four years old and it has always been assumed, though I can find no supporting evidence, that her mother was Mary Bodel, daughter of the labouring man in whose cottage on the Cave Hill Harry had so often sheltered. Be that as it may, and the assumption is probably correct, the news of that brief interview changed the world for Mary. The child was, she records, " left to our care " and brought home to Rosemary Lane, but she makes no mention of the family tussle that ensued. It was one thing to welcome to the family roof little Atty Bunting, but in John McCracken's eyes, at any rate, there were more convenient and perfectly usual methods of disposing of this reminder of Harry's impetuosity. " We have got " he wrote to Frank in September [then on his way to the Barbadoes], " an addition to the family since you were here, it is a little Girl said to be a daughter of poor Harry's, it was bro' very much against my inclinations." Harry's secret, it is evident, had been divulged only to Mary ; instantly she had made up her mind, the child was to be cared for as her own, loved and treasured " as an only and affectionate daughter." She was called Maria. No doubt memories of Mary Wollstonecraft fortified Mary Ann in her decision, for it was no light matter, in the circumstances, to bring this child into the family circle ; but it was her own deep love for Harry that made any other action impossible. From that moment all the affection that his memory evoked was lavished on his little daughter who, so soon, was to merit in her own right.* Fearing, no doubt, the gibes and taunts that might be hurled at this dearly loved child by children at a local school, Mary sent her niece to a boarding school at Ballycraigy, near Antrim, where she was very happy, and we may be sure her studies were followed with close interest by an aunt so enthusiastic for the education of women. We may be sure, too, that holidays were the occasion of joyous re-unions.

Meanwhile the affairs of state went on. On October 6th the Irish Parliament was prorogued, Lord Castlereagh declaring in a notable speech that " the dangerous and wicked rebellion " had been suppressed and that Sir Horatio Nelson had won a glorious victory over the French in the Mediterranean. [The battle of the Nile.] But the Government was taking no chances. Martial law continued, troops were still quartered on civilians, spies were everywhere, arrests were frequent, and methods of gruesome cruelty were, at times, employed against any who came under suspicion. Prisons were full, and hundreds of the rank and file of the United Irishmen and Defenders were transported to the newly established penal settlement of Botany Bay ;[4] others were permitted to serve in the army and navy in dangerous climates, or to join the armies of the King of Prussia. The chief leaders were still confined in Dublin, and in the spring of 1799 no less than twenty, including Robert Simms, Thomas Russell and Samuel Neilson, Wm. Tennent, Rev. Steele Dickson, and others from Belfast, were removed to the lonely fortress of Fort George in Inverness-shire for safe keeping till the war should end.

Exhausted and dispirited, a strange apathy fell on the politically-minded in the North, while, led by the new Marquis of Donegall and his lady, a wild and extravagant gaiety dominated the scene. Dancing till eight in the morning, excessive gambling, masquerades and private

*The child's mother and her family were assisted by Mary to go to America.

theatricals filled night after night of the calendar, and pages of Mrs. McTier's letters—

> This town is at present one continued scene of gaity, in private houses and of hours you may judge when I tell you that at Greg's* Ball Genl. Goldie and his party kept their seats at the Brag table from 9 'till three when supper was sent to them, from that till they breakfasted next Day and broke up at 5 of it on Cunningham sending them word that he was sorry his being engaged prevented his requesting their company to dinner.[5]

And so it went on.

Side by side with this hilarious extravagance there was increasing hardship for the poor. While a good harvest in 1798 did much to restore tranquility in the country districts, the following two years were disastrous. 1799 was unusually wet, heavy snow falling in April with floods on the River Lagan exceeding anything that could be remembered. Food was so scarce that by Proclamation the baking of other than brown bread was prohibited, and the soldiers were deprived of their hair-powder which was manufactured in Belfast and largely composed of flour. The exportation of all foodstuffs was forbidden and the free entry of Indian corn and meal allowed—arrangements that stand out in glaring contrast to those at the time of the potato famine half a century later. The year following was exceptionally dry, and again the harvest was bad. Prices soared and there was widespread unemployment owing to the dislocation of trade and to the many bankruptcies that occurred in Belfast.[6] Old Mrs. Drennan, writing to her son in January 1799 bemoans

> . . . there is no living here on small incomes, everything you can name double the price . . . everything in the nice way of eating is banished my home, it takes all I can muster for the plainest meat[6]

*Cunningham Greg was a brother of Jane Greg who took such a poor view of Hannah More [p. 110].

And, exclaims Mrs. McTier, thinking apprehensively of her fixed income,

> the very paper I write on is to-day raised for the 2nd time—Bread, Potatoes and every necessary doubled—unless my bequest increases what am I to do?[7]

For the poor these conditions were disastrous, and efforts were made to mitigate suffering. The gay rich were reasonably generous and a public kitchen and a public bakery were opened, and some of the charitably minded ladies established the Cheap Repository in Skippers' Lane where garments, made or collected by them, were sold very cheaply to the deserving poor. The Strangers' Friend Society was the pleasant-sounding title of the organization that endeavoured to find work for the growing number of unemployed who swarmed in from the country. At this time the population of Belfast was estimated at approximately 19,000. Unusually severe recurrences of fever were the inevitable result of misery and starvation, and what must have been a frequent happening is thus related by Mrs. McTier:

> Doctor Thompson of Colerain lies ill in a fever got in his attendance on the fever Hospital where the patients are crouded & attendants all ill, yet crouds and familys rejected every day—The Town subscribes above 200 guineas a month to *one* charity the Soup house & yet our streets and the habitations of our lanes present scenes of vice & wretchedness unequall'd in former times, a habitation which I visited yesterday fill'd by 4 generations of females—two confined on their straw by sickness—without a remnant of Linen, a chair, stool, or board to sit on, the wheel* at the Pawn brokers & all they once possessed—for once they were decent, this scene has suggested to me the idea of charitable *dry* Drums once a week, where open'd cards are to be played with & the usual card money go to the poor—The lady at whose house the party is, to have the distributing of the money—*Provided* she enters in a book for that purpose, the names, circumstances, & places of abode of those she relieves . . . On Saturday I make the first attempt.[8]

*The spinning wheel.

The poor were not the only victims of fever. Well-to-do families were smitten and, in many cases, so great was the fear of infection, friends would not even call to make inquiries at the door.

Whilst in Dublin the burning topic of the proposed legislative union between Ireland and Gt. Britain occupied every mind, it could neither pierce the apathy nor interrupt the gaiety in Belfast—" union or no union seems equally disregarded."[9] In general the merchants were opposed to it as likely to worsen rather than improve the prospects of trade, though some of the linen manufacturers saw possibilities of benefit. In October 1799 His Excellency the Lord Lieutenant [Lord Cornwallis] arrived on a short visit to Belfast, with a view, no doubt, to influencing the inhabitants in favour of proposed union. It was natural enough that the Sovereign and burgesses, still the nominees of the Donegall family, should present him with the freedom of their Corporation, but that Mr. and Mrs. William Sinclaire should entertain His Lordship to breakfast and later take him to the " Green ", shows just how far in the opposite direction the pendulum had now swung.

Nine years previously Wm. Sinclaire—nick-named by Tone " The Draper "—had been a prominent advocate of extreme reform and an outstanding opponent of Henry Joy jun.'s policy of gradual constitutional change. He had been one of the first to befriend Russell when he arrived in Belfast in 1791 to join his regiment, and to introduce him to the political views for which, at that moment, he [Russell] was languishing in Fort George. Tone's diary abounds in references to Sinclaire's leadership both in politics and industry, and his description of the bleach green deserves to be quoted :

> Oct. 24 [1791] Breakfast at Wm. Sinclaire's, per engagement ; could not eat. Mrs. Sinclaire nursed me with French drams, etc. Rode out with P.P. [Russell] and Sinclaire to see his bleach green. A noble concern ; extensive machinery. Sinclair's improvements laughed at by his neighbors, who said he was mad. The first man who introduced American

> potash ;* followed only by three or four, but creeping on. The rest use Barilla. Almost all work done by machinery ; done thirty years ago by hand, and all improvement regularly resisted by the people. Mr. Sinclair, sen. often obliged to hire one, and sometimes two companies of the garrison, to execute what is now done by one mill . . . Sinclair a man of very superior understanding. Anecdotes of the linen trade . . . Ireland able to beat any foreign linens for quality and cheapness, as appears by the American market, which gives no preference by duties, and is supplied entirely by Ireland. If England were disposed she might, for a time, check the trade of Ireland in linens ; but she would soon give up that system for her own sake, because she could not be supplied elsewhere so good and cheap.[10]

Gradually, however, Sinclaire disappears from the political scene, and we may assume that he was one of the not inconsiderable section of the Presbyterian reformers previously mentioned [p. 169], who modified their republicanism in the interests of trade. It was of such that Henry Alexander wrote to Pelham in June 1798 " The Northerners do not like the Papists. They feel the injuries [by the French] to America. . . . They possess the escheated counties ; and their bleachers, though they would huckster with any man who would promise to govern them cheapest, will not like the destruction of their greens."[11] Now, one year later, we have William Sinclaire, the eminently successful bleacher and once the ardent United Irishman, taking the Lord Lieutenant to visit his still famous " green ", aware, no doubt, that concessions for the linen and cotton industries might be negotiated as the price of support of the Union. How true had been Jemmy Hope's prognostication [p. 169].

If no instance better illustrates the varying and changing motives behind some sections of the Northern movement, none throws into greater relief the disinterested idealism that to the very end inspired Neilson, Russell and McCracken. To these three it was the principles of Liberty, Equality and Fraternity alone that mattered, and for which each of them sacrificed glowing possibilities of material advancement.

*For bleaching.

Such then was the Belfast that surrounded Mary Ann in the months immediately following her brother's death. How desolate she must have felt without Harry, how lonely without the companionship of others with whom she had been in close and continuous contact, and how cut off from those who formerly had been pleasant acquaintances; for we may be sure that very many besides the Sinclaires avoided those extreme McCrackens whose devotion to their principles had run them into serious trouble. Mary's stout heart may sometimes have been daunted, but she never faltered. There was still the friendship of Eliza Templeton; the sufferings of the poor would be a constant concern, and so, if for no other reason than to provide employment, the muslin industry must be kept going at all costs; at the same time she allowed no political apathy to blunt her keen perception into the Union controversy.

Fortunately some letters of these years remain, written between Mary Ann and her cousin Grizzel Joy, one of the "warm-hearted Belfast girls" who kept house in Dublin for their brother the Counsellor. The first is written from Dublin on Nov. 10th 1798 after Grizzel, her sister Harriet and her brother had been on a visit to Belfast. Grizzel acknowledges the receipt of a piece of plaid muslin, which was greatly admired, and goes on to say that the trial of the unfortunate Mr. Tone* had started that day. He appeared in Court, dressed as a French officer in a superb uniform, and behaved in a most "firm and dignified manner." He read his defence which was both "inflammatory and eloquent." Harry [the Counsellor] had meant to attend the trial but arrived as it was ending, and these particulars had been furnished by a gentleman who was present. She continues:

If I can procure a copy of Mr. Tone's defence I will send

*In 1796 Tone returned to France from America. The next two years had been spent in ceaselessly urging the French to send aid to Ireland. After disappointing Irish hopes so disastrously in the spring of 1798 a French expedition landed at Killala in August of that year to be quickly repulsed. In October another small French force, with Tone as one of the officers, was intercepted off the Donegal coast. Tone was taken prisoner and brought to Dublin for trial.

it to you as I suppose it will not be published. You will not allow me to say I *pity* such a man, I certainly feel the greatest regret at his unhappy fate, and the sincerest commiseration for his wife and family.

Harry and Harriet join me in love to my Uncle and Aunt and all the family, don't forget to give Kissy Joy's love to Mary and Ann, and believe me, dear Mary, with warmest affection

Yours

G. Joy.[12]

Ann was John's toddler daughter, the subject of Mary's early letter ; one wonders if Mary was, perhaps, the little Maria.

Two days later Grizzey sends Mary Ann the " sketch " of Mr. Tone's trial, and adds

You have doubtless heard before this of the attempt he made on his life, he however, suffered the wound in his throat to be dressed, and is so much better to-day that little doubt is entertained of his recovery.[13]

Probably there was another letter when Tone's self-inflicted wound proved fatal, but it has not survived.

The plaid muslin had been very successful, and the next letter carries an order for Grizzey's friend Mrs. Echlin :

If you have none exactly the same send me patterns of those you have that she may choose. Some time ago you sent me patterns of Cambric muslin. We liked the one marked 6/6d. extremely, and thought it quite thick enough. I would have begged of you to keep that piece for us, but as we had no immediate opportunity of getting it I thought you might get it sold in Belfast and we would get the next you would make. If that piece, however is still on hand we shall be glad to have it, or if not as soon as possible a piece of the same kind. Mr. Waring, the atty. would I am sure bring it up for us.[14]

Grizzey then embarks on politics :

I enclose you the Anti-Union of to-day, in it is a short address of Harry's* to the electors of Ulster. I am astonished

*The Counsellor.

> that on a subject of such importance to the country the people of Ulster, and particularly the Inhabitants of Belfast have not expressed their sentiments, a measure on which the very existance of Ireland as a Nation depends. My pride as a Irishwoman would lead me to detest it, if I were not, as I am, convinced that it will be destructive to the interests of Ireland, our manufactures it will annihilate, and our taxes will be increased beyond calculation. Parliament sits on Tuesday next when it is expected the question will be brought forward. I can scarce give you an idea of the agitation of the public mind here on this subject. I have no patience with Belfast.[15]

The letter is undated, but was obviously written just before Jan. 22nd 1799, the day on which Parliament reassembled to hear the Speech from the Throne that introduced the momentous proposal. One can almost see a weary smile pass over Mary Ann's face as she read the pamphlet and Grizzey's remarks. Why, oh why, all this vehemence now ? Indeed it is she who turns impatiently on the Counsellor :

> I thank you, [she replied] for Harry's address which afforded me much pleasure ; if any publication were to be issued here, written with such spirit and boldness, both writer and publisher would run a great risque of having their houses demolished, besides being committed to the military prison.
>
> Tho' it is with extreme pleasure I observe such an unexpected change has taken place in Harry's political opinion, yet I can scarcely think it possible that it is he who so strenuously recommends the consideration of public measures to general attention, he who so lately appeared to think it sacriligious to oppose any of the measures of Government or infringe any of the laws, which he thought sufficiently obligatory in being generally known, and who seemed also to disapprove so highly of individuals not connected with Government, neglecting their own [affairs] to meddle with politics. The motto of his address is perfectly applicable to the present situation of the country ; but in a sense quite the reverse of which he means. Is there no other argument against this union, than ' that it will lessen the property of the rich ' ? The question I ask myself is, Can it increase the sufferings of the poor ?—of

those especially who are entitled to our commiseration? Let us turn our eyes to the wretched cottagers of the south, whose labour can scarcely procure them a single meal of potatoes in the day, and whose almost total want of clothing make them fly the approach of strangers. Yet how insensible did we all appear to that accumulation of injuries and oppressions under which they have so long groaned, and by which they were finally driven to their late unhappy insurrection;—I say unhappy because unsuccessful [for] long before resistance came the most shocking cruelties were practised on the people though on a less extensive scale than subsequently to the insurrection. I do not make this assertion on slight grounds, or on hearsay authority, but from the perusal of a great number of affidavits sworn by the actual sufferers, and collected by one whose exertions in behalf of humanity are now at an end; by one who, in neglect of every personal consideration uninfluenced by every motive of individual advantage, set danger and difficulty at defiance, in prosecuting an investigation into the complaints of the unfortunate people in a neighbouring county, where a licensed horde of ruffians, under the denomination of Orangemen, were allowed, unpunished, to commit atrocities which humanity recoils to think on.* It is not every man can look on every law of justice and humanity trampled on, openly and daily, and that with impunity. And yet we were told that justice even then rested on an immutable basis. The Habeas Corpus Act, the Indemnity Act, have long since proved that these foundations might be shaken or removed at the pleasure of a British Minister. As there are two distinct bodies in the North, I know not which of them Harry means to address. Is it that body, who once vainly imagining that they were in possession of an independent Parliament, whose laws were sufficient to protect their liberty, and stepped boldly forward, and were willing to hazard life, property, and everything they held dear in support of it? But the delusion is now vanished; the intrigues of the British minister weakened, by dividing the country; it is now no longer necessary to deceive the people; they are left without the means of resistance, if they had the inclination or temerity to have recourse to it, and must patiently submit to the new wrong that is now in meditation for them. All, it is true, do

*She alludes of course to her brother Harry.

not feel this to be their situation ; some having deserted their early principles, and adopted those they enrolled themselves among the volunteers to oppose. What is there left to contend for, now the substance is gone ? shall we quarrel for the shadow ? for the shadow alone of nationality remains in this unfortunate land.[16]

In spite of the general apathy in Belfast, here was someone who knew what she thought, and she did not scruple to let the Counsellor know just where she stood.

There was nothing original in Castlereagh's proposal, a legislative union had repeatedly been suggested as the only solution for the recurring difficulties between the two islands, indeed, the Rebellion itself may have been intentionally stimulated by the British Government to achieve that very end. When the great proposition was made it was opposed, not as one might at first imagine, by the remnants of the liberal groups, but, with a blast of fury, by the Ascendancy party itself, who saw, firstly, that the proposal would end their enormous prestige, power and privilege, but, on second thoughts, that they could commute that misfortune at a very good price. How that opposition was broken down is well known and need not concern us here. It was supported, though on rather more disinterested grounds, by the whole body of the Law, and Henry Joy, K.C., hustled for once out of his legal decorum, took a prominent part in organising the opinion of the Irish Bar. A great meeting of lawyers took place on December 9th 1798 when a resolution denouncing the Union was carried by 166 votes to 82. On the other hand, the opinion of the old liberal groups was divided. To all of them the autocratic power of the Irish Ascendancy party was the great enemy, but while the many still hoped for an Irish Parliament truly representative of the people, others, disillusioned by the results of 1782 and 1798, were ready to think that if complete separation from England were not at the moment possible, then representation at Westminster might be preferable to the concentrated corruption of College Green. Such thoughts were shortly to be expressed by Neilson in Fort George.[17]

For Mary the immediate prospect was dark indeed, but to fight for the maintenance of an Irish Parliament in Dublin without any guarantee that it would concern itself with the welfare of the humble people, made no appeal to her. She must have realised too, that the Catholics, raised by Tone and Harry and Russell from their state of silent servitude, had now their own ideas as to the struggle they were prepared to make for freedom. At any rate in spite of the Law and because of the Nobility* the Parliament in Dublin voted away its birthright, and the Act of Union was passed. On Jan. 1st 1801 a new flag was hoisted on the Old Market House in Belfast—it bore the cross of St. Patrick superimposed on the crosses of St. George and St. Andrew.

But to get back to muslin. Regarding the order for Mrs. Echlin, Mary replied that

> . . . a piece of Cambric Muslin of the same web, tho' not the very same piece off which the pattern you liked best was taken [had already been despatched by Mr. Wright.] I wrote to Magain desiring him to send you two pieces of Plaid Muslin, but not having since heard from him I apprehended they have both been sold. I therefore shall write to Coile and tell him to send you with this the only piece he has of it on hand.[18]

These details, written within a few months of her brother's death give some idea of the extent to which Margaret and Mary Ann had developed their business in spite of all other preoccupations, and of the care with which they carried out their transactions. It is likely enough that David Manson's progressive educational syllabus included the rudiments of business methods, but wherever she learnt it Mary Ann knew all about proper office routine. Half a century later, writing to Dr. Madden, when she was eighty-eight, she casually remarks that, on looking up her " letter-book ", she finds that several months had elapsed since she had last written—the early habits stayed with her to the end ! In spite of the disturbed state of trade, which incidentally had

*There were many notable and honourable exceptions.

prevented William McCracken from restarting work at his cotton mill in Smithfield, the sisters had been extremely successful. Their connection with Dublin required at least two agents there, and business in Belfast must have been equally satisfactory—Belfast gaiety would at any rate create a local demand for finery, and the Peace of Amiens (1802) produced optimism and gaiety everywhere. Furthermore the sisters were pioneers in the production of patterned and checked muslin, and in this they took great pride, Mary herself admitting that she "excelled in the beauty of our manufacture." So popular was this novelty that they were unable to meet the demand and "some others in the business sent to me for information on the subject which I gave them." Too generous to contemplate any form of monopoly, she and Margaret were obviously in the first rank of muslin manufacturers.

In the *Belfast News-Letter* of May 17, 1803, there appears a letter signed "Subscriber", which, for reasons that will be obvious to those who have studied her letters and writings, I have not the slightest hesitation in attributing to Mary Ann McCracken. It runs as follows:

To the Editor of *The Belfast News-Letter*.
Sir,

Actuated by a sincere regard for the happiness of my fellow creatures, I am induced through the medium of your valuable paper, to address to the Proprietors of Cotton Mills, and other Factories, the following hints, which from long experience have been found conducive to the preservation of health and of morality:—

The passages, stairs, floors and inner doors should be constantly kept clean, by sweeping, washing with soap and water, and scouring with sand, the walls whitewashed once a month, especially during summer, and for those parts most likely to rub off, the lime should be mixed with skim milk.

The above operations appear best adapted for destroying effluvia or miasmate, the concommitant of all crowded rooms.

Quicklime should daily be thrown into the houses of Convenience attached to large factories, which will effectively destroy all *fetid effluvia,* and produce a most valuable manure. As much air as is convenient should be allowed into the rooms both day and night, and particular attention should be paid to the cleanness of the workers' hands, faces, etc. who ought to be provided with warm coats and cloaths so as to be protected against the evil effects of wet and cold, when going to and returning from their work ; sufficient time should be allowed for amusement in the open air during fine weather, especially after the dinner hour.

A very serious responsibility attaches to those who employ children ; for if the morals of children become depraved, from what sources are we to procure virtuous men and virtuous women ? Those, therefore, who draw children from the superintending care of their parents, ought to consider themselves as accountable for their conduct, consequently very circumspect in the choice of their overseers, and in the men and women employed with the children ; keeping the sexes as separate as possible, offering premiums and every other source of encouragement for good behaviour, discouraging improper conduct, by levying fines for swearing, obscene expressions, etc., and holding out such inducements as will procure a strict attendance at Sunday Schools.

In short the proprietor of a Factory is in duty bound to consider himself as the parent of a numerous family, and to do all those things which a sensible and virtuous parent would do ; for it is obvious that nothing short of such conduct will prevent *emaciation*, *ignorance*, and *vice*, or e'er long the following exclamation—*Live Morality* ! —*Perish Factories* !

I am, Sir, etc.
A Subscriber.

Here we have, as well as her passion for the general welfare of workers; her interest in health, her never-satisfied clamour for education, and a clear grasp of the responsibilities created by these new forms of industry. She rejoiced in the scientific developments of her day, they aroused in her the courage and imagination of the explorer. Of all her characteristics this deep interest in industry and in the new methods of production, is one of the most striking. Inherited it may have been, but she had no inhibitions about extending it. At the same time she was acutely aware of the increased responsibilities devolving upon employers, and of the calamitous effects of bad conditions of employment on the defenceless workers. In all this she was greatly in advance of her day. One wonders if she knew that three years earlier Robert Owen had started his famous experiment at the New Lanark cotton mills, where he set himself to improve conditions of work in order to improve the characters of his workers. Owen was only one year junior to Mary McCracken, there is no mention of him in any of her writings; if he and his work did not influence her then she was simultaneously proclaiming comparable ideas. This letter was written a quarter of a century before textile workers in Britain, banding themselves together under the leadership of Doherty and Robert Owen, prepared the way for the Chartist risings, and almost half a century before Lord Shaftesbury's crusade which ushered in the whole sequence of factory legislation. Still in her early thirties, Mary saw clearly the basis on which alone satisfactory industrial relations could be established; to her it was the same as that on which every kind of human relationship must rest. To maintain these principles she had followed Harry into the arena of political strife; had they been born a decade or two later their sphere of action would, in all probability, have been industrial.

Though the Rebellion had been suppressed and the Union accomplished there had been, while the war with France lasted, constant rumours in Ireland of threatened invasion, and fears that the revolutionary element had not completely abandoned hope. Mrs. McTier remarked that large quantities of handcuffs had arrived in Belfast from Birmingham,[19] and her brother sensed that "the leven of republicanism which still rests among the Northerners will still meet with political and personal publication."[20] But generally speaking Ireland was wearied of war and civil war. The Peace of Amiens [1802] was welcomed here, as elsewhere, and to the weary prisoners in Fort George liberation seemed near. All were released, but on varying terms. William Tennent, Robert Simms and the Rev. Steele Dickson returned to Belfast, but Russell, Samuel Neilson and Thomas Addis Emmet, with others, were obliged to accept banishment as the price of freedom.

As one reads the meagre reports of the release of the prisoners one feels the chilling blast of anti-climax. The Governor of Fort George was a humane and likeable person, who, by his consideration for the welfare of the internees had won their gratitude and admiration. More than that, the failure of the Rebellion had been a soul-searing experience. For those in the North who had persevered to the bitter end it had been a venture of sheer idealism, an entirely disinterested effort to gain parliamentary reform and to alleviate the burdens and sufferings of the lowest classes of society in town and country, Catholic and Protestant alike. It had failed, tragically failed,—in the short view through lack of support from those on whom they had depended, but longer reflection disclosed more fundamental causes. So, men who had risked and lost everything for an ideal suffered, for the most part, either deep disillusionment or bitter resentment. It is said that Government spies penetrated even the fastness of Fort George, and that all this was known. The disillusioned were allowed to return to Ireland and there they endeavoured to adjust themselves quickly to the new regime. Robert Simms took up his business in Belfast and bought a house in the country; William Tennent quickly resumed his place as a most progressive merchant and was shortly to be connected with the founding of one of the first Banks in the town; and the Rev. Steele Dickson continued his vocation as a presbyterian minister. The majority, however, had to face the loneliness of banishment. Neilson, after one fleeting clandestine visit to his family and friends in Ireland, set sail, as did many of his companions, for America.* Others, including Russell, wandered from

*He died in 1803 near New York. In fairness to the Rev. Wm. Bristow [again Sovereign of Belfast] it must be recorded that while he was perfectly aware of Neilson's unauthorised visit he permitted him to bid farewell unmolested.

place to place on the Continent, brooding on failure, and yearning for an opportunity to avenge defeat. To the old ideals was now added the urge to shatter the Act of Union.

Thomas Russell had borne the longest internment of any of the political prisoners. For five years and nine months he had been continuously confined without any trial, indeed in the words of the Chief Secretary, Pelham, who spoke "handsomely" of his character, "the government had no specific charge against him."[21] Now he was thrown on the world penniless, and unable to return to his country and friends. Immediately before his release he had written thus to John Templeton:

> Fort George. June 5, 1802.
>
> I must now speak of myself. The situation must excuse the egotism:—So far from conceiving the cause of Ireland lost, or being weary of its pursuit, I am more than ever, if possible, inflexibly bent on it, for that, I stay (if I can stay) in Europe; all the faculties I possess shall be exercised for its advancement, for that I wished to go to Ireland not to reside, but to see how I shall be able to serve it, and this I can only do when at large. Every motive exists to stimulate the generous mind—the widows & orphans of my friends, the memory of the heroes who fell, & the sufferings of the heroes who survive. My very soul is on fire. I can say no more—[22]

After his release he joined the group of Irish exiles in Paris, and there in the autumn of 1802 met young Robert Emmet, who had travelled from Dublin to see his brother Thomas, living then in exile in Amsterdam.

The Peace that for one year halted the war with France was strangely unreal: Napoleon was merely gathering his strength for further action, and Britain accordingly increased her armies and strengthened her defences. It was generally accepted that if hostilities were resumed the invasion of England would once more be a possibility, and it was believed that the French could count on a still disaffected minority in Ireland, should they decide to attempt a landing there. This was the situation that Robert Emmet and his collaborators intended to exploit.

When Emmet returned to Dublin early in 1803 he left in Paris a group of United Irishmen directed by Thomas Russell and closely in touch with Napoleon and Tallyrand. Sometime in the spring of 1803 Russell also made his way back to Ireland; in May England was again at war with France.

It is impossible to say how closely Mary Ann had kept in touch with Russell since the day in October 1796 when he was arrested in Belfast after breakfasting with the McCracken family, or how much she knew of what was happening. In the Kilmainham correspondence his name occurs from time to time, once in connection with some shirts that Mary was making for him, and again in the charming reference to the place he held in the affections of the Tomb family. But apart from the letter that she wrote to him at Harry's death Russell's papers contain no correspondence at all from Mary Ann, though he kept a goodly number of letters from other friends, especially from John Templeton. In 1800 Russell enclosed in a letter to this friend " a tune for my friend Bunting, which I beg you to give to him."[23]—it seems curious that he did not send it direct to Rosemary Lane. Again, writing to Templeton before his release and setting out his plans for the future, Russell sends " his kindest and warmest regards to Miss Mary McCracken, and all the good family. Remember me to Bunting. I have a copy of his music with me, and will do all I can to introduce it to notice."[24] Altogether it would seem that the Templetons were at this time Russell's closest friends, and that he was still unaware of the deep affection Mary felt for him, her shy, proud, nature disdaining any possible demonstration of her feelings.

As is frequent with idealists, Russell had a curiously unpractical attitude towards the mundane things of life. Not only was he penniless himself, and under the necessity of appealing to his friends for funds, but no provision having been made for his sister Margaret, to whom he was devoted, she was frequently the recipient of generous support from individuals in Belfast and Dublin, and her brother seemed quite content that it should be so. "Russell" remarks Drennan in 1802 "writes to his friends in the true spirit of a martyr, and demands a supply of £50 in the spirit of the poor Grecian Philosophers who used to leave the support of their Widows and daughters to some of their rich neighbours. Russell, in the same stile, leaves the support of his Sister to his friends."[25]

In the scant records of his movements there is no indication as to how soon Russell got in touch with the McCrackens after his return to Ireland. Emmet had put him in charge of the northern section of the projected rising and there was one brief visit to Ulster in May, but, from the accounts in Madden, it would seem that it was not until his second visit, towards the middle of July, that he met Francis McCracken, William and Robert Simms, and that Mary Ann and Margaret and Atty Bunting visited him in his hiding in the Castlereagh Hills. Yet Francis and the sisters must have known something of his plans, for it was Margaret who recommended to him a safe place of lodging, and there are two rough notes scribbled by an informer in Dublin to the Castle officials dated May 23rd, 1803. They run as follows:

> The Exultation last week in every party I met was excessive on account of the news from the Continent . . . As to the Ex. it is a thing next to impossible to ascertain the names—for the North I think it probable that either Tennant, the Sugar Baker, Francis McCracken, Rope and Sail Maker, or the Rev. Steele Dickson, forms part of it. No meetings have as yet taken place, nor are they even so much as talked of—nor is it probable they will be called on till they see or hear of the French making good a landing . . .
>
> I met by accident on Sunday last William Tennant and Francis McCracken of Belfast. Their being in town at this juncture is somewhat extraordinary, as they bore very conspicuous characters in fomenting the late Rebellion.[26]

"Their being in town" may, however, have been for a purpose very different to that inferred by the informer; it is possible that they had travelled to Dublin to do what they could to prevent a rising.

In the beginning of July, Mary forwarded the second instalment of a collection of 25 guineas that she had made for the destitute Margaret Russell in Dublin. Apparently she was endeavouring to get promises of annual contributions sufficient to support the unfortunate lady, and complains bitterly in an accompanying letter of the "little benevolence and spirit shown in the town of Belfast."[27] If, at the time of making the collection, she knew nothing of Russell's movements [which I find it hard to believe] she must certainly have been aware of the rumours current everywhere consequent on the renewal of war with France. When some busybody informed the authorities that Miss McCracken was collecting money for, it was *said*, Miss Russell, they reasonably enough regarded the whole thing with the utmost suspicion and Mary Ann was forced to curtail her efforts. Never did she allow personal convenience to influence her conduct, but on this occasion her sense of need and distress seems to have outrun all considerations of ordinary prudence.

Russell came north, as has been said, about the middle of July accompanied, as on the previous occasion, by Jemmy Hope, and he took up his position on the outskirts of Belfast, living with a weaver who worked for the McCracken sisters, and it was in his cottage that, so far as we know, the first meeting for seven years between Russell and the sisters took place. As Margaret and Mary Ann set out on that summer day for their journey across the Lagan and up into the Castlereagh Hills what memories would fill their thoughts—Harry's dearest friend—the family confidences that he had shared—the joy and mirth that he had done so much to heighten—would the "manly beauty" be still unaltered? Doubtless Mary's heart beat fast in bewildering anticipation, but it was Margaret, retiring, coldly proud and sensitive, who suggested that they should take ten guineas and "the ring that had been bespoke for Francis when he was going to America with Harry's hair in it" as gifts for the cherished outlaw.[28] We know nothing else about the visit.

The meeting already mentioned, between Russell, William and Robert Simms, Francis McCracken and others, was vital. All dissuaded Russell from an enterprise that could end only in disaster. No record has been left of the arguments they used—doubtless they pointed out the vast changes in the revolutionary movement owing to the loss of leaders, the wholesale transportations by the government and the exile of many prominent figures. The government measures for suppressing the Rebellion of '98 had been ruthless and effective—those former leaders who were permitted to return to the country had been obliged to give enormous bail.[29] The military strength of Britain was apparent, so was the utter futility of placing any confidence in France. But in addition to all this, these Northerners had been forced to realise that the traditional divisions in Irish life were still stronger than the bonds the United Irishmen had sought to forge. In the bloody battles of the Rebellion that took place in Wexford the old religious and social alignments had swept the county, and the men of Belfast refused to contemplate further action on such a basis. False and exaggerated though many of the reports from the South may have been, the happenings there were, I think, one of the most potent causes of the speedy decline of the insurgent element in Ulster.

Whatever was said, the counsel of the ex-leaders prevailed, and Russell realised with bitter anguish that a rising in the North was impossible. Until this renewed contact with his former companions, he was unaware how completely the situation had altered since his arrest in 1796—how widespread had been the disillusionment. Broken-hearted, he decided to quit the North, and on July 15th he wrote to Francis McCracken :

> I go this moment for the purpose of, if in my power, rectifying the mistakes that have taken place. Whether I fail or succeed is in the hands of God, but the cause I will never relinquish. He has for the moment stopt our progress no doubt wisely—courage alone was wanting here as far as I can see to render our success not only certain but easy . . . I am going to join any body I can find in arms in support

> of their rights and that of mankind. Let me request of you not to suffer your . . . to be dispirited, the cause shall succeed tho' individuals may fall . . . I beg it may be stated that I have no anger to the country. I have no doubt committed faults but I acted for the best, and hope I may be able to repay and set all right. I received from a lady* on Wednesday what you sent me, for that and all your kindness accept all I can give my thanks.[30]

Had he got back to Emmet would the rising have been postponed? The answer to that question will never be given, for before Russell could set out on his journey news reached him that Emmet had been forced to change his plans and that the attack had opened in Dublin on July 23rd. There was now no alternative. In desperation he issued his Proclamation, hoping against hope for support. He sent his messengers here and there, but except for a few isolated, leaderless groups, the North failed to respond, and before it had rightly started the rising in Dublin had collapsed—though not until tragic occurrences had taken place. Fantastic as the whole situation was, the Government took no chances. Belfast and Dublin were heavily garrisoned with troops and the hated yeomanry, and rewards were offered for Russell's apprehension. From the hiding place in the Castlereagh Hills came a strange little note to Mary Ann, expressing confidence even yet of ultimate success, and requesting that ten guineas be sent at once.[31] It was written—not in ink—but with the blue used by the linen weavers to stamp their webs.

To-day the Rising of 1803 appears as incredible folly—the planning was totally inadequate, there was no hope of support from the French, there was nothing but the impelling conviction of two leaders. Close though it was in point of time to '98, and often considered as its delayed conclusion, in point of fact it was the opening of a new era, for in ideology the two risings were worlds apart. The Rebellion of 1798 had been fundamentally a great struggle for social justice, the nearest thing to the French Revolution to happen in these islands, and it is

*Presumably Mary McCracken.

significant that it occurred in that one of them where conditions, in some respects, closely resembled pre-Revolution France. With Emmet's Rising, on the other hand, modern Irish nationalism was born, and the long struggle centring on nationalism had begun.

We can only guess at the anguish for Mary Ann. Once again she embarked on the business of aiding an outlaw. To the government's award of £500 the Sovereign of Belfast added another £500—subscribed by the citizens. It may seem strange that in the town where Russell had been such a favourite companion this sum should have been so speedily raised, but it is stranger still that when Mr. Skeffington, a magistrate, accompanied by the Rev. Wm. Bristow, Sovereign, called on Dr. James McDonnell they were promised a donation by the man who had been Russell's intimate and generous friend, and who, even during the Fort George captivity, had been his regular correspondent. McDonnell later endeavoured to explain away this strange behaviour—this second failing of his friends—but the sad fact remains that influential opinion always swayed his actions. " Three friends of mine " he wrote years afterwards " John Templeton, his sister and Miss Mary McCracken refused soon after to speak well of me. . . . These things vexed me more than I can express ; but without any explanation on my part, all these persons returned to my friendship."[32] The following extract from John Templeton's diary dated 4 April 1825 provides the " explanation " :

> To-day Dr. McDonnell and I met and shook hands. This renewal of our intercourse was brought about by my sister Eliza. Disagreeable sensations yet pass across my mind when I recollect the deed of 1804 [sic] and with what affection, yes apparently brotherly affection Russel looked upon McDonnell. I cannot think of his subscription of £50 to induce some wretch to capture his friend without thinking what a sacrifice of every principle of Hospitality, Honour and Friendship he committed and how such an act would be reprobated by every man in whom the selfishness of Party Spirit had not obliterated every humane and benevolent feeling, and raised that of an interested and

> Savage ferocity in its place. But the Cloak of Royalty at that period covered every atrocity however despicable. I hope the thoughts which must have intruded themselves in the midnight hour have made him repent of the deed. Time has perhaps softened a little my feelings but I cannot forget the amiable Russel.*

It is not too much to suppose that Eliza's action was supported, perhaps even instigated, by Mary Ann.

In spite of tempting rewards, "posted on every corner" round his hiding place Russell stayed in safety with John Rabb and his wife, friends of the McCrackens, in the hills above Holywood for almost a month, a neighbourhood well known to Thomas and to Mary Ann, for Harry had been sent to the lough-side village to recuperate from an illness in 1794. The citizens of Belfast might subscribe for Russell's apprehension, but no one on the North would betray him for reward. Then word came of Emmet's arrest, and immediately Russell determined to set out for Dublin, in the hope of assisting his friend's escape. He had an overpowering admiration for young Robert. It was the Rabbs who found two fishermen in Bangor to take the outlaw in an open boat to Drogheda, and it was Mary Ann who financed the undertaking.[33] From Drogheda he made his way to Dublin, arriving perhaps too late to see his hero alive. Plans were next made for him to fly the country, but he was arrested on September 9th and lodged in Kilmainham Jail.

The news sped back to friends in Belfast, and efforts to effect his escape were instantly afoot. Negotiations were carried on through the McCrackens' agent in Dublin, who was instructed to draw on the sisters' account for funds. £200 were thus appropriated, of which a bank note for £100 was conveyed to an accomplice in the prison as a bribe for the turnkey. Gone were the days of Mary's passive devotion : sorrow and danger swept away all reserve. It may well be that Mary went herself to Dublin. She has left no record of such a journey, but a

*I am indebted to Mr. John Hewitt for bringing this extract to my notice.

persistent tradition has been preserved that " a young woman named McCracken had been allowed to visit Thomas Russell about the expense of his trial, and that they met in the Governor's office in the presence of the Gaoler and the turnkey".[34] Spies were again at work and on the morning of the day on which the escape was to be carried out, Russell was moved without warning to Downpatrick to stand his trial for high treason. Once more plans had to be remade. John McCracken induced young James Ramsey, a Belfast attorney, to offer his services without charge and he was immediately dispatched to Downpatrick. At first Russell refused to have any legal defence, but when it was pointed out that others awaiting trial might benefit if his case was properly conducted, he consented, and Mary Ann engaged the services of Counsellors Bell and Joy, at fees of 100 guineas each. It may have been an indication of the Counsellor's hatred of the Union with England that he should have undertaken the defence of a rebel. There was another hurried collection among friends—all her life Mary was to be found collecting money for someone or something—which produced £80 towards these legal expenses: the balance was met by the sisters. The resources of the muslin business were recklessly plundered, Mary regarding it as nothing short of providential when, at a most critical moment, a man who had been sent to sell muslins through the country arrived back with £90.

> How was it possible [she wrote] to shrink back when told that human lives were at stake, which my exertion might be instrumental in saving, and that no other person dare make the attempt . . . and, we having undertaken it, there was no question of drawing back for pecuniary risk.[35]

But that was not all. Mary determined to go to Downpatrick herself to see Russell. The trial was expected within a day or so and there were matters he might not wish to commit to writing, there was, for example, that ever present problem of his sister's future; there was also, we may assume, her own compelling longing to see him once more. Unfortunately she mentioned her scheme to Mr. Teeling, an old friend of the family, and he, poor man, horrified at the suggestion, went fussing along to Rosemary Lane, telling everyone of the dangers involved, and thoroughly frightening Mrs. McCracken. Mary Ann, neither to bind nor to hold with rage, seized her pen, and in the greatest haste, dashed off a note to Eliza Templeton her " dear enthusiastic friend "—the writing itself declaring her red hot indignation :

> My dear Eliza. I was never so completely vexed and perplexed in all my life as at present owing to [an] absurd and ridiculous indescretion in mentioning my intention to Mr. Teeling never supposing it possible that any person would think of opposing what I considered so natural and so much my duty. I should have . . . . but no matter. It is an injury I can never forgive from whatever motive it proceeded to have my liberty of action confined and circumscribed, had Mr. Teeling kept his advice for my own private ear, or communicated his opinion on the subject to no one else but my sister I could have easily have brought her over as I have already, but not satisfied with that he had mentioned it to Frank and called himself just as I was at breakfast. I cannot however blame him altogether for introducing the subject as Frank first mentioned it, and after I had prepared my mother by despising cowardly friends and various other preliminary conversation—Mr. Teeling got her completely intimidated by his plausible arguments of involving the family of my Father, Mother, Brothers. Etc. the house being marked and numerous other absurdities, that she had declared her determination that if I do go her and I should part for ever, not that I would attend to that silly threat, only as it shows the degree of fear she labours under. I am not certain that I should [cause] her serious uneasiness without a probability of doing some real good. I am just at a loss what course to pursue, but this I know that I will henceforth renounce all such cowardly friends and shall take particular care never to hold any confidential communications with anyone of that family again, or give them an opportunity of influencing my conduct by their maddening officiousness, but in the present instance of what use are these determinations. I know of no other course I can pursue than writing by Mr. Ramsey tomorrow to know if

> it be possible to do any good by going, and ifso to defy all prohibition. I hate such half measures, but I know not what I ought to do—farewell. I do not ask your advice because I know you would not wish to give it and yet I would like to have it—only this I know that the greatest enemy I could possibly have could not have caused me the same degree of uneasiness that a professed friend has done whom I wish now that I had never considered as such—[36]

No ending—no signature! "Confining her liberty of action" indeed! One wonders what kind of a reception the unfortunate old gentleman received on his next call at Rosemary Lane, and how indeed poor Francis fared during the next few days at the hands of his small, slight and generally so reasonable sister.

To this torrent of wrath Eliza composed what she hoped would be a calming reply, from which it is evident that she also had been considerably perturbed by the scheme. Knowing her Mary too well to offer straightforward opposition, she suggested that if Margaret would go too it might ease the situation, and would Mary not think of writing to Counsellor Joy for his advice? She concludes her letter thus: "if you and Margaret go, I go also."

Notwithstanding Mary's anger she knew well enough that the journey was dangerous and that there were real grounds for concern. In that same month Mrs. McTier wrote "women have certainly been taken up, lodged in the Prevot and bail refused—one of them is a Miss Munroe, sister to the man who was hanged,* and others of the name of Shaw, 'tis said they are charged with high treason. . . . they are sent to C. Fergus at least Miss M. on a common car—there is something too like France in this."[37] The McCrackens were still suspect and carefully shadowed, and old Mr. Teeling had every right to conclude that if the sister of Henry Munroe could be "taken up", so also could the sister of Hen Joy McCracken, more especially if she was found on her way to Downpatrick Jail. The old gentleman had lost one son in the recent Rebellion, another had been in Kilmain-

*Henry Munroe, the rebel leader at Ballynahinch, p. 173.

ham with Harry and he had himself been confined in the prison ship in the Lough ; with others he had refused to associate himself with this affair of Emmet's, now he could not bear that further trouble should fall on this dear family.

Without waiting for any advice that might come from Eliza, Mary wrote off to Thomas Russell :

> The first intention of both my sister and me was to visit you immediately on yr. arrival at Downpatrick to learn if there was any means left of serving you, to this we were equally prompted by inclination & sense of the duty we owed the memory of our beloved departed brother. It is not therefore without the most poignant regret we are obliged to postpone at least, if not to relinquish our design, as from the well meant tho' ill judged officiousness of a friend my mother's fears have been excited to such a degree that I am apprehensive we shall have some difficulty in allaying them. If, however, we can be of any real use to you I am sure she will not object to our going, do not, therefore, hesitate to command us in any manner we can be of use to you. It wd. be to us a source of continual regret & self reproach were we to suffer ourself to be deterred from doing any [thing] which wd. either essentially serve you or even contribute in the smallest degree to your satisfaction.
>
> Fearing you might be short of cash, I have taken the liberty of enclosing you a small supply. I entreat you will inform us in what manner we can best serve you. Joined by my sister in the most anxious wishes for your safety & hapiness I remain yours with the truest esteem & affection
>
> [It is not signed.]
>
> Belfast. 15.10.1803.[38]

" Inclination " and " sense of duty " must have pressed hard and inextricably in Mary's heart. Thomas Russell had been Harry's dearest friend, on account of that alone mere duty would have been transformed into a debt of love. But it is not difficult to imagine that the renewed contact with him had rekindled her own long-controlled devotion. Now he too was going from her—nothing of Harry would be left at all : there would be no one who would completely understand, no one on whom she could lavish adoration, though there were still many who needed her love and care. Whether or not she had longed for marriage we do not know, but the strongly emotional side of her nature hungered for the beauty, the idealism, the gaiety of Thomas Russell.

This, then, we may suppose was the cause of her despairing rage, and it is a measure of her heroism that the iron discipline so quickly reasserted itself and that concern for her mother's peace of mind prevailed.

Meanwhile Frank had arranged that Tom Hughes, one of his clerks, should go to Downpatrick, ostensibly to collect debts due to the firm, but, as Mary wrote to Eliza :

> He knows the Gaol and the Gaoler well, and can perhaps assist if anyting can be done . . . and if these hopes were realised of which there is scarcely a possibility there would be more ground for my mother's fears. I have scarcely slept last night contriving plans and schemes, but all to no purpose.[39]

Obviously they were still hoping that some means would be found to effect Russell's escape.

Following Eliza's suggestion Mary had written to Counsellor Joy. A copy of the letter remains for, as Mary noted on it years later : " I wrote that over again as I could not bear to address [him] Dear Harry as I was thus used to begin my letters to my brother and substituted the formal Dear Sir."[40] His reply, as one would expect, came down heavily on the side of prudence—but he was a kindly, if unimaginative person, and promised that he himself would do all he possibly could for the prisoner—surely, he thought, that should satisfy Mary Ann ! But before this reached her she had, out of deference to her mother's wishes, practically abandoned her cherished project, writing thus to Eliza : " Should I be the cause of unhappiness to her and my Father I should never forgive myself."[41]

What in the end reconciled her to the bitter disappointment was a letter from Russell himself, written to her brother Francis almost on the eve of his trial :

> To the more than friendship I owe to you and your sister it is impossible to be sufficiently grateful, nor will I wound your feelings by attempting to thank you. I would not wish you to make an attempt to see me, which would be fruitless and could only serve to draw suspicion on you and your family. As to me I shall only say that to the last moment of my Liberty I was not thinking of myself or acting for myself but for my Country and though what I was engaged in with the Immortal Hero* who has fallen is considered as perhaps wild yet I could show and it will be showed that the failure was alone surprising, with some of the reasons I am still unacquainted. [He then speaks of his trial and accepts counsel for the reasons already given, but continues] —I intend to speak in conclusion myself on my political and religious opinions. I perfectly know that not a hair of my head is in the power of man without the permission of God and am perfectly resigned to his pleasure. He can and perhaps may deliver me, but whatever he wills is best . . . I have no wish to die . . . but had I a thousand lives I would willingly risk or loose them in it, and be assured Liberty will in the midst of these storms be established . . . I do most sincerely hope and earnestly recommend that when Freedom comes my country may be merciful. Politically I have done nothing but what I glory in, morally I acknowledge myself a grievous sinner. I trust for pardon and mercy thro' my saviour as I do most sincerely forgive all those who are about to take my life—to his protection I recommend you and your and my friends. I need not recommend my sister to you I am satisfied. May God Almighty bless you all is the wish and prayer of your sincere and affectionate friend. T.R.[42]

He can be judged by no ordinary standards : this was the man that Mary loved—these were the convictions she understood. With a burning heart she had already written to him once more—as always, without any formal opening, though this time she concludes with her initials :

> I hoped to have had the pleasure of seeing you once more but as that satisfaction seems now improbable I feel most

*Robert Emmet.

deeply at the disappointment, not that I supposed your mind required the support of any human consolation, possessing as you do that comfort which the world can neither give nor take away—but I wished to have assured you of my intentions of continual friendship to your sister & also to request if there are any others who have claims on your affection, that you will not thro' motives of false delicacy scruple to mention them that those who shall ever venerate your memory may know how to show it that respect of which it is so truly deserving—it is impious and certainly cruel in us to repine at the prospect of your removal from a world every way so unworthy of you, yet it is impossible to divest oneself so entirely of selfishness as not to feel the deepest regret for the loss society will sustain in being deprived of one of its most valuable members—a firm reliance on the wisdom and goodness of that Providence that governs the universe & who does not permit afflictions in vain, can alone reconcile us to such a melancholy event—if there is anything I can do either now or hereafter that would in the least degree contribute to your satisfaction you cannot gratify me more highly than by naming your wishes—I have no doubt but that the day will arrive when your loss & such as yours will be universally deplored even by those who are at present most active against you. May I request that you will indulge me with another lock of your hair, that I received already & for wh. I am particularly obliged I had to divide with my sister & my friend Eliza, each of us shall preserve our [torn] invaluable treasure as a memento of virtue seldom equalled & worthy of affection [torn] of imitation. Forgive me imposing so long on your so very precious time, [torn] to be considered worthy of your friendship is an honour which we shall ever most highly value. I am joined by my sister in every sentiment of attachment & veneration.

I remain,

Yours most truly,

M. McC.[43]

Thomas Russell never read that letter. On the draft of it, which Mary Ann kept, she wrote this sentence :

The letter of which this is a copy Mr. Ramsey handed T.R. the morning of his death but having then made up his mind for the event wh. he fully expected tho' not then brought to trial, he did not read it lest as he sayd it disturbed his mind, but as the gentleman (Trevor I think was his name) who had been sent from Dublin to watch him was present he might fear he would insist on seeing it he put it on the fire.

The trial before Baron George began on the morning of October 20th, and lasted till 8 p.m.; the Solicitor General and the Attorney General prosecuted for the Crown. Many were called to give evidence that Russell had travelled through the county Down inciting to rebellion, among them Patrick Lynch, home from one of his song collecting expeditions in the West. A refusal to act as witness for the Crown would have been fraught with grave danger, and there is a touch of genuine sadness in what Lynch had to say: " He knew the prisoner, and he was sorry to see him there, he had first met him in the library in Belfast and had given him lessons in the Irish language. On a day in July the prisoner had come up to him to shake hands with him, but he, Lynch, had refused, knowing him to be an outlaw, but not wishing to hurt him."[44] When the witnesses had finished Russell made his moving speech which the faithful Ramsey carefully reported. It contained many of the sentiments already expressed in the letter to Francis, and concluded by exhorting the gentlemen of the jury " to pay attention to the poor, and to spread comfort and happiness around their dwellings." Counsellor Joy made a strenuous defence, admitting afterwards " that he never in his life felt so interested for any man ", —the matter-of-fact lawyer was Russell's last conquest. Next morning, facing death with all the dignity and a touch of the gaiety that had ever endeared him to his friends, this visionary-patriot, and one of the most remarkable of the United Irishmen, was hanged and then decapitated at Downpatrick Jail. He was not yet thirty-six years of age. He had entered the scene as the gay young officer with the world at his feet, the darling of hostesses, the welcomed club man, and " a very madman in love."[45] All had been renounced for the principles of brotherhood and liberty learnt first in Belfast, and for which years of imprisonment had been endured. When the sentence had been pronounced he asked the judge that he might be allowed three days longer to live so that he could complete the work upon which he was engaged—the translation from the Greek of the Revelation of St. John—a request which was not granted.[46]

The whirl of gaiety in Belfast must surely have paused, and many a heart must have felt an uneasy stirring of conscience, an upsurge of admiration. In her grief his old friend Mrs. McTier wrote:

> Enthusiastic he did indeed appear, religious he always was since I knew him, and in his last confinement it was not to be wondered at that such a mind as his might have grown even flighty.* I rejoice in it, and that whatever it was—enthusiasm, fortitude or Error, that it bore him up to the last. Few, few have I known like him. Heart and enthusiasm is laughed to scorn now and fares the same fate of patriotism, yet the two former we may presume will have a place in Heaven, tho' so dangerous here.[47]

*unbalanced.

CHAPTER XII

INTERLUDE

1803–1810

If Mary treasured in that precious draft [p. 223] the last expression of her feeling for Thomas Russell, she left no record of the devastating loneliness that his death must have brought to her. In just over five years the two she most loved had been publically executed for their adherance to principles that were the mainspring of her own life—a truly terrible experience. But there was no giving way, no bitter resentment, no self-pity; her ideals remained unshaken, and the rest of her life was dedicated to those same principles that had driven both Harry and Thomas to the scaffold.

Very soon after the execution at Downpatrick she wrote a long letter of condolence to Margaret Russell:

> Dear Madam [she began]
>
> Fearful of intruding unseasonably I have hitherto foreborne to write, & perhaps even yet will be unsuccessful in attempting to offer any consolation. None but those who have been taught by experience can know how inefficacious all human comfort is & that nothing but a strong sense of religion and the hope of meeting again in a happier State can support us under those trying separations from friends dear to us as our own existence and in loosing whom we seem to have lost a part of ourselves . . .

After warning Miss Russell not to believe the misleading reports regarding her brother's trial circulated in the daily papers, and telling her that Mr. Ramsey will be in Dublin in the course of eight or ten days and will himself give her full details, she continues:

> In the meantime it will perhaps gratify you to hear what you would no doubt know without being told that the composure, dignity and firmness of our beloved friend both at his trial and at the last awful scene commanded the

esteem, admiration and astonishment of all who beheld him, and those who had never before had the pleasure of his acquaintance and who had only for a few days an opportunity of conversing with him found themselves attached by an extraordinary and irresistable impulse, such as they never held for any man before . . . It will also be a satisfaction to you to know [of the] respectful treatment which he received and also that his remains were properly attended to and decently interred in the churchyard of Downpatrick by one who had formerly the pleasure of his acquaintance and with whose kind attentions he expressed himself most gratified. All the articles he had in his possession are taken care of by a gentleman of the strictest integrity* and will be delivered to you shortly, excepting his letter to you and the book he had been occupied in writing which were taken in charge by the Rev. I. Taylor . . . I shall always esteem it an honour of the highest value to have been considered worthy a place in the friendship of one whose memory I shall ever . . . so it will still be my greatest pleasure to serve in any manner the sister of that friend who was by him so tenderly beloved . . .[1]

Practical help was immediately forthcoming. As Harry had bequeathed to her the care of the little Maria, so, in Mary's view, had Thomas laid on her the charge of his sister. For several years the McCrackens' agent in Dublin kept in touch with the destitute lady, and in Belfast Mary continued to collect money to eke out the miserable pittance that Margaret Russell earned by the little school that met in her room over a " dram shop " in one of the long Georgian streets in Dublin. Later, through Mary Ann's exertions she was admitted to The Retreat at Drumcondra where, in 1834, she died at the age of eighty-two, bequeathing to her benefactress such of Thomas Russell's papers as had been retrieved from prison officials.[2] Over the years Mary maintained close touch with other members of the Russell connection, helping them financially and following their careers with affectionate interest.

For Thomas himself her last act of service was to

*Probably Thomas Ramsey.

cover his grave with the plain stone slab on which she had his name engraved and which to this day marks his resting-place in the graveyard of the Parish Church in Downpatrick.[3]

At home, her father, long in failing health, died in December of that sad year [1803]. More silent and retiring than his busy, practical little wife, Captain McCracken had had an abiding influence on his family, endowing them all, but perhaps most especially his son Harry, with qualities which warmed and enlivened the less romantic characteristics of the Joys. The long obituary notice which appeared in the *Belfast Newsletter* speaks of him thus :

> . . . The name of master was at all times rather heard than felt ; an interest in the welfare and happiness of all those placed under his authority, created an attachment which produced promptitude of obedience ; it was love, not fear, and a thorough conviction of his skill, which made the hardy sailor spring with alacrity to the post of danger and of trial. During 28 years of his life his conduct as master of a vessell met with the perfect approbation of his employers whose interest he never neglected, while he at the same time respected himself. By foresight or caution he may be said to have commanded fortune : Never did his countenance appear more animated than when he related that, from the time he first commanded, he had only to regret the loss of one poor sailor, which, unfortunately happened during his last voyage. To the duties of a sea faring life may be added his character as a merchant, which has scarcely ever been excelled, an integrity incorruptible, and rigid adherence to truth, made all who knew him place the most implicit [confidence] in his honour and his word. To him is Belfast indebted for the establishment of the Ropewalk Company in 1758, now an extensive and flourishing branch of commerce ; and through his unremitting assiduity was formed the Marine Charitable Society from which so many distressed sailors and their families have received both comfort and support. His ever active mind led him to enquiries not immediately connected with his profession, and to the enquirers into the manners, customs and commerce of the countries he had visited he was a constant source of information. Kind and benevolent

> to all, with a particular gentleness which rendered him a desirable companion, his loss will be long felt in those social circles in which he was accustomed to appear.[4]

But in spite of mourning, the house in Rosemary Lane resounded with children's voices — there were the nephews and nieces, and little Maria. John and his growing family were established in Donegall Street, a newly developed residential area, on the outskirts of the town. William's family were in Castle Street, where Rose Ann had started a haberdashery business, to which she later added a lending library—copies of her book plates can still be seen.

As for Mary Ann—one would like to think that she had some share in the discussions that centred round an ambitious project initiated about this time by John Templeton. Recalling a suggestion made years earlier by Thomas Russell that there should be in Belfast an educational establishment offering to young men and women of the Province facilities to pursue the various branches of higher learning, Templeton now set himself, with the help of others in the town, to realise Russell's plan. As a result the foundation, known to-day far beyond the confines of Ulster as the Royal Belfast Academical Institution, was opened in 1810 in the building which it still occupies. It was indeed a notable achievement, comprising a school department for boys and a collegiate department open to both young men and women where eminent professors lectured in the natural sciences, classics, modern languages and English literature, and where the foundations of the Belfast School of Medicine were laid. The collegiate end was subsequently taken over by the Queen's College of Belfast [now Queen's University], when it was opened in 1849. This would be a project dear to Mary's heart, as a memorial to Russell, and as an outcome of the discussions in those happy days at Orange Grove when, we may be sure, education had a foremost place and when Mary would, no doubt, have voiced her constant desire " that the female part of the Creation as well as the male should throw off the fetters with which they have been so long mentally bound and, conscious of the dignity and importance of their nature, rise to the situation for which they were designed." [See p. 127.] Did the idea of the new school and college, one wonders, originate in some degree with her?

We are sure, however, of one absorbing interest—Bunting's continued work on Irish music.

Through the difficult years before and during the Rebellion Atty had sedulously avoided any entanglement in the political affairs of the McCrackens, indeed it speaks volumes for their tolerant attitude that he was able to live so completely as one of the family, and yet be so unresponsive to their dominant activities. John was his constant companion. Encouraged no doubt by the great success of his first publication of Irish airs, and indeed not a little envious of the rapid popularity of Tom Moore's Irish Melodies with accompanying words, Bunting decided to embark as soon as possible on a systematic study of the harp and harp music from the earliest times, together with a further collection of native airs to which he would set translations of ancient Gaelic poems. Such a comprehensive scheme could not possibly be undertaken single-handed, and from the beginning Mary Ann and John McCracken were deeply involved. During 1798 and '99 journeys to remote districts were impossible, and Bunting was obliged to confine himself to the duties of an organist and teacher and to his recently acquired agency for Mr. Broadwood's pianofortes, but with the opening of the new century conditions improved and he set off once again on his travels. Before long it was obvious that still more help would be required and in 1802 Patrick Lynch [see p. 225] was employed and financed by the McCrackens to assist in the collection of native poems. Lynch had been known to them and to Thomas Russell as a teacher of Irish in the language classes that had been started in pursuance of the joint intention of the Festival promoters. Many of Lynch's letters remain, some addressed to John from the wilds of Mayo and elsewhere reporting progress—one mentions the discovery of 150 songs—and acknowledging payments, but when payment failed to arrive the stranded collector turned in despair to Mary Ann—" My dear Miss Mary I hope you will see me relieved out of this hobble."[15]

Mary it was who kept in touch with Bunting during his continual absences, maintaining, in spite of her own occupations and her great sorrow, a watchful eye on everything that concerned his interest, acting in fact as his secretary. Many of Atty's letters to her have been preserved. They were written from every corner of Ireland and from London, and he kept her informed in detail about the people he met and the discoveries he made, sending her information to be passed on to others, notably to Henry Joy jun. who gave much assistance to Bunting at this time, and receiving through her contributions for his scholarly " dissertation " which was to form the first part of this work. " I received your letter " he wrote on one occasion " and shall take care to have the paper enclosed relative to the brass trumpets, etc. inserted in its proper place." It is sad that nothing remains of her share in what must have been a long and interesting correspondence. We know that over the years she had come to occupy a special place in Atty's life. Exacting, even exasperating, though she must often have seemed to this sociable, enthusiastic young man, he found himself relying more and more on her sound judgment, and the many references to her in other letters to Bunting describe her continually as " Your friend Mary."

It was one thing for Lynch to collect and translate the Gaelic poems, but quite another to shape the translations into songs, and here Mary Balfour enters the scene. She was the daughter of the incumbent of the parish church of Limavady, a small town in County Derry, where she and her sisters kept a school, but poetry and music provided the real interest of her life. Her father had received his living from the hands of the erratic and magnificent Bishop of Derry, Frederick Augustus Hervey, Earl of Bristol, whose liberality Miss Balfour commemorated in one of her poems. A patron of the arts in the grand manner, the Earl Bishop was already benefactor to Denis Hempson, doyen of the Harpists at the Festival in Belfast, providing the blind centenarian with a cottage near his magnificent residence at Downhill, where with his family he would visit the old man and dance to his music—a curious environment for this noted epicure. It is likely that Mary Balfour frequently travelled the few miles from her home to Magilligan to visit Hempson, and that it was through him that she became acquainted with Bunting. At any rate she became Bunting's most enthusiastic collaborator in the matter of song writing, and Mary Ann McCracken was the point of contact. To her Miss Balfour wrote for advice and direction, asking if such and such a song had given satisfaction, begging for criticism, which she assures "dear Miss McCracken" will be taken in the best possible part, and mentioning how much easier it would be if she knew the air to which each song would be set, as she could then choose her words accordingly, a very important point, she adds, in song writing. In 1810 Mary Balfour published a collection of her poems, some of which are based on Irish translations. Her interest in Gaelic is so noticeable that one wonders how much of the language she knew herself, and to what extent she was indeed one of the pioneers of the Gaelic revival

Unfortunately only fragments remain of the correspodence between the two Marys: what little there is includes transactions regarding muslins, a reminder that in spite of all other undertakings Mary McCracken did not neglect her business. It is clear, too, that Mary Balfour had been quickly received into the circle of family friends, one of her letters ending thus :

> Adieu my dear Miss McCracken, with love to your Mother, your sister and to Miss Templeton
>
> Your most obliged Friend
>
> Mary Balfour[6]

Atty, meanwhile, was roaming over "the four green fields" of Ireland collecting music, or battling in London with publishers and attending to orders for pianos. In

London his genial temperament found ample scope, and at the Broadwoods' home he met many of the leading literary and musical figures, including Dr. Burney. The appreciative interest of these eminent men greatly encouraged and delighted Bunting, and he in his turn delighted them with performances of his Irish music.[7] So pleasant was this sociableness that Mary Ann, at home in Belfast, wondered anxiously if Atty's friendly, self-indulgent nature was tempting him to spend rather more time on enjoyment than on the matter in hand, and it must have been something near a reprimand that drew from him this vehement retort :

> I can assure you, my dear Mary, I have not the least intention of wasting my time with nonsense in London—but am determined any little ability I may have in the line of my profession . . . [torn] although I am almost petrified at the expense of the letter press, but it must be done at all costs.[8]

She may indeed have been too severe, but a wasting of time, or for that matter of anything, she could not tolerate. As for Atty, he had sacrificed his once promising prospects of comparative affluence as a successful musician and teacher, in order to engage in the hazards of research—it was unreasonable of Mary Ann, so he thought to himself, to deny him such few opportunities of advancement and professional enjoyment as came his way.

At home John McCracken was busy preparing illustrations. The lovely drawing of the Dolway harp, and that of Arthur O'Neill, together with the other delicate illustrations in this volume are thus acknowledged by Bunting in his introduction :

> The accurate and elegant drawings from which the engravings of the frontispiece and the other plates in this volume have been taken, were made by Mr. John McCracken, Esq., of Belfast, and presented to the Editor for this work.

At last, after twelve years of detailed and most laborious research Bunting's second volume—the " General Collection of the Ancient Music of Ireland " was published in 1809 by Messrs. Clementi & Co. of London. The evolution of the harp and harp music is traced not only in Ireland, but in the various countries of antiquity where it had been known. And then follows a collection of seventy-seven ancient Irish airs arranged for the piano, twenty of them being accompanied by words. Altogether, it represented a formidable undertaking in days when there were no typewriters, no tape-recorders, no easy methods of communication, none, in fact, of the modern aids to such research, and when the author himself had no academic qualifications for his task.

It is easy to picture the exultation in the McCracken household ; Atty's friends in the town gave him a public dinner. In the background, but so closely connected with the whole great undertaking, was old Mrs. McCracken. Years afterwards, when he himself was an old man thinking back on those days of pioneering effort, Bunting gave vent in one short significant expression—" Your dear, dear departed mother "—to the abiding love and indebtedness he felt for her, who by her patience, sympathy and practical interest had done so much to fit him for his life work. How glad they all were that in her eightieth year she shared in these triumphant rejoicings.

On St. Patrick's Day of the previous year the Belfast Harp Society had been inaugurated, with Bunting as musical director, and Mary McCracken and Mary Balfour among the 191 original members. Though the Society was short-lived, its contribution to the revival of interest in the Irish language, poetry and literature was considerable, and it took its place in the wider romantic movement. Irish legends began to replace classical stories as inspiration for the rising poets. Sir Samuel Ferguson, born in Belfast in 1810, was to be an outstanding exponent of this development and was later to be closely associated with Bunting's third publication. Lady Morgan and her " Wild Irish Girl " represented another aspect of the same trend. The old tradition that harp playing was a congenial and profitable profession for the blind was carried on by the Harp Society through its scheme to give instruction to sightless people ; Arthur O'Neill was put in charge of a small school for such pupils.[9] All sorts of plans were made to collect money for this venture, among them a series of subscription balls with which John McCracken was closely connected, but the school proved too great a strain on the financial resources of the Society which had to be abandoned in 1813, having spent £1,000 in the five years of its existence. Through the generosity of Dr. McDonnell an annuity of £30 was paid to Arthur O'Neill for the remaining years of his life.[10]

In 1813 Bunting launched another considerable enterprise from the McCracken headquarters. On May 29th he waited on the committee of the Poorhouse,

> and stated that he intended to have a Musical Festival in the Town sometime in August or September next if sufficient support could be procured, and that he was disposed to allow the surplus, which might remain after paying the performers, to be applied to the funds of the Poor House.[11]

His scheme materialised and for a week the citizens of Belfast revelled in musical entertainment. The concerts were held in the theatre, though when an organ was necessary the audience repaired to the church of the 2nd Presbyterian congregation, where Bunting at the time was organist. Distinguished artists were engaged at very high fees—so high indeed, that the " surplus " for the Poorhouse was negligible—and the festival is memorable as being the occasion of the first performance in Belfast of Handel's *Messiah*. The oratorio was conducted by Bunting, and the chorus was provided by the choir of Christ Church Cathedral, Dublin.[12]

In 1815, Atty, now a portly and sophisticated bachelor of forty, set off on an extensive tour in Europe, Waterloo having put an end to Napoleon's activities. Everywhere he made the acquaintance of eminent musicians and was received with enthusiasm. In Paris, after playing some of his Irish music to a delighted audience, he sprang from the stool and, slapping his thigh in excitement, exclaimed to the astonished Frenchmen " Match me that." The great Catalini was enchanted with his music and on one occasion took from her finger a beautiful ring which she presented to Bunting to mark her appreciation of his work. From France he travelled to Belgium and Holland, meeting with, and learning from, the famous organists of the Low Countries. And so back to Rosemary Lane. Very shortly the jovial figure was to leave the family that had sheltered him since 1784. He moved to Dublin and married, but to the end of his life Atty maintained a continuous correspondence with Mary Ann. Writing to her after the birth of his first child he said :

> We cannot live for ourselves alone and I hope I shall grow better every day, at least as to those notions of propriety which all sensible folks practise and which I never did, to my shame be it spoken, till now. I for the first time received the Sacrament at St. Patrick's Cathedral on Christmas Day with my lady . . . My little darling son, she and I take the greatest delight in . . . I intend to be in Belfast on Thursday by day mail so I shall soon see you all once more, hearty and well.
>
> I am with true affection ever yours sincerely,
>
> E. Bunting.[13]

How greatly the household must have missed his lively, if turbulent presence.

The social life of Belfast went on apace. Mrs. McTier writes of the " gambling, variety and ruin of our society already so much changed that, in this trading Town, you might frequently suppose yourself in the midnight revels of the nobility."[14] The theatre was immensely popular. Not only were leading actors and actresses attracted from London—Mrs. Siddons played for the last time in Belfast in 1809—but local talent reached unprecedented heights. These were the days of Master Batty—better known as " Young Roscius "—the gifted boy from Dromore, County Down, who, while still in his early teens, became so celebrated that on one occasion Pitt moved an adjournment at Westminster to enable members to see him play Hamlet. There was Thomas Romney Robinson, writing poetry at the age of six, and publishing a collection of his works at thirteen, in order to raise the funds necessary to enable him to proceed forthwith to Trinity College. There was also little Miss Mudie, aged six, playing to crowded audiences on many nights in the character of Norval, and reciting a long address and epilogue composed by the aforementioned young poet, in which, according to the *Belfast News-Letter* "the Child united humour, archness, irony, elocution and dramatic finesse."[15]

Mme. Catalini and other celebrated musicians performed at concerts, and there was an early visit of Mme. Tassaud's waxworks. When one remembers that the Irish Sea still had to be crossed in sailing vessels dependent on the vagaries of the wind, and that theatres and halls were lit only by candles, one wonders how these events were ever successfully carried through. The Belfast Literary Society, founded in 1801 largely through the exertions of Henry Joy, jun., met the needs of the more serious minded, and Mrs. McTier gives an amusing description of how some of the leisured gentlemen occupied their time.

> Some time ago, there was a bet taken between Stewart Bruce and some other gentleman (perhaps M . . . dy) who wd. produce themselves the best dressed Man. Much no doubt depended on the awful decision—but tho' Bruce's pocket handkerchief was cambrick at a guinea a yd. two rows of quaker hemming with dresden between and his name cyphered in the middle, these were his *common* ones—he gained the award by having his *Boots* perfumed with otto [sic] of Roses. Now what a pity it is to the public at large these geniuses of the body had not been made taylors. Dublin might then have boasted of them, and Erin's sons had their rough angles polished off.[16]

This facade of gaiety hid, to some extent, grave uncertainty in industry. There were many bankruptcies and such conditions meant increasing hardship for the poor. In order to mitigate suffering the House of Industry was established in 1809 to take the place of the Strangers' Friend Society, no longer able to cope with the situation.

The aim of the new organisation was to provide raw materials and a centre in which the poor could work while still living in their homes. Appeals were made for subscriptions and the loan of " wheels ", for spinning was to be the principal source of employment.

There were signs too, that the town was becoming aware of its responsibility for educating the worker as well as providing him with work. Fifteen years earlier Harry McCracken's classes for boys and girls had been terminated by the vicar and his band of ladies. In the years preceding the Rebellion, reading societies, regarded with the greatest suspicion by the Tory element, had sprung up in the towns and country, where tradesmen and workers, avid for information, met to read, or to have read to them, the public prints and other stirring literature. With the new century, however, the outlook was changing, and in 1802 the Belfast Sunday School was started by voluntary subscriptions, where secular instruction was given by a staff of regular teachers, Sunday being the only day on which workers were free to attend. By 1810 over a thousand pupils had been admitted, and hundreds were waiting to get in : it was obvious that such success called for development. An article on " Belfast Sunday & Lancastrian Schools ", appearing in the *Belfast Magazine* the following year, reports as follows :

> To give permanence to the institution and render it of that public utility required in such a town as Belfast, it has long been the ardent wish of the persons concerned, to accomplish the building of a suitable house, and to graft on their system that of a daily school on the Lancastrian plan. It is with great pleasure, therefore, they can announce that the liberality of the public last year has enabled them nearly to carry this object into effect, the house being now almost prepared for reception of upwards of 500 children, to be taught in the Lancastrian manner, and the Sunday School, much increased in number, having been held in it for some months past.[17]

Joseph Lancaster, himself, was to visit Belfast in the immediate future and would help the committee in the choice of a head teacher and with other matters. Thus began the Lancastrian School, which for many a long year Mary Ann visited weekly, and which continued as a voluntary undertaking till merged in the Belfast Education Authority in 1935.

Other philanthropic enterprises were started; but, though she must have been interested in all of them, this was for her a period of silence. Her own wounded spirit must recover, and, as far as the public was concerned, it would take some time to live down a reputation for political unorthodoxy in a society that was quickly modifying its opinions.

CHAPTER XIII

THE TURNING POINT

1810–1827

ALL this—gaiety and philanthropy alike—was built on a foundation of cotton : Belfast had begun its headlong, but not unchequered, career of industrial development. In the three decades that had gone by since Robert Joy set up his new machines the economic outlook of the town had altered completely and fundamentally. In the streams flowing down from the hills over which Mary Ann had searched for Harry, there was abundant water to turn the wheels of spindles and looms, and, more important still, there were workers starving for want of employment. Local industrialists soon found themselves competing with enterprising employers from England and Scotland who were lured to Belfast by the prospects of cheap and abundant labour which was the basis of the town's rapid growth.

As for the workers—during the spells of more plentiful work they made their own efforts to cope with the nightmare of unemployment by combining to demand uniform wages and a limitation to the number of apprentices to be taken by any one employer, the first indication of the modern trade union movement. Needless to say, these tactics were strenuously resisted even by enlightened employers. In May 1803 the *Belfast News-Letter* printed a long statement condemning such illegal combinations " which of late years have been frequently manifested by *turning out*, and the cessation of work by said Tradesmen, as is at present the case with Carpenters and Taylors." This, the statement declared had " the baleful effect of putting all descriptions of workmen on a [like] footing as the Idler and Botch." The signatories, and there were one hundred and forty five of them including Francis and John McCracken, agreed to resist such practices and, at the same time, to give every encouragement to well conducted workers and young apprentices.

With all these developments the McCracken family was closely concerned, though the Joys had by now forsaken industry to carry on the legal traditions in which their family had been raised. While Captain McCracken had been able to provide for each of his sons a seemingly secure position in cotton, John turned out by far the most successful. Shrewd and very enterprising, by 1811 he employed 200 workers, a large number for those days, and had a fleet of ten vessels to convey across the Irish Sea the 600 tons of coal that his mill annually consumed. Already water was being superceded by steam—"that great new applied power."[1] Whatever may have been in the mind of Uncle Robert Joy, and was most certainly in the mind of Mary Ann, business for John was no philanthropic undertaking for the benefit of poor creatures who needed work, it was a keen, grim, but enjoyable contest for gain. He had many of his father's gifts including his ability to handle men easily—there remains a poem written in his praise by one of his workers, a blind man,[2] but there remains also a sad and touching letter written by Jemmy Hope in 1808 to Mary Ann:

> Dear Miss Mary,—I wished to have called on you some time past, but never had time when you would be at Leisure, and now wrtie to tell you that on Saturday Evening I was obliged to tell Mr. John that I must Leave his Employment for want of wages, not being able Longer to support my family out of my small salary; and now, in Consequence of the interest you have allwise in my welfare, I will Describe to you what has been the nature of my situation since I went to my present place. For the first year I was treated by Mr. Plunket (whom I consider to be a blunt, honest man) with the Greatest Rigor, under the Idea that, having been an old Sufferer, I was what he Calls a follower of your family, and might be Corrupt Enough (as he had observed several others) to take improper Liberty. However, by a subordination that Required some strength of Body and mind, I Conquered his prejudice, and completely secured his friendship and Confidence. But as to Mr. John, although he never Checked me much, he allwise treated me (when Ever I spoke to him about my

own Situation) with a silence which in another I would have taken for Contempt: but imputing it to his usual temper and press of business, and Coniceous of never having given any Cause for it, I over Looked it as a thing for which I Could not fully account, and which time Certainly would. I have at Lingth, through all the bustle and inconvenience of the place in which I was obleeged to do business, acquired such improvement in the practice of writing and Keeping accounts as will Enable me to a considerable Share of Business in any office where I may hereafter find Employment. This last assercion is the only one I would expect Mr. John to Contradict; unless he would consider that if he was me and I somebody else, he Could not at all times answer for his own Correctness. As to my future views, there is but one Employment at present in my Reach, which is to apply to the men who conduct the Cart Business for Belfast and Dublin to Employ me as Guard, which, although it will afford me a Considerable salery, is a Long Road to Either Ease or Credit, and an Employment as different from my Inclination as many other I have thought of, but if I could stand it for one year, I hope I am still possessed of Resolution to save what money will Discharge a few small accounts which I ow, and Enable me again to Join my Little family with the fair Chance of another tradesman, without being troublesome to any whom I call friend; and this being at present my highest ambition, I will Risk the last power of my Constitution to attain it. One thing more I mention, and I hope it will not hurt your feelings. I thought between winding and warping to have paid what I am indebted to you, which, although I know you do not think of it, does not make me forget. I think my work is entitled to some Credit, and I can assure you that the piece that was warped in our house was finished and taken off the mill by my own hand, and if I was on my oath could freely disclose that it is my Belief there was not a broken or Latched End in it Leaving our house, whatever what may have been said to the Contrary. Let no friend of mine grieve at my situation; it is a Litle hard, but does not discourage me, I am determined to deserve success. Dr. Miss Mary, your Much Obliged Well-wisher,

James Hoope [sic][3]

One imagines that her heart bled for the Hopes: Jemmy—who more than any man now living had been dear to Harry, could not one of the foremost cotton manufacturers assist this faithful soul to better himself instead of turning him off with a cold, unfriendly glance? The price of success for John was a growing isolation from his sister and all that she represented.

No such success attended Francis. The sail-cloth factory and the rope walk, amalgamated in one company, are reported bankrupt in 1812 and again 1815, two of the very " depressed " years, when war with America upset the imports of raw cotton. After paying his creditors, as Mary Ann is careful to point out, he was somehow able to start again, and remained in control of the business till his death.

Of William and his family only the barest details remain. He continued in business, probably in partnership with his cousin Francis Joy, the lineal descendants of the original firm of Joy, McCabe and McCracken.

The sisters' undertaking appears in Holden's Belfast Directory for 1809 as Margaret McCracken & Co., Muslin Manufacturers, 37, Waring Street. The next door premises were tenanted by Francis. Probably the move to this important commercial area close to the quays took place in the beginning of the century, and it seems likely that at this stage the sisters launched into production on a factory basis, continuing at the same time to employ weavers who worked in their own homes. The depression years brought great anxieties to the firm, for not only was Margaret's and Mary's money completely tied up in it, but their workers must, if possible, be safeguarded against the dire results of unemployment. " I could not think of dismissing our workers [wrote Mary later], because nobody would give them employment, and then we could not tell when a revival should take place, what would be most required."[4] These worries, on top of years of anxiety, conquered even her indomitable will, and somewhere about 1813 she had a serious and prolonged illness. When we recall her delicate childhood, we can only be amazed at the strains both physical and emotional which she had endured. Those were the great days of "spas" and "waters", and Mary was advised to go for her convalescence to one of the renowned resorts. But her mother was ailing, and she would venture no farther afield than the Spa at Ballynahinch in County Down, then a locally fashionable and pleasant centre with its Pump-Room and Maze, and here she seems to have completely regained her health.

In 1814 old Mrs. McCracken died, the last of the three remarkable children of Francis Joy. There is a hint in one of Eliza Templeton's letters that, of all her dearly loved children, Mary Ann held a special place in her mother's affections.

Within a fortnight William too died, very suddenly: it is recorded of him that he never really recovered from the sorrow of Harry's death.

At some stage before the eighteen-twenties the house in Rosemary Lane was given up, and Francis with Margaret, Mary Ann and Maria, moved to No. 79 Donegall Street, close to their brother John.

Margaret was now over fifty, business difficulties were increasing alarmingly and the sisters decided, sometime about 1815, that they must retire. They were indeed faced with ruin, for the continued bankruptcies in all branches of the cotton industry had widespread repercussions. In writing to Dr. Madden years later Mary refers frequently to their business, and reproaches herself bitterly for some supposedly rash action on her part which, she avers, precipitated the crisis. This may have related to an advance of £300 which they made to their Dublin agent who was in financial difficulties. The loan was of no avail, he went bankrupt and Margaret and Mary never retrieved their money. She had always been venturesome and ready to take a risk, particularly if someone else would benefit thereby. There was also another heavy loss when a mill owner, who owed them a considerable sum, was accidentally killed by his own machinery—a poignant reminder of the hazards accompanying the development of mechanised industry. Clearly the business had been a major interest in Mary's life; it was no spare time hobby, but a serious undertaking built up by years of hard work and capable direction, and it had been extremely successful. She delighted in it, because of her inborn ability, because of the employment it created, but perhaps most of all because it expressed, as nothing else did, her independence.

A fragmentary notice, relating to one of the frequent labour disputes in the town at this time, includes an illuminating reference to the sisters :

> But to the great credit of the Miss McCrackens, they kept the set full six months after the rest took it off ; and if they were under the necessity of paying them in notes, they always paid the discount with it.*[5]

In a letter to a friend Mary Ann writes :

> I have indeed been daily thinking of you, and reproaching myself for not writing to you these several months past ; but my time has been so entirely occupied, and my mind so perplexed in winding up our affairs that we may quit a business in which all who have been engaged these two years past have lost heavily, that I could not command a tranquil half hour in the four and twenty, and now that we are getting clear by degrees I trust that the little which we got by my dear mother will enable us to pay all we owe, which is a great comfort, even if we have nothing left. Doubtless if riches would have contributed to our ultimate happiness, they would have been bestowed on us ; and while Providence is pleased to bless us with health and a capacity for industry, we should be thankful and contented ; but the sphere of a woman's industry is so confined, and so few roads lie open to her, and those so thorny, it is difficult to fix on any . . .[6]

It must have been a bitter sorrow to relinquish her hold on their enterprise—to give up yet another vital interest. She had never faltered because of the thorniness of any path she had had to tread, but were they *all* closing before her ? What road now lay open ? Life had been so pitifully empty without Harry and Thomas ; active participation in Atty's great work had ended with his

*There was a discount of 2/– on cashing bank notes.

recent move to Dublin; now her business had gone. Did she realise that she was indeed at a decisive turning point in her life? If there was a moment of despondency no trace of it has come down to us: very soon she knew again where she was to go.

Meanwhile she surveyed a political scene strangely altered, and to the twentieth century student the glaring contrast between the Belfast of the late eighteenth century and the opening nineteenth presents a problem of fascinating interest. In the first place, nowhere in Ireland was the Act of Union accepted with greater complacency than in Belfast, the former stronghold of insurrection. In the main industry prospered, due, principally, to the resuscitation of linen, though as we have seen there were many tragic casualties by the way: furthermore, the manner in which it did prosper created new ties and extensive intercourse with Britain, so that for the first time Belfast became an outpost of industrial Britain rather than an indigenous part of the Irish economy.[7] John McCracken's little fleet transporting coal across the Channel was but one instance of this new trend.

Secondly, the failure of the '98 Rebellion resulted in the virtual disappearance of Belfast radicalism, and, following on the legislative union with Britain, the liberal element became attached to English liberalism, thereby losing much of its local flavour and all of its national characteristics, and becoming subject to party trends at Westminster.

It is true that, following on the Union, the British Parliament introduced measures which alleviated, to some extent, the distress and poverty in Ireland and secured a better administration of justice. Grand juries were instructed to provide asylums for the insane and infirmaries for the sick; stipendiary magistrates were appointed, and the maintenance of law and order was committed to the newly established Constabulary; an annual grant of £2,000 was expended on the provision of schools, and in 1824 a Royal Commission was appointed to consider "means which can be adopted for extending generally for all classes of the people the benefits of education." Whatever may have been Mary's personal reaction to the Act of Union these were measures which she could not but welcome. In 183?[7] she wrote quite excitedly of a visit of the Lord Lieutenant to Belfast: some people she said were upset at trifling mismanagements:

> but I was too much gratified with the present to feel any annoyance—not merely with the beauty of the scene, but in looking forty years back, and in thinking, too, of those who were gone, and how delighted they would have been at the political changes that have taken place—which could not possibly in their day, have been anticipated by peaceable means—and of the improved prospects of their country now that the English in general, and particularly the present Ministry, have such just feelings towards Ireland and the Irish people . . .
>
> And now a better day has dawned. The old prophecy—'that these countries would never be well ruled until a virgin queen should come to the throne' seems to be realised, as there have been greater improvements since she came to the throne than for a much longer period before; and she is so truly amiable and feminine that she is universally beloved.[8]

These altered tactics involved no change of ideals for Mary Ann. Everything that she and Harry had done had been actuated by the desire for social justice—nationalism, as it was to be known in Ireland later, played no part. Now, if a better mode of life for the common people was to be had by a legislative union with Britain, then she would be content with the Union.

Though political life had become centred at Westminster, there were local religious and political controversies that stirred Belfast profoundly from 1820 onwards. We have no indication that Mary took any part at all in the various efforts to complete Catholic emancipation, or in the Repeal movement: indeed she later expressed the opinion that O'Connell should have devoted himself first to the abolition of tithes rather than to the repeal of the Union, thereby expressing once more her predominant interest in the welfare of the poor.[9] We have no record of her reaction to the Rev. Henry Cooke, the powerful presbyterian leader who dominated religious and political life, and whose thunderous voice echoed through the Province in such strange contradiction to the exhortations of Neilson, Russell and Harry McCracken. Gone were the scattered groups of thoughtful men, typified by Jemmy Hope, who struggled—perhaps inadequately—with such fundamental questions as the rights of ownership, a living wage, and so forth: in their place were the dictates of the Moderator of the Presbyterian Synod of Ulster, in full-blasted support of entrenched authority. As we have seen, Mary McCracken, her family and her circle, had been part and parcel of the great Northern crusade for religious freedom, political responsibility and social betterment; she had no attachment at all to the movements now afoot, and there is no necessity to recount them here in any detail. She had no interest in the Arian controversy that split so tragically the presbyterian community; she must have been puzzled by the alliance of influential presbyterians with the leaders of the Established Church; she must have regarded with dismay Cooke's strenuous opposition to the plans for a national system of education acceptable to all creeds, as formulated by the Chief Secretary for Ireland in 1830; and she, who was to write that she would never seek to change the religious beliefs of Roman Catholics lest she only "turn them from being Christians to infidels", must have been deeply distressed by Cooke's passionate denunciation of what he called "fierce democracy on the one hand, and the more terrible Popery on the other", thus violently expressing his hatred of the memory of '98.

So far as we know she had nothing to do with all this and the reason, indeed, is plain. Shortly after giving up the muslin business another path *did* present itself. She saw a road opening up before her where political weapons would be of little account, but along which she could work effectively for the ideals she never ceased to cherish: she was, in fact, on the threshold of her career as a pioneer social reformer. It was a course far less dramatic than dashing up to Kilmainham or arranging for the defence of political prisoners on trial for their lives, and Mary by no means despised a dramatic situation. It was, nevertheless, more unique, more revolutionary, and more fundamental to the ultimate welfare of the under-privileged members of the community, and it would demand from her the same persistence, the same passion for justice, the same dominating concern for the dignity of the human person that had characterised her partnership with Harry. Very shortly she was to meet another woman who, in different circumstances, was pursuing comparable ends : if, in the annals of social history, the name of Elizabeth Fry is more famous than that of Mary McCracken it is due to accidents of birth and environment rather than to any difference in sincerity and purpose.

It is necessary at this stage to review the development of the Belfast Poorhouse. Originally intended as an infirmary and shelter for the aged poor, its functions had expanded with the rapidly changing conditions in the town. Within a few years of its foundation children had to be accepted, for the simple reason that there was nowhere else for destitute children to go. On one occasion, for example, Mr. Mills, a Church Warden, reported to a meeting of the Poorhouse Committee " that on the evening of Sunday last a Rap was made at his door, and it being opened by the servant, a child named Mary West, which was pinned on her back, about two years, walked in but no other person appeared."[10] And so little Mary West was admitted to an already overcrowded establishment.

Nothing is more indicative of the social upheaval in the country at the close of the 18th and the opening of the 19th centuries than the numbers who clamoured for admission to the Poorhouse. The economy of the rural areas had collapsed, largely owing to the deterioration of the linen industry, and there was a continual drift of workless people to Belfast which, because of failures in the normal trading enterprises, was unable to provide employment for its own labouring population, much less for these hungry migrants. The applicants at the Poorhouse were carefully checked, and only those who had been resident in the town over a number of years were admitted, nevertheless by 1802 more than 130 people were accommodated in the building originally intended for half that number. Moreover, the House was obliged to shelter yet another type of sufferer ; mental deficiency and mental disorders were well known to the committee as they considered their charges. " Weak intellect " is a common enough description of children and adults, who in general were given the indulgence due to their incapacity, and Andrew Cochrane is typical of a number of " lunaticks " for whom there was no other refuge but the Poorhouse :

> Andrew Cochrane who is in a deranged state of mind was admitted here on Sunday last by order of the Committee. After having him chained (which we had to do by force) in one of the Spire Rooms, he broke the chain and came down the stairs. I then had him confined in the room where Livingstone [another lunatic] was. [And later] Andrew Cochrane having again fallen into that deranged state of mind for which he has been so often detained in this House was admitted on Saturday last by order of the committee. Yesterday he appeared to be much better, but at night he found means to get loose from his chain and made his escape. This morning I sent a Man to where he lives who found him walking in his Garden and apparently very quiet—he told him he found himself much recovered and that he intended to begin his work.[11]

This poor man's name recurs in the records with pitiful regularity every few months.

When the Poorhouse was released by the military in 1800 and resumed its normal functions the experiment in weaving was discontinued. As far as possible the old people were expected to work—spinning and knitting were the usual occupations for the women, oakum picking for the men, and a school had been instituted for the children, with a master and mistress in charge of two separate departments. Dreary and rigorous though it probably was, this school gave instruction of a sort at a time when the children of the poor received no formal education at all, and apparently it called forth the traditional reaction, for the committee from time to time were forced to deal with " absconders " :

> That the three boys who had absconded be readmitted and severely flogged and McAllister and Close be put in solitary confinement for two weeks and afterwards logged for a fortnight. Augustus to be logged for a fortnight.[12]

It is cheering to read that ten years later " Thomas Augustus returned from his apprenticeship with a good character from his Master, who sent with him 2 guineas, the amount due to him at the end of his apprenticeship."[13] Corporal punishment was never ordered for the girls ; solitary confinement and logging were considered adequate deterrents for them.

Schooling ended with the eleventh year when every endeavour was made by the Poorhouse committee to apprentice the children. Advertisements to the effect that so many boys and girls were ready for apprenticeship were inserted in the newspapers, and inquiries to discover the character of intending masters and mistresses were made. It was a formidable proceeding, the apprentice was bound to his master by papers of indenture for a stated number of years, generally five or six, during which time he was to be fed, clothed and housed by his employer, and taught his trade. At the satisfactory conclusion of the apprenticeship the lad was due a fixed sum from his master, and, in theory at any rate, was in a position to make his own way in the world. During the whole time of his apprenticeship the committee considered itself responsible for his welfare. There are frequent references in the minutes to complaints by a child that his master was " treating him ill ", and complaints from masters about the conduct of the apprentices. On such occasions the child and the employer were summoned to attend before the committee, when the complaint was investigated. The findings were by no means uniform, at times the master was ordered to fulfil his contract or the indenture would be cancelled, while at other times the child was admonished and sent back. If the allegations against the master were more serious, he was summoned to the petty sessions court.

It is obvious that, so far as was possible, the committee considered the individual needs of the children. Indentures were not completed without, if possible, obtaining the consent of the parents, and there are several instances where a boy did not want to be apprenticed and was allowed to look for work for himself. Domestic service provided work for most of the girls—who were apprenticed for " 5 years to learn the business of a servant "—though a fair proportion of them became spinners or weavers ; and, while occasionally a boy was apprenticed to a shoemaker, carpenter, hairdresser and a blacksmith, the great majority of them went to hand-loom weavers, men who still worked in their own homes, and gave employment to two or three additional hands. At one time so many of these lads were apprenticed in Carrickfergus that the committee committed them " to the care and superintendence of the Revd Messrs Dobbs and Savage, and Mr. Johns, Storekeeper to the Castle. . . . to inquire into the tasks appointed to them and take care that they should be suited to the age and state of the boys. These gentlemen are to report the result of their enquiries to the Committee of the Poorhouse through Mr. Johns."[14] Later a similar arrangement was made for the apprentices at Ballymacarrett.

But children were only a part of this vast undertaking, and one is filled with admiration for these eight or ten Belfast clergymen, doctors and merchants, who, week after week on Saturday mornings, met to transact every aspect of the business, and who in turn acted as orderly, attending daily at the House for seven days to supervise each detail of management. Henry Joy, jun. was, perhaps on account of his father if not indeed for his own zeal, regarded as the senior member amongst a group which included a Bruce, a Suffern, a Sinclaire, a Tennent, a Drummond, a Macartney and other well-known Belfast names. We are apt to think that voluntary charitable work was invented by the Victorians, but in Belfast, at any rate, it was the rational Georgians who set this extremely high standard for posterity.

With the years of acute industrial depression around 1812 the task became increasingly difficult. Between three and four hundred souls were now crowded into the original building, with, it is true, the addition of one or two " cabbins " that had been left standing on the Poorhouse ground. The descriptions in the orderlies' reports of the consequences of this fearful congestion show that at any rate they were aware of the seriousness of the situation. Totally inadequate sanitary arrangements, drunkenness and the depravity that instantly asserts itself when too many people are herded together, the difficulty of caring for the old and infirm, vermin, rampant ringworm and the " itch " among the children, the need for an extra stove to dry the sheets of the boys' beds, the public bakery sending bread of inferior quality and bad weight ; such were some of the problems that were dealt with faithfully week after week, and against, at this time, a crippling background of lack of funds.

In their extremity, the Gentlemen of the Committee bethought themselves of their practical wives and daughters, and in March 1814 a small Ladies' Committee was inaugurated to concern itself with the welfare of the women and children. It consisted of Mrs. Ballentine, Mrs. Ramsey and the Misses McKedy and McCracken. Mary had always been in touch with the Poorhouse, and before this date her name appears in the minutes from time to time with suggestions about the girls being taught to embroider on muslin, and to plait straw for hats and bonnets.

The ladies met : there seemed so much to suggest that they wrote in their first report that " they can better recommend their opinions by conversing with the Gentlemen, whom they would be glad to meet here, at Eleven o'clock on Saturday next." They had many opinions to express over the next months; with a little rearranging an extra sleeping room could be found for the girls; they were "most decidedly against" moving the girls' school to another room, and felt it "incumbent upon them to make a strong remonstrance to the Gentlemen of the Committee on this subject. . . . the present schoolroom might be enlarged at a small expense, & where so much evil may be prevented, a little expense ought not to be regarded"—this to the penniless committee!—; the classes should be smaller, and staggered, "for the purpose of better subordination under the School Mistress." Already Mary Ann had decided that Mrs. Gilpin, the mistress, was worth a little cossetting: so

> The Ladies take the liberty of requesting the Gentlemen's attention to the propriety of procuring Mrs. Gilpin a better Bedstead than that she sleeps on at present, which is too short, the head so low that it is impossible to sit up in it, & the closeness obstructs the air too much.
> The Ladies should not presume to dictate, but think a small field bed with curtains would not be very expensive, and would be much more comfortable and more respectable.[15]

There were also vigorous protests about cleanliness and the need to have two sheets on all the beds:

> It is impossible otherwise to eradicate any infectious disease, as the infection remains in the Blankets, which cannot be so easily or so frequently washed as Sheets.[16]

The "opinion" about the schoolroom was going too far, the Gentlemen shelved "the memorial from the Ladies" from week to week, and after two years we hear no more of that Ladies' Committee. Probably Mary Ann had discovered that, for the present, they could attain their ends by less formal methods. The Ladies still had a "right of entry"; from time to time the Gentlemen asked them to find employment for girls who needed special consideration, and doubtless they made themselves felt in other directions, for on one occasion the Rev. Dr. Hanna and Mr. Joy were requested to wait upon Miss McCracken and explain to her "why the Committee cannot admit Ellen Murray again into the

House." Notwithstanding their visit and all their good reasons Miss McCracken prevailed, for in the Poorhouse Ellen Murray continued to reside, in spite of repeated outbursts of a most unruly temper.

Meanwhile the Gentlemen struggled with their ever increasing difficulties. Unemployment was widespread in Gt. Britain, and it would seem that in addition to the local problem the charitable public in Belfast was confronted with an influx of beggars from across the water, for the Committee of the Poorhouse agreed "to the suggestion from the Sovereign to meet him with the committees of the other charitable institutions at the House of Correction on Friday next at 12 o'c to take into consideration the late transportation of Paupers from England."[17] Some financial easement must have come to the harassed committee, for in 1821 and 1824 the first additions to Robert Joy's building were made, two wings for men and women respectively being erected. By this time the name of Dr. McCluney appears on committee lists, presumably the apothecary whom Mary McCracken had called to her aid on the day of Harry's execution. His frequent comments in the Orderly Book show him to be a practical person, and in time he begs "leave to suggest the propriety of reviving the Ladies' Committee, a number of whom I know are ready to attend if invited." He was charged with conveying the invitation, but for some reason the ladies, as a body, did not respond, though Mary Ann continued her activities and is next heard of sponsoring the case of an apprentice against her employer.

Such, briefly, was the situation in the Poorhouse and Mary Ann's connection with it, prior to 1827.

Note: Sometime about 1830, Nicholas Crowley painted a picture entitled "Cup-tossing". Its interest for us lies in the fact that Mary McCracken is said to have posed for the gipsy woman, and that the young girl eagerly awaiting the interpretation, is a grand-daughter of the once "infuriating" Luke Teeling. As a portrait of Mary Ann in middle age it is welcome, and as an indication that something of the fun and gaiety of family life in Rosemary Lane still continued, it is most re-assuring. In spite of all her serious undertakings, Mary McCracken never lost sympathy with the lighter side of life.

CHAPTER XIV

THE LADIES' COMMITTEE

1827–1851

EARLY in February 1827 Elizabeth Fry, accompanied by her brother Joseph John Gurney, braved the elements and set out on a visit to Ireland. Though the journey was undertaken in the Quaker tradition " primarily for the purpose of paying a religious visit to the Society of Friends ", Mrs. Fry had acquainted Sir Robert Peel of her " intention to visit such of the prisons in that country as she might be permitted to see." The Home Secretary " in the most handsome manner sent her a letter which would cause the doors of every prison in Ireland to be thrown open to her, and he moreover, gave instructions that all her letters and parcels should be transmitted postage free."[1] Houses of Correction, Houses of Industry and Infirmaries, all came within the purview of these " philanthropic strangers."

An eager welcome awaited Elizabeth Fry in Ireland, her arrival being heralded by a poem* of salutation in the *Belfast News-Letter* beginning thus :

> Far nobler subject than the praise
> Of Hero crowned with laurel bays
>   Invigorates my mind
> I hail the sea—the bark—the oar—
> The winds of Heaven that wafted o'er,
> From Albion's cliffs to Erin's shore,
>   The friend of human kind.[2]

In due course the little party made its way north from Dublin, and on the 12th March visited the House of Correction in Belfast.

> The Inspector, Protestant, Presbyterian and Roman Catholic Chaplains and the Surgeon of the establishment were in attendance together with several Clergymen of the

*By William McComb.

town, Professors of the Institution*, and a number of the most active and intelligent members of several of our charitable foundations. After minutely examining the past and present state of the prison calendar, and inquiring into the kind of employment provided for the prisoners, the stated periods of attendance at school, the character of the works employed in education, and the nature of the religious instruction afforded by the respective chaplains, it became necessary to adjourn to the Court House. Mr. Gurney expressed the great satisfaction he had felt in visiting the House of Correction. He averted to the general prevalence of cleanliness, order and regularity among the prisoners; and to the watchful administration of the individuals to whom the moral and spiritual instruction of the inmates was entrusted.

Mrs. Fry then stated the high gratification she had received from her visit; pointed out in the most plain and perspicuous manner the importance of a well regulated system of prison discipline, as calculated not only to coerce, but to improve human beings, and concluded a very impressive address by observing that before visiting the prison she had intended to have recommended the formation of a Committee of females, who might lend their aid in promoting the reformation of the prisoners, particularly the females; but from the assiduity and cordial co-operation of all the regularly appointed officers, she did not deem it necessary to submit such a resolution to the meeting.[3]

We may assume that Mary McCracken was present, and can imagine her extreme interest in this famous visitor. Here was someone exhibiting that most desirable feminine independence, and who, while fulfilling the duties of a wife and mother, was yet able to devote herself so successfully to the service of the most unfortunate of human sufferers. Recalling her own tragic acquaintance with prison life, her knowledge of the trials of the poor, the sick and the workless, Mary McCracken must have been deeply moved as she listened to this renowned expert, who reiterated what she herself had so often proclaimed, and who based all she did on a foundation of sincere, personal religion. The House of Correction

*The Belfast Academical Institution, see p. 230.

and the Court House have long since been swept away, but it is easy to visualise the tall, serene, commanding figure of Mrs. Fry as she addressed the meeting, attired in her Quaker cap and gown, precisely ten years younger than Mary Ann.* Wherever she went Elizabeth Fry impressed on those responsible the need not only for suitable and up-to-date buildings, but also for the proper care and instruction of the inmates ; and, furthermore, the desirability of creating in connection with the "female" department of such institutions, be they prisons, hospitals or poorhouses, an association of ladies who would, in co-operation with the matron, undertake to visit the women, read to them, arrange for their education, and by every suitable means endeavour to help and befriend them.

At the conclusion of the three months' tour of Ireland, during which forty prisons were visited, as well as other institutions, Elizabeth Fry and Joseph John Gurney presented a report to the Lord Lieutenant, which, after more than a century, still rings with unusual sincerity and vigour.[4] Since this is a story of Belfast two references from it are included here. Firstly : the mention of the House of Correction in Belfast along with the Bridewell in Dublin as being "two of the best managed prisons in Ireland", and secondly : "the house of industry at Belfast. . . . may also be mentioned as [an] orderly and well managed establishment." The comments on the County Jail at Carrickfergus, where Henry Joy McCracken had been detained thirty years previously, were very different.

Though there is no record in the minutes of the Belfast Charitable Society or elsewhere, that Elizabeth Fry visited the Poorhouse, it is likely that she did so, for on May 13th 1827 some ladies gathered in the Friends' Meeting House and agreed to devote their attention to the women and children in the institution. The list of the twenty-seven present is headed by the name of Miss Mary McCracken, then in her fifty-seventh

*In that same year Florence Nightingale celebrated her seventh birthday.

year, the younger generation being represented by Miss Joy, probably the daughter of Henry Joy, jun.; by Isabella and Letitia, the two gay daughters of William Tennent, once the fellow prisoner with Russell and Neilson at Fort George; by Miss Macartney, daughter of the Vicar of Belfast and a one-time school friend of Maria's; and by young Mrs. Henry Purdon, wife of the first of five physicians of that name to be continuously connected with the Poorhouse for over one hundred years. Most of the "Ladies" were in some way related to the "Gentlemen" to whom the following tactful communication was addressed:

> At a meeting held on Tuesday Evening, 13th March at the desire of Mrs. Fry, it was proposed that some Ladies should form themselves into a Committee for the purpose of superintending the female department in the Poor House, and to divide their attention amongst the female children, the aged women, those confined to the Hospital, and the children after their removal from the Institution, who may be apprenticed in the town and neighbourhood.
>
> The Ladies wish to submit this proposal to the Committee of Gentlemen, in the hope of obtaining their approbation and support to enable them to effect their object, and beg most earnestly to assure them that there shall be no interference whatever with any of their arrangements or regulations.[5]

Just how they hoped to carry out their aims according to these lady-like rules it is difficult to imagine, and doubtless the Gentlemen were under no delusion as far as Miss McCracken was concerned. After considering the proposition for a week they recorded that: "The proposal from the Ladies to form a committee to superintend the female department of this House, agreeable to their letter entered last Saturday, was agreed to."[6]

In spite of their enthusiasm the Ladies took some little time to get into their stride, but by August the efficient Isabella Tennent was secretary, and the organisation on its feet. In the early stages Mary Ann appears to have kept in the background from where she made her influence felt.

The first matter for consideration was " the propriety of having these [Poorhouse] girls instructed in several modes of obtaining a livelihood ", and straw plaiting and " tambouring " were obvious lines to follow. Bonnets in those days were made locally, and the white embroidery for which the north of Ireland was so shortly to become famous, was already in great demand on muslin and cambric, as we have seen in the case of Stewart Bruce's handkerchiefs ! The Gentlemen provided a grant of thirty shillings with which the experienced Miss McCracken was to purchase the necessary tambour frames, piercers and muslin. The Ladies suggested that Helena Kelly, one of the inmates, be retained in the House to teach embroidery—" she is an expert at plain work and might without any expense obtain instruction from the Mistress of the Lancastrian School, who has been in Dublin learning a variety of useful and ornamental kinds of work " ; and some of the girls who had been attending straw plaiting classes in the House of Industry would now be able to teach others. Mrs. Gilpin was still in charge of the girls' school and loyally supported the Ladies in these efforts towards improvement.

Realising the limitations of the Poorhouse facilities, the next idea of the Ladies' Committee was to arrange for such of the girls as were ready for apprenticing to go to private houses for a few hours a day, to assist in any household occupation " for the purpose of making them familiar with work they may be expected to do when in service and in which the Poor House establishment does not offer any practice." The " Gentlemen " were agreeable provided the girls were not permitted to leave the House " before daylight ", and along with their permission sent a list of the " grown girls capable of going out." One learns with something of a shock that the ages of these " grown girls " ranged from eleven to fifteen, the majority being around twelve and thirteen ! At this stage Miss McCracken became treasurer for the committee and the Ladies set about collecting funds to provide blinds for the hospital windows, the full rays of the sun being very distressing to those who were lying ill in bed. The Ladies noticed, too, that many of the old wooden beds had been replaced by iron ones. Straw mats were therefore necessary " as the iron is found when in immediate contact with the ticking of the beds to cut and wear them, and the cold proceeding from an iron bedstead requires some intervening substance to mitigate that effect." The need for adequate fire-guards in the children's rooms was another detail that did not escape their vigilant " superintendence."

Before long the Ladies directed their attention to the children who had left the House. Armed with a list of apprentices, Isabella Tennent undertook the first round of after-care visits. Jane Allison, she reported, was doing very well with Miss Higginson the dress-maker " and has made great proficiency." Jane was one of the lame girls for whom places had been found by the former Ladies' Committee. Her apprenticeship would be completed, wrote Miss Tennent,

> . . . on the first day of May next, and as she would be rather unfit to commence business on her own account, from not being able to stand to take measures, I would earnestly entreat the Ladies of this Committee to exert themselves to procure for this deserving girl a situation in a family who would have no objection to sit beside her while engaged in trying on their dresses. She is well fitted for any department of sewing . . . She is 17 years of age, and appears intelligent and active.

Martha McAuley was giving general satisfaction, but her mistress found fault with her ignorance :

> The girl herself seemed smart and was very clean, but I had no conversation with her alone, and I would recommend the Lady appointed for visiting next month to endeavour to speak to her in private if possible.

> Called at Mr. Thos. Ewart's. Grace Hunter a most interesting child of 13 years is apprenticed here as servant. She says she is quite happy where she is and her master expressed

> himself in the warmest terms of her good temper and good conduct, she has yet two years of her apprenticeship to fulfil, and there is every prospect of her performing it with credit. Her brother has also been apprenticed out of the Poor House, he is a shoe-maker, and the relation of affection that subsists between these two orphan children, and the exemplary conduct of each must be gratifying to everyone at all interested in this excellent Institution.[7]

By present day standards of welfare visiting, Isabella Tennent had done her work admirably. The next visitor succeeded in interviewing Martha McAuley by herself and found everything satisfactory, but it was decided by the Ladies that as monthly visits "may be deemed intrusive" they should call in future at three monthly intervals.

Some of the visitors wrote their reports in great detail, and from them it is clear that present-day difficulties are not exclusive to the 20th century. Miss McCracken found that one girl "objected to some occupations to which her mistress had put her on the plea that they were not in her agreement. I tried to convince her that it was equally her duty and interest to learn every kind of work." The mistress of another girl complained of her temper. "I spoke to the girl apart, who promised amendment, she wept and acknowledged the kindness of the family, but she did not look happy." On the other hand Mary Robinson she found "busy in the weaving shop winding pirns, the picture of health, cheerfulness and contentment."[8]

Obviously this was work that interested the Ladies greatly and the reports are full of interest, but there were other jobs as well; they inspected the combing of dirty heads, they arranged for the boys to be taught to mend and knit, there were constant appeals to the Gentlemen for adequate clothing, and the perennial problem of vermin was not avoided:

> Having found in an old receipt book (which accompanies this for the inspection of the Gentlemen) that deal shavings present a great encouragement to *bugs*, affording them their favourite food in abundance. The Ladies of the

> Committee, aware that many of the beds of the establishment are at present composed of that material, and that the House is dreadfully infested with bugs, request the Gentlemen's attention to the subject, and also the suggestion that the dried leaves of the Beech tree gathered in autumn, or the Goslera Maritima called also Ulva Marina (which is found abundantly on our shores) when washed and dried, afford an excellent substitute for shavings or straw, and that many of the old men or boys might be advantageously employed in the summer in gathering either of these cheap articles and preparing them for use.[9]

The Gentlemen replied that they would appoint three of their number " to make experiments with the view of getting rid of the bugs " but the Ladies were forced to return to the subject again and again :

> Fear of the vermin prevents many Ladies from coming to the House—some of the Ladies have known a solution of arsenic prove effectual, applied with a brush to the walls and ceilings and floors, as well as to every article of furniture—others recommend gas water, also Tobacco water, . . . Were one or two of the old men set to each room in the House at once, the whole might be finished in one forenoon and thereby prove much more effectual than if done by degrees.[10]

The Gentlemen were silent on the question of arsenic, but the problem of bugs remained with them for many years. Indeed the place of vermin in society is perhaps one of the more outstanding differences between the 18th and 20th centuries. The extremely refined Mrs. Glasse in her " Receipt Book " gives instructions for destroying bugs : " Where only the bedstead swarms pull to pieces and let them lie in cold water four and twenty hours."[11]

In 1832 the fine hand-writing of Isabella Tennent disappears from the Minute Book, due in all probability to her marriage,* and Mary Ann McCracken became

*Letitia Tennent had likewise vanished to become the wife of that uprising young barrister James Emerson who, willing to take his wife's name along with her fortune, was later to achieve distinction as Sir James Emerson Tennent, Governor of Ceylon and later President of the Board of Trade.

secretary. From the beginning she had been the directing force on the Committee, through all its activities can be traced the ideas long dominant in her mind.

Firstly, there was the need for education, whether for life or for work. After attacking the immediate problem by starting the classes for needlework and straw plaiting and giving the girls some idea of household duties in order to equip them more adequately for the business of earning their living, the Ladies proceeded to a much more revolutionary notion—the establishment within the Poorhouse of an Infant School for the many children not yet old enough for the more formal instruction of Mrs. Gilpin or the school-master. Infant schools were, at this time, a new departure in the general effort to provide suitable education for younger children — in some instances perhaps little more than a sub-division of existing classes according to age. In the hands of Mary McCracken, however, the development was to go far in the direction of the twentieth century pioneer nursery school movement associated with the great names of Rachel and Margaret Macmillan. Mary knew that the Lancastrian school nearby was considering the new idea, and, to quote the minute :

> The Ladies beg to inform the Gentlemen that there is about to be formed in town an *Infant School*, and fully impressed with the importance of these establishments, and the great advantage of introducing the system into the Infant department of the Poor House, they *earnestly* solicit permission to select *two girls* out of the House, for the purpose of having them educated (which can be done without any expense at the new school above mentioned) so that they may be qualified to pursue the same system in the Poor House.[12]

The Ladies were determined that the children in their care should lack none of the benefits provided for children elsewhere. But the Gentlemen thought otherwise—this was going too far, surely a clear case of " interference with arrangements ", such excessive zeal must be repressed. So they replied that they were " very sensible of the advantage of Infant Schools, and may, at a proper time consider of establishing one in the House, but think the present proposal premature."[13] To accept the principle, but declare that it could not be carried out in the Poorhouse was precisely the argument to arouse the fighting spirit in Miss McCracken and her Ladies: had she not already earmarked two possible girls for training? For nine months the idea smouldered, the ladies watching with sympathetic envy the success of the experiment across the road. Then they returned to the subject:

> The Ladies Committee having had long in contemplation the introduction of an Infant School into the Poor House and an institution of this kind having been now in operation in the town for nearly a twelvemonth, offering a proof of the excellence and success of the system, they would respectfully beg the Gentlemen to take into consideration the propriety of improving the condition of the nursery by this means. There are at present under the entire care of *one old woman nineteen* babies, many under three years who require the superintendence of a more *active* and more *enlightened* person, and in Mrs. Gilpin's school there are 13 more, too young not to be injured by the sedentary habits of the old mode of instruction.[14]

The underlining is in the minute book and the whole has a strikingly modern ring for an age that ante-dated by at least a decade the misfortunes of Oliver Twist. Here is a true appreciation of the fundamental educational needs of the very young child.

But again the Gentlemen were adamant: they resolved "that the Committee upon mature deliberation do not think it advisable to establish an Infant School in this House."[15] Mature the deliberation may have been, but the Ladies would have none of it. They said no more until June 1830, when the following statement was set out for the Gentlemen to read:

> The Ladies beg to inform the Gentlemen's Committee that an exertion has been made, in the midst of many difficulties, to establish an Infant School in the House. This has been

practically effected for more than a fortnight and, even in its present imperfect state, has given much satisfaction to many who have had opportunity of seeing it. They now respectfully call on the Gentlemen to aid them in completing what they have commenced—and for this end request they will permit the carpenter of the House to make the following articles for the use of the School: 4 *Lesson Posts*, 12 *Boards* for lessons and a Box for holding metals and various other articles . . . The Ladies would also suggest to the Gentlemen that Hannah Murray, who has been selected as Mistress for the Infant School should receive some small reward for the very laudable efforts she has made to fit herself (as far as her capabilities will permit) for the situation, and the unremitting attention she has paid since the children were placed under her care. They think that the usual proportion of Tea and Bread which is given to other individuals who are making themselves useful in the House, would be a proper remuneration for the present, and a stimulus to future exertion.[16]

In face of this " fait accompli " what could the Gentlemen do? At a special meeting the carpenter was instructed to make the necessary equipment, and even Hannah Murray's tea and bread were officially sanctioned. Lesson posts and boards may sound formidable, but was not Montessori to have her counting frames and letters?

The Ladies must be pardoned if, in exultation, they threw their Regency bonnets in the air. Flushed with success, they fluttered round Hannah and her infants—clean, tidy and happy, and no doubt many toys from the nurseries of their friends found their way to this Poorhouse venture. But—

. . . there are still a few little articles wanting, such as a few pictures, reading lessons and a numeral frame. The sum of *Twenty Shillings* would amply suffice for the purchase. The Ladies would feel most grateful should the Gentlemen deem it proper to grant them this sum.[17]

The £1 was forthcoming: one feels that some of the Ladies had, over the past months, done a good deal of lobbying with their friends on the Gentlemen's Committee!

Soon a larger room had to be found, the Ladies suggested one

> . . . which in its size and distance from the Hospital (as the noise of the children must be irksome to the patients) will fit it. The Ladies will feel grateful if this improvement be immediately entered upon, as a serious inconvenience attends the school in its present limited situation.[18]

Frequent references to play and noise abolish any fears that the children were unduly repressed. Hannah Murray was giving continued satisfaction, and it was agreed "that she should be rewarded for her praiseworthy exertions in this department by receiving a Stuff gown out of the Ladies' fund for the encouragement of industry in the Poor House."

The next observations are most interesting :

> The Ladies who attend the Infant School discovering a remarkable deficiency in information upon common objects, among the children of the Poorhouse, compared with others of the same age in the other schools in town, and ascribing this to a total confinement within the walls of the establishment, which prevents them from seeing anything save that what the House presents, request the Gentlemen will authorize them to send these children out to walk *one day* in the week under the Superintendence of Hannah Murray, their Teacher, and if she and her assistant be not found equal to the task of taking care of them, one or two of the steadiest girls out of the large School, might be selected to assist with great profit to themselves, by accustoming them even for this limited time to take charge of young children.[19]

And, two weeks later :

> The Ladies being of opinion that to want of exercise more than to any other cause may be attributed the unhealthy appearance of the children in the Poorhouse, beg the Gentlemen will permit the erection of a *Pole* and some other *little wooden structures* in the playground, for the purpose of exercising and giving robustness to the frame.[20]

They had nothing to learn from Pestalozzi and Montessori as to the value of experience in education, and "poles" and "little wooden structures" foreshadow the most modern nursery school equipment. Always there was the desire to give the Poorhouse children every possible advantage. Hannah Murray must have been a very capable girl, probably she was no more than fifteen when she was put in charge of the infants; that she was also ambitious was accepted as natural by the Ladies, who reported to the Gentlemen that:

> . . . this young person from her successful exertions in the Infant School has imbibed the laudable desire of placing herself on a more respectable footing than a mere ordinary inmate of the House, and for this purpose she has memorialed the Ladies' Committee to intercede for her with the Gentlemen to obtain, *in lieu of the present supply of clothes from the establishment*, a small salary, the receiving of which will add to her consequence as a Teacher and enable her to appear in a costume suited to her office. The Ladies with deference name the sum of *Five Pounds per Annum* as a suitable salary for H. Murray, and beg the Gentlemen's attention to her request.[21]

The Gentlemen agreed, and it is a pity that very shortly Hannah should have got herself embroiled in a misunderstanding with the teacher of the girls' school. Possibly others were jealous of Hannah's "consequence as a teacher", and in a fit of temper she seems to have walked out of the House. In spite of her own contrition, and the Ladies intervention on her behalf "as from her kindness to the children and her qualifications as an Infant School mistress it may be difficult to find another equally fit for the situation",[22] the Gentlemen would not tolerate such behaviour. Hannah was offered a post as Infant school mistress in Omagh, which, according to the Ladies minutes "by the advice of her friends she accepted, the matter now to be considered is the appointment of another and on what terms."[23]

The Ladies were extremely particular regarding the person to whom they would entrust their precious experiment, and, while there was no shortage of applicants "not one of them is adequate to the business."

An offer of temporary help from a teacher in a nearby school was gratefully accepted, and in due course the appointment of a Mrs. Porter was recommended to the Gentlemen, as a person " superiorly qualified for the situation." This applicant requested a salary of £20 per annum, " that she should be permitted to have her child, a fine boy of about four years old (whom she would support at her own expense), be allowed a room to herself for which she has furniture of her own, and also be allowed to be one of the choir of St. George's Church."[24] Alas ! such a salary was completely beyond the range of the Gentlemen. Mrs. Porter applied again, and again the Ladies pled for her appointment on account of her kind and affectionate disposition, her superior abilities, and her exemplary character, and " with all due deference to the Gentlemen " they recommended that " she should be permitted to have her child with her, in order to render her mind more free from care and anxiety and better fitted to attend to the duties of her situation." Say what they would, the answer came back that the Infant School must be run by one of the girl inmates as no salary at all could be paid. In desperation the Ladies arranged to conduct the school themselves and were horrified to discover

> . . . that the very modest remuneration which they recommended for the [temporary teacher's] services should be considered too much by the Gentlemen, as it was the very lowest sum the Ladies thought could be offered to her, and considered too little by some of them . . . the girl made no agreement, trusting to the justice of the committee for a suitable recompence, not only for her time, but also for the shoes and clothes worn in the service coming out in all kinds of weather now for 45 weeks, which ought to be considered—the Gentlemen will please to say if they wish her service to be discontinued which if she is not to expect any remuneration in future cannot be looked for.[25]

In time the harassed Ladies discovered in Mary Kelly, a lame girl, a possible successor to Hannah. She was allowed to attend the school in Brown Street, " for the purpose of improving herself in the art of education" and turned out a most successful teacher. After many months the Gentlemen were induced to give her a "cloak wide enough to cover her crutch", and a straw bonnet—"the price with ribbon 5/s"[26] —and there are constant references to her ability. But alas! she too was offered a position elsewhere, with a salary of £5 per annum and consequences that can be gathered from the following minute:

> Resolved unanimously to request the Gentlemen may reconsider their offer of £2 as a salary to Mary Kelly as it is not reasonable to expect that the girl would prefer £2 to £5, particularly as £2 would not be sufficient to provide her with respectable clothing and also where she got £5 she also got animal food which is necessary to support strength sufficient for the duties of an Infant School which is much more arduous and fatiguing than the business of any other school—if Mary Kelly be parted with, the Gentlemen will not easily find another who is competent for the business in every respect at so low a salary as £5—and in addition, to understanding the system Mary Kelly [has] a kind and affectionate disposition and good principles—so that the children under her care are neither subject to capricious treatment, nor to an example of falsehood.[27]

One is impressed again and again by the sympathetic understanding of the needs of little children implicit in these minutes of Mary McCracken; it was not merely a question of having the children taught, or even "minded", it was their training, their education in the widest sense, and their happiness that was at stake. No less did she sympathise with the aspirations of the young teacher, and nothing enraged her more than any suggestion that, out of a sense of gratitude for charity, the inmates of the Poorhouse, young or old, should willingly accept disadvantage or indignity—against such treatment she was their constant protector. Indeed one imagines that in this she was far more liberal than even Elizabeth Fry.

As for Mary Kelly—if £2 did not satisfy her, the

Gentlemen said she was free to accept the offer made to her, and so another of Mary Ann's protégées departed.

It is possible on this occasion to advance some apology for the Gentlemen's action. It was now 1839, the Irish Poor Law administration had just been established, a momentous happening in a country where, until then, the relief of poverty had been practically entirely in the hands of voluntary charitable societies. The Union Workhouse in Belfast was already planned, and the Committee of the Poorhouse was perplexed and uncertain as to its future. Would applicants continue to seek admission when the great new workhouse was completed, and if they did could a heavily taxed community be expected to provide the necessary funds to maintain a voluntary institution, —problems raised again by the passing of Welfare legislation one hundred years later.

Meanwhile the Ladies searched for a successor to Mary Kelly; two girls were found, and the school continued for a time, but the children in the Poor-house were soon to feel the impact of the new regime. In 1841 Mary Ann wrote in the Minutes:

> The Ladies request the Gentlemen will seriously consider whether it would not be more advisable to remove such of the children as have neither father or mother to the new Poorhouse, than to turn out any more of the old and infirm—the pain of the former would be of much less duration than to the latter, and their ultimate good in no respect risked while to the old it seems misery for life—at the same time retaining any very sickly or helpless child, who appears attached to those under whose care it is placed.[28]

It is interesting to find with what confidence the socially minded welcomed the inauguration of the workhouse system!

Nothing more is heard of the Infant School. The struggle to establish it, the continued insistence on teachers of high quality and special ability and their right to adequate remuneration [according to existing

THE POORHOUSE, BELFAST, *c.* 1820

standards], show clearly how advanced were the views of Mary McCracken and her Ladies with regard to the care of little children, and how fully they appreciated every implication. Recalling all that she had already experienced of hard work, sorrow, tribulation, joy and love, there is something unusually touching in the sincerity and success with which, at the onset of old age, [she was now seventy-one] she championed the needs of the very young child.

The Girls' school, though not their own creation, came also within the terms of reference of the Ladies' Committee. While Mrs. Gilpin was in charge they were assured of co-operation, and their attention was largely devoted to improving vocational instruction, for the stark necessity of earning a living could never be disregarded. Little Mary Arnold, aged 11, was allowed to go for some days a week to help a " respectable washerwoman " recommended by Miss Tennent, and so long as a " very well-conducted woman from whom they could receive no injury " was in charge of the " little kitchen " in the Poorhouse the older girls were allowed to assist her, " particularly in washing and doing up linen for their improvement . . . At the same time the Ladies would not recommend the children being employed in the washhouse, where they might receive much injury and no improvement ".

Happily, there was a lighter side to instruction. " Miss McCracken was appointed to procure a few story books to be added to the library of the girls' school. Miss Edgeworth's Popular Tales might also be very useful ",[29] and while the following request was made in the name of the Infant School it was probably an omnibus order to be shared by all :

> The Glasgow Magazine, Some Birds of Prey, The Eagle and the Raven with lessons, also some lessons for such birds as are in the School at present—metallic minerals and Pinnock's Geography, the whole not exceeding 10/6.[30]

There are constant requests for Grammars for the girls :

> . . . that they may be taught a thorough knowledge of the

English language and thereby be prepared for future usefulness in a higher sphere, should any such occur, and even as nursery maid a good education is very desirable.[31]

If education was important so also was the wise use of leisure, in Mary McCracken's view time was far too precious either to be arbitrarily filled or to be frivolously wasted :

We would recommend that the girls should be allowed the free use of their time during play hours so that such as are of industrious and sedentary dispositions may have an opportunity of acquiring expertness and habits of diligence —there is little occasion to force children to take exercise in the way of amusements ; all that is necessary is to supply them with inducements ; and [in] the present case skipping ropes would be very useful, also the repair of the pole swing in the yard.[32]

Again :

. . . that Nancy Rice and Mary Kelly be allowed to spend their leisure hours in any kind of industry by which they may be able to supply themselves in a variety of necessities which the House does not supply, and which, tho' trifling, are necessary to comfort and respectability . . . [and] that they [the Gentlemen] will at least allow them candles sufficient for the hours of darkness, when not in bed, and supply them with books for their moral and intellectual improvement, and not doom them in winter to spend several hours daily in darkness, and consequently in idleness—the injurious consequences of which are too obvious to require comment.[33]

Similarly a request is made for five or six " wheels " for a few of the old women who would spin :

The Gentlemen will please to recollect that the uneducated have few resources within themselves and of course are the more in want of some employment in which they feel an interest as an antidote to ennui and the present quarrelling and discontent with each other.[34]

Behind all these arrangements was the urgent desire to stimulate in the girls, and even in the old women, self-respect and " resources within themselves ", and every encouragement in the way of " premiums " and " remuneration " was given. The subject recurs many times, but one characteristic minute must be quoted at some length :

> The Ladies have heard with infinite surprise and regret that the Gentlemen are opposed to promoting industry in the House by the only means, that of allowing individuals to derive some little advantage from their own exertions. At the same time the Ladies are aware of the argument that may be used on the occasion, viz, that it is the duty of the inmates of the House to devote all their abilities to the general good of the institution by which they are supported —yet as it is an incontrovertible fact that the highest and best-educated classes of society require some additional stimulus to exertion, besides a sense of duty and the public good, it is too much therefore to expect that those of inferior advantages should rise higher in the scale of perfection. The Ladies therefore respectfully request the Gentlemen may reconsider the matter and examine it in every point of view. In the first place they will please to recollect that every human being whatever may be their station in life ought to have some leisure daily, at their own disposal which is the case with the servants in all well-regulated families, besides in this House at this season of the year the greatest portion of the time which those who are engaged in active duties (particularly in attending to the children) have at their disposal, they would be obliged to spend in darkness and therefore idleness if not allowed to earn the means of purchasing candles for themselves, as what they get from the House does not afford light for more than one hour out of the twenty-four . . . The Gentlemen will also please to observe that it would have the appearance of partiality and inconsistency to allow some to derive profit from their industry, particularly those receiving salaries and deny the same indulgence to others who receive none . . . respecting the old women and the trifle they have earned the arrangement has preserved peace and harmony . . . while the work has been remarkably well done—had these old women been told they must do the work whether they could or not, they might have made the attempt but, wanting the proper stimulus, the work would

> most probably have been too ill done for a continuance of their labours to be required. The Ladies are quite sorry at having to trespass so long on the time and attention of the Gentlemen, but before concluding must take the liberty of recommending . . . that the children should be washed at night in tepid water in the school-room in place of in the morning in the open air.[35]

This was written in the month of January ! Here is Mary Ann, as we have seen her before, goaded to fury by frustration and pigheadedness. These are no ordinary minutes.

But to this tireless, though now ageing, secretary sheer play had its own importance. One of the first observations of the Ladies was to beg that permission " be given for the girls to spend the play hours of one or two days in the week in the front court " where there was more room and a " freer circulation of air ". Hoops, balls, tops and skipping ropes are requested for the boys so that they too may have " active sport ", indeed it is over this question of outdoor play that one of the most vehement entries occurs.

The principle of allowing the girls to play in front of the House having been conceded, they were expected to reach it by a circuitous route through the kitchen and the back door. This was all very well until the Ladies discovered that " the man who keeps the kitchen door is brutally harsh in his manner ", and in order to avoid this unpleasant creature they asked the Gentlemen's permission for the girls to use the main entrance " one or two monitors might be appointed to see that they make their feet clean on returning and passed in an orderly quiet manner ". This request was completely ignored, and when two reminders had elicited no response and five precious months had gone by, the Gentlemen found themselves confronted with the following :

> . . . if the nicety of the front hall be considered of more importance than securing the children from ill-usage and coarse language a door might be opened between the women's yard and the green, the key of which might be kept by Miss Ryder.[36]

It is only necessary to picture Robert Joy's lovely flagged entrance hall, approached by a gracious flight of steps, up which the children returning from the green would romp, to realise the piquancy of this thrust. The Gentlemen's minutes remain silent, and contain no reference to any door being opened from the women's yard, so we may assume that Mary Ann had been successful.

One can almost see her—rummaging in the back of her mind and unearthing one after another the principles by which David Manson had educated her when she herself was a little girl. Exercise in the open air, a sense of dignity and responsibility, rewards, reading from worthwhile books, the proper use of words, adequate play material for all ages, and suitable equipment to aid even the youngest child to learn—all of his precepts that her long life had taught her to prize so highly, were now evoked for the benefit of the Poorhouse children from whom nothing of value must be witheld.

It could not be supposed that this system of supervision by the Ladies would always run smoothly, and hitches were most noticeable in connection with the Girls' School. Miss Ferris, who succeeded the worthy Mrs. Gilpin and had been the cause of Hannah Murray's departure, was herself dismissed by the Gentlemen for " unnecessary harshness toward the children under her care ". The Ladies apparently had doubts as to the ability of Miss Ryder, her successor, and suggested that " some of the best works on education " should be procured for Miss Ryder " who had a great desire for improvement ", particularly *The Teacher, or Moral Influences* by Abbott. Trouble again flared up. Nancy Rice, who looked after the children at night and when they were not in school, was another of the Ladies' discoveries and completely trusted by them. Judge of their indignation when they learned that Miss Ryder had accused her of " introducing ardent spirits into the House, and of using, on occasion, improper and impertinent remarks ". The Gentlemen ordered that Nancy should be confined to the House for three months, and " if during that period Miss Ryder can substantiate any just complaint against her she will be dismissed" : at the same time they warned Miss Ryder "that she would have to be more close in her attention to her duties". Very shortly the harsh measures against Nancy were relaxed—it would seem that this was another case of professional jealousy. Ten years later, Mary Ann, remembering a gross injustice, was constrained to write this minute :

> No business came before the Ladies to-day—the children were all preparing to attend the funeral of Nancy Rice, who died on Sunday morning, she had been an inmate of the house from a child for a period of about thirty years, except for nine or ten months from April 1834 till June 1835, having accompanied the late Mrs. Gilpin, who had been schoolmistress in the House for near 20 years, when ill health obliged her to give up the situation and go to her daughter in England. Nancy accompanied her as her attendant but returned on Mrs. Gilpin's decease and tho' in ill-health from early childhood, rendered herself useful, in acting as nursery maid and caretaker of the children, by all of whom she was much beloved, being kind, affectionate and considerate, she was strictly well-principled and attentive to her religious duties, this tribute is due to her memory.[37]

Allied to education was the whole question of work and apprenticeship. No twentieth century Personnel Officer is more alive to the importance of wise selection and placing, where juveniles are concerned, than was Mary McCracken and here she spoke from first-hand experience. If, like the other Ladies she knew all about running a house and "the business of a servant", she appreciated, perhaps more than most, the endless drudgery that this could mean for some temperaments, and from her personal knowledge of the spinning and weaving industries she understood far better than many of the Gentlemen just what those trades demanded. As we have seen, the first concern of the Ladies was to provide for the children as wide an experience as possible of the few occupations open to them, and repeated instances could be quoted where the needs of individual children were carefully considered. For example :

> The Ladies request the Gentlemen's attention to their recommendation of 3rd Jan. respecting Mary Kelly and also that Anne Dick may be allowed to accompany her daily in her attendance on Mrs. Gorman, as the girl does not appear sufficiently strong for hard labour and has a taste for needlework, and Mrs. Gorman, who is a conscientious woman promises to give both the girls all the improvement in her power and by cutting out work in their presence, by this means Anne Dick, who is but 11 years of age, will require a shorter apprenticeship to some eminent dressmaker and by understanding various kinds of work will be qualified for a situation in a respectable family. Mrs. Gorman, tho' not a fashionable dressmaker understands plain dressmaking and staymaking and can make boys' clothes. [38]

As well as seeking for suitable employment there was the constant problem of the dead-end job :

> . . . they take the liberty of recommending . . . not to apprentice girls to weavers, if other places can be had, as the sedentary occupation of winding pirns from morn till night in close damp weaving shops is highly injurious to health and spirits (particularly to those of active habits) and by no means qualifies them for earning their bread hereafter. [39]

But the greatest struggle centred round the Ladies plan for some period of probation :

> . . . they take the liberty of requesting the Gentlemen may take into consideration the propriety of allowing the children, previous to their being bound, to go for a month or two on trial that the master or mistress may be able to choose in one that answers them, otherwise when they cannot get rid of a boy or girl who is not fit for their employment they treat the child in such a manner that it is obliged to leave the place and is thereby exposed to the danger of utter ruin—many children have given satisfaction in a second place that have not answered in the first.[40]

They return to this subject again and again, giving instances of girls who had been in four or five places before they could finally settle. They request the Gentlemen to consider how very unwilling they themselves would be to take an apprentice of whom they knew nothing, and how irksome they would find it to keep an unsuitable one for five years; not to speak of sparing children the suffering and " destruction incident on being driven away by ill usage from places in consequence of their not answering ".

The Gentlemen would give no decision, adopting the time honoured device of deferring the matter from one meeting to another. They were, it is true, at that moment struggling with problems presented by the advent of the Poor Law Commissioners; with their responsibilities in connection with The Spring Water Commissioners; with requests to establish a Female Penitentiary; with boys breaking windows and men stealing lead from the roof.[41] But the Ladies come back yet again to the " old subject "; it was a crucial issue for Mary Ann. True, the Gentlemen were always prepared to stand by their apprentices and repair wrongs that had been inflicted, but how much more reasonable, she urged, not to let wrongs occur " for damage to character can seldom be entirely obliterated ". " If the Gentlemen dread the additional trouble, the Ladies would undertake to make the experiment with the girls." For some reason this offer won the day. It was agreed that the Ladies

> . . . shall have permission to grant a trial of one month for girls prior to Indentures being signed. This liberty to be restricted to the Town, and to last till November, on the understanding that the Ladies will superintend and report on the issue of the Experiment.[42]

When November arrived the experiment was continued for another three months, and thereafter seems to have become an accepted fact as far as the girls were concerned.

A further problem arose when it became no longer customary " in Belfast for respectable tradespeople to receive apprentices into their houses as boarders . . . it will therefore be necessary [the Ladies pointed out] to allow the girls to remain inmates of this house during the term of their apprenticeship ",[43] an arrangement which would naturally involve the alteration of regulations. Meanwhile the visiting of apprentices living with their employers continued, entailing long walks to Ballymacarrett and to the Falls. Many of them were weavers and these visits were " a stimulous to good conduct and a protection to them from ill treatment by the employer,"—the unofficial beginnings of factory inspection. The exploitation of child labour, that awful concomitant of the Industrial Revolution, was already rife in Britain—how vulnerable, reflected Mary, were the Poorhouse children.

Always on the look out for new modes of encouragement the Ladies suggested that there should be an annual gathering of the apprentices on—say, Lord Belfast's birthday :

> . . . to give them a dinner, and make trifling useful presents to such as brought good characters : . . . it would have the effect of stimulating the children to good conduct and inspiring self respect and thereby raise them from their present degraded state of neglected outcasts . . . with which they are frequently upbraided.[44]

The idea was not taken up, but it underlines once again the constant endeavour to retrieve these children from the stigma of pauperism, and restore them to an honourable place in society.

Health and cleanliness comprised the third main concern of the Ladies. All her life Mary Ann had the highest regard for soap and water and the fundamental rules of hygiene, and in this respect the Poorhouse presented many difficulties. Years of overcrowding and filthy habits had wrought havoc with the rooms of the old people, and scrofulous ailments were rife among the children. Apparently in the very early days the Ladies had secured an allocation of soap for distribution amongst the old women, for we find them requesting an increase to " enable them to supply the old men, who have earnestly petitioned for a small bit to keep their hands and faces clean ". The Gentlemen were certainly niggardly with this commodity :

> . . . the quantity of soap allowed for the nursery and the hospitals is by no means sufficient for the purpose of cleanliness [and the ladies] request the Gentlemen to take into consideration how very essential cleanliness is to health and comfort and beg [they] may consult the females of their own families and enquire if two pounds of soap per month, that is half a pound in the week, be sufficient to wash the wearing apparrel, sheets, blankets, etc. for twenty-seven children, the number in the nursery. The Ladies present would consider double the quantity a very stinted allowance—a sufficient quantity of coals is also requisite to warm the water—nothing can be made sufficiently clean with cold water.[45]

The distribution of soap to the old people was carried on by the Ladies throughout the life of the committee and Mary Ann inscribed directions in the minute book as to how it should be done :

> Distributed 42 lbs of soap, 235 pieces. 119 pieces to the women 9 longer to the married people and 9 smaller to the men 2 pieces to the men at the gate six to the men in the graveyard and one to the women . . . Cut each wedge in 8 pieces and divide each piece in two for the women the men to get half as much. Two small pieces left over, one of the two given to Mr. Lemon.[46]

Inspection of the personal cleanliness of the girls was undertaken in rotation. Miss McCracken, after attending to that " department " for a month gave a most satisfactory report. Again, in a bleak December it is recommended

> . . . that the morning school (that is from 8 till 9 o'clock) be discontinued till the days get longer; as it is scarcely daylight before 8 and it is quite impossible for one person to wash and comb seventy children in an hour and still more so to comb them properly in the dark.[47]

And as the days get brighter they ask the Gentlemen to consider

> . . . whether the mornings before breakfast might not be better employed by the girls at play in front of the house than at work, or lessons; health being of so much importance.[48]

Dormitories were regularly and carefully visited :

> . . . the girls' rooms were remarkably clean, the boys' as much the worse—quiery, might not sprinkling the floor with Cloride of lime have a better effect than throwing quantities of lime under the beds, which serves as an excuse for slovenliness in not dusting under the beds ; the Ladies, however, observed that under the beds where there was no lime there was much dust—the floors, walls and ceilings were all very dirty.[49]

A few months later " a tolerable improvement in the boys' rooms " is reported " except in corners and behind the doors where there was dust and cobwebs ". The Gentlemen's attention is directed

> . . . to a superior mode of cleaning the floors which is by substituting black soap in place of freestone, the soap to be used with a scouring brush and if done carefully is not more expensive than freestone, cleans the boards better and is an antidote to fleas, the most economical plan is to purchase a barrel at once which costs 14/0. Mrs. Mattear speaks from experience as she always makes use of it herself, it is also useful in washing clothes in the first scald.[50]

Washing clothes ! This was the problem that above all drove Mary Ann to despair. Constantly there are requests for more frequent changes of sheets [the Gentlemen still controlled such domestic concerns]—" the difficulty of eradicating the itch is greatly increased by keeping the bed-linen too long unwashed " ; covers were needed for bolsters and clean shifts should be given oftener, all of which meant more work for the already overburdened women in the laundry. Again and again she pleaded that some encouragement may be given to the women in the House to assist in washing :

> . . . this might be done by doubling the allowance of tea and sugar and allowing tobacco to those who have been accustomed to it. The Ladies beg to refer the Gentlemen to those who understand housekeeping and know something of the labouriousness of washing whether seven or eight old women who are past their labour (the head

> washerwoman being above eighty) are sufficient to wash for upwards of four hundred people, and also whether two ounces of tea and half a pound of brown sugar be too liberal an allowance to those so employed, the Gentlemen might also enquire whether there be any new constructed washing machines, or any for wringing which might lessen labour and beg to remind them that parsimony and economy are widely different, and that what is expended in promoting the children's health and preparing them for earning their bread may be a saving to the public hereafter.[51]

Parsimony and economy! How infuriating that she could not go straight to the hardware shop and discover which of these "new constructed washing machines" would best answer the purpose.

If a better laundry was essential so also was better food. By present day standards the diet was astonishingly unvaried. According to the accounts so carefully scrutinised by the Gentlemen, it consisted almost entirely of oatmeal, potatoes and buttermilk, and the quantities consumed in one particular quarter, when the population of the Poorhouse was about 450, amounted to twenty tons, forty tons, and 2,600 qts. respectively.[52] Generally a meat stew was given once a week—"Lob-course" it was called, and cows' heads were one of the main ingredients—but in times of financial stress this delicacy was withdrawn. Bread was an almost negligible item. It must be remembered, however, that potatoes, butter-milk and oatmeal constituted the staple diet of the labouring class all over the country.

On all this the Ladies make the following observations: they

> . . . take the liberty to recommend that the Nursery children be allowed half a pint of sweet milk per day as conducive to health and strength. The Gentlemen are no doubt aware that there is but little nourishment in butter-milk and that every child's stomach does not agree with acid particularly as an ingredient in every meal . . . the health and consequent comfort and well-being thro' life depend in a great measure on proper nourishment and treatment during the period of infancy.[53]

The half pint of sweet milk was granted, and the same concession was soon allowed for the children in the hospital. Later the Ladies note "the allowance of bread for dinner to the Nursery children not near sufficient, considering that they get only three meals per day and no pieces". There were constant requests for a more generous allowance of "animal food" for teachers and those who were performing any service to the institution, and—another reason, "the Gentlemen are no doubt aware that scrofulous patients require nourishing food."

It is tantalising to have thus ruthlessly to summarise the Ladies' activities, but this survey will give an indication of their attitude to the needs of deprived children. It would be unfair both to the Gentlemen and to Miss McCracken, to leave the impression that the relationship between the two committees was one of intermittent warfare. The Gentlemen had much to occupy their thought—their property, their finance, the new burying ground that they had opened to augment their funds, and a host of administrative details, and their own minutes record the many tasks they eagerly handed over. To the Ladies, concerned only with the welfare and comfort of the women and children, everything was viewed on a personal basis, and no lady-like politeness was allowed to lessen their efforts on behalf of those who stood in need of help and protection. All through her life Mary Ann's hasty temper had been roused by distress, want and frustration, but when she died it was "her ardent charity, her large and tender sympathy, her sweet humility and self-forgetfulness" that were put on record.[54]

From 1848 the attendance of the Ladies began to dwindle, occasionally there could be "No meeting of Committee to-day, only one member attended. Signed M. A. McCracken." No doubt this decline in interest was due to the changes occasioned by the Poor Law legislation already mentioned. The new Workhouse had been opened in Belfast and numbers in the Poorhouse were rapidly falling, so that in this year there were approximately 120 adults and 80 children as compared with a total of 450 in 1839. Indeed in the Gentlemen's minutes we find arrangements being made to lend iron bedsteads to the Fever Hospital, and later to sell them to the Antrim and Ballymena Union. A great effort was made in 1851 to recruit new members, and a list of a dozen names is recorded, but in October of that year, for some cause unknown, the minutes of the Ladies' Committee come abruptly to an end. In almost her last entry Miss McCracken writes:

> Visited the schoolroom and some other rooms and were much pleased with the cleanliness and regularity of all we saw. Distributed soap to 119 people.[55]

and in the Gentlemen's minutes there occurs a few months earlier the following ungrudging testimony:

> The Committee appointed for examining the children's apartments and schools . . . report that they find the Boys are able to read and spell well but their minds appear greatly neglected as they did not comprehend the simple questions put to them . . . It appears the Schoolmaster is not capable of expounding their minds beyond a certain extent . . . The Committee are glad to be able to report favourably of the Female School as the spelling and reading was very creditable and the children understood the questions put to them and answered very well. The writing and arithmetic was very good.[56]

Practically a quarter of a century had passed since that great day in 1827 when the Ladies, spell-bound by the enthusiasm of Elizabeth Fry, had resolved to form their committee, and without a doubt it was the determined leadership of Mary McCracken that had kept them together through the years. Page after page of minutes are written in her plain, sensible handwriting in two very ordinary foolscap jotters, the lines on every page being ruled in pencil.

Dr. Drennan, referring to another set of minutes and their readers, declares that ". . . through these windows of the breast they might see the purity of their intentions and the singleness of their object,"[57] and this graceful comment can be applied with all sincerity to the records of the Ladies Committee. Not even her Uncle Robert, who in his day had done so much for the Poorhouse, could have matched his niece's fierce determination to provide for these lonely children, health, nurture and education, the rightful heritage of all human beings. Such were the principles which in the young happy days had impelled Harry and herself to serious action ; for Mary there had remained these long years of relentless service.

She was over eighty-one when she wrote the last entry in the minute book. Elizabeth Fry had died six years earlier.

CHAPTER XV

THE LAST YEARS

1851–1866

Let each of us remember that he has been created by God for the purpose of labouring, and of being vigorously employed in his work ; and that not only for a limited time, but till death itself.

—Calvin. *Commentary on St. Luke* 17.7.

NOTHING has so far been said, except in passing, of what was after all the driving force behind everything that Mary McCracken did, namely her religious faith. She came of a stock which, on both sides, maintained opinions at the cost of sacrifice and suffering. The uncompromising convictions of old Grandmother McCracken, the gentler but no less real dependence on Providence of Francis Joy, were part of her upbringing, as was the influence of her own godly parents—she inherited both the fire and the reasonableness that characterised religious expression in the eighteenth century. In her youth all the influences had encouraged a rational outlook, but when rationalism attacked religion, as did Paine in *The Age of Reason*, then Paine, and to that extent rationalism, had to go, and in this Mary was but following the trend of general opinion in Belfast. The Calvinist doctrine of society as governed by the teaching in the Word of God, and the solemn right and responsibility of the people to choose the human instruments of that government, was deeply implanted in all the McCrackens; it was their unquestioned heritage and it ruled their lives, imbuing them with a profound belief in the democratic principle and in the essentialness of liberty. There was also for Mary Ann the dominating sense of stewardship—everything in life, wealth, talents, position, etc., were divinely given, not only for personal enjoyment but for the service of all. From her girlhood the recognition of this obligation was evident, and in old

MARY ANN McCRACKEN

age the blessing of, for example, continued health was subject to it :

> I know many . . . not one of whom is so entirely free from pain as I am and consequently it is my very peculiar duty to endeavour to be useful while I can.[1]

Strict disciplinarian where she herself was concerned, there was in her nature a compassion so boundless that neither doctrinaire rationalism nor calvinist rigidity could ever quench its flow.

There was, nevertheless, nothing speculative about her religion, indeed it was the firm, fixed base from which all other adventures were undertaken. The great principles having been accepted, there remained only " the [to her obvious] duty of entire resignation to the divine will ". Everything else in life could be, and was, questioned ; but not that. The intensity of the " New Light " controversy in the preceding generations had fixed for a time theological thought. Mary, and her contemporaries, accepted the decisions thus made, though in the generation that followed doubts once more arose. We may assume that it was by deliberate choice that her father and the Joy uncles were members of the Third Presbyterian congregation, the congregation that had been formed to uphold the traditional presbyterianism of the Westminster Confession in the face of other views. In this church their children worshipped. But, orthodox presbyterian though she was, there was little of the puritan in her make-up. Reasonable enjoyment of the pleasures of life she never shunned. There is every indication that in the early, happy days she had, with the rest of the family, delighted in the arts and in the many good things that came their way ; and, in spite of the stern path to which duty summoned her, she never lost sympathy with those, in any walk of life, who cared for beauty and legitimate luxury, be it only a bonnet " with ribbon " or an extra ounce of tea !

In the account of Harry's trial and execution, [see p. 173] that Mary Ann wrote for Dr. Madden about

1840 she says, after alluding to the new developments in democratic government:

> Religion also should be called to aid the regeneration (if I may use the term) of our political as well as our social and individual character. Its Divine precepts are simple and easily comprehended—to do to others as we would wish others to do to us; to do no evil that good may come of it; to love our neighbour as ourselves, and to be guided by the parable of the good Samaritan, to consider all who are within reach of our kindness as our neighbours, however they may differ from us in our religious belief; thus endeavouring to become in reality what we profess to be, true and sincere Christians; for then indeed would this world become a paradise of peace.
>
> Some object to joining religion and politics together; but surely religion should be the ruling principle of every action and of every thought. With such an unerring guide how could we go wrong? The same golden rule that should regulate the conduct of private individuals, should direct the acts of public men; and with such direction no government could inflict the wrongs on a people which ours have endured, and found to be intolerable in 1798.[2]

Perhaps she oversimplified the issue, but it was by such rules that her own actions were directed. One incident may be recalled here. During Harry's brief imprisonment in Belfast before his trial, one of his guard called at the McCracken's house saying that Harry had sent him to get half a guinea and a bottle of whiskey, and these he was immediately given. It was a bogus message, and, as such, no doubt vexed the family. In a few days the man was charged before a court martial and, thinking to console his aunt, Henry Joy jun. sent round the following note to Mrs. McCracken:

> Dear Aunt,
>
> I drop this to say that the fellow who committed the robbery of the half guinea was last night flogged, getting 300 lashes, and ordered to be sent to the West Indies—He preferred going there to risque the yellow fever, rather than

receive 800 lashes which the Court Martial of the Regiment, the Fifeshire, were to have inflicted on him.

Yours truly,
H. Joy.

Sunday Morn.
One of his officers stays in the house with us.[3]

On the back Mary wrote the following :

This note we felt as an insult, in supposing that we would delight in the suffering of others.

Deep and driving as was her sense of religion, it is a fact that religion remained the one thing that did not rouse that hasty temper. No mere wish to avoid controversy, but a fundamental respect for the convictions of others, created in her a tolerance that must never be confused with agreement or indifference. The penal enactments against Catholics wounded her with a personal intensity, as an affront to that liberty she held so dear for all—they must, at whatever cost, be ended. The old Roman Catholic servant whom she taught to read and write was given a Douay Bible, and together, " every evening one or two chapters were read, each in her own Bible ". [4] The heat and fury of the mid-nineteenth century religious Revivals in Ulster swept by her ; she would judge them, she wrote to Dr. Madden, by their results. The night constables, she hears, have now little to do, many public houses have been closed and people are making restitution for past wrongs, and " all this family have observed a great improvement in the manners of the girls coming out of the mills which we pass almost daily going through Bedford Street . . . formerly their dress was immodest and their language and manners had been bold and offensive, now they appear modest and quiet which is proof of a change for the better."[5] So far, so good : but these emotional experiences roused feelings of resentment between Catholics and Protestants, so Mary continues :

> We never make it a subject of discourse to our Catholic servants whom we look on as friends and would not wish to hurt their feelings, neither would I think of attempting to change their religious opinions lest I should only turn them from being Christian to be infidels . . . we look on our servants as our treasures.[6]

But if opinions are to be respected the young must be instructed in order that they may have opinions to hold, and the following minute of the Ladies Committee may be taken as Mary's mature views, and is an interesting deviation from the youthful rationalism that inspired Harry's school [p. 56] in the old Market House, with which she had so greatly sympathised:

> They [the Ladies] also take the liberty of suggesting that some efficient means should be adopted for affording the children the advantage of religious instruction suited to their capacities either by allowing them to attend their respective congregational Sabbath Schools, or by procuring the attendance of teachers in the House.[7]

Such instruction the Ladies regarded " as an auxiliary to and for the purpose of enabling [the children] to understand what they would hear in their respective Churches ". She herself taught for many years in an undenominational " Sabbath School " held in the Lancastrian School in Frederick Street.

It was indeed her religion that, in spite of sorrow, loneliness and disillusionment, made Mary McCracken the great woman she was and brought her life to its serene and confident conclusion.

As well as her long interest in the Poorhouse, Mary Ann was intimately connected with The Ladies Industrial School from its inception. This school was established in 1847 by " a Belfast Ladies Association for the Relief of Irish Destitution " as an effort to assist directly some of those stricken by the Famine. Nothing that she wrote during the years of this great national catastrophe remains, but her heart must have been wrung with pity, and at the age of seventy-seven she threw herself with her accustomed energy into this practical expression of sorrow. Every annual report of the School from the year of its foundation till that of her death includes her name as a member of committee, and the obituary notice, already quoted [p. 285], refers to her " as a beloved friend . . . whose place was never vacant at our weekly meetings so long as she was able to attend ". In appreciation of her interest in the school, she was made its President, a position she held at her death.[8]

She was also one of the earliest workers for the Belfast Ladies Clothing Society, and was an ardent collector of funds for the Society for the Relief of the Destitute Sick. In connection with the latter she used to say that the committee would not allow her to visit the cases as she was too easily imposed upon, never being able to refuse any who appeared to be in distress. We are so accustomed to think of her fortitude and outspoken directness, that the cost of this courage to a sensitive nature might have gone unnoticed had not the following revealing comment been recorded in connection with a family for whom she felt constrained again and again to collect money : " so disagreeable was the task that she said she felt it sometimes a reprieve when the person for whom she asked was not at home ".[9]

She was one of a committee set up in Belfast to abolish the use of climbing boys in chimney sweeping, and she shared the strong reaction to intemperate drinking that marked the opening years of Victoria's reign, a reaction strengthened no doubt in her case by vivid recollections of the tragic indiscretions into which extreme conviviality had so often lured the United Irishmen.

But her interests were never merely parochial, and it is not surprising that all her life the anti-Slavery movement had claimed her deepest sympathy, a sympathy shared in the pre '98 days by most of the circle in which she and Harry and Thomas Russell moved. The Belfast public, because of manifold trading connections with the West Indies and the eastern seaboard of America, was fully aware of the position of the negro in the New World, and advertisements like the following, which appeared not infrequently in the papers, suggest that traders did not always return empty handed :

> Runaway from John Cawden Princes Street Belfast a young negro manservant named John Moore a reward of three guineas straight and well made has two remarkably broad teeth in upper jaw.[10]

> A most beautiful black Negro girl, just brought from Carolina, aged eleven or twelve years who understands and speaks English, very fit to wait on a lady, to be disposed of. Applications to be made to James Carolan, Carrickmacross, or to Mr. Gavan in Bridge Street, Dublin.[11]

In " just abhorance " at an advertisement in the *Belfast News-Letter* offering a reward for the return of a run-away " Indian Black ", the Amicable Society of Belfast, in 1781, pledged themselves " to our unfortunate fellow creature the aforesaid Indian Black . . . that we will not only harbour him, but enable him, by pecuniary donations, to carry on a legal prosecution against his intended enslaver . . . If the aforesaid Indian Black will apply at Mrs. Hervey's, at the Phoenix, High Street, Belfast, he will meet with the necessary assistance."[12]

The citizens of Belfast were well aware of the great fortunes then being made in Liverpool, Bristol and elsewhere from the traffic in slaves, and in 1786 Waddell Cunningham, that enterprising merchant, actually proposed to his fellow-townsmen the formation of a Belfast Slave-Ship Company. The scheme was vehemently denounced by Thomas McCabe—the friend of Robert Joy and Captain McCracken—in these words :

> May God wither the hand and consign the name to eternal infamy of the man who will sign that document.

Nothing came of the project, though one imagines that Waddell Cunningham must have had some grounds for anticipating success.[13]

So, when Wilberforce started in England the great crusade for the Abolition of Slavery, his efforts were supported with enthusiasm by the strong opinion already vocal in Belfast. Writing to Dr. Madden in 1859 Mary Ann recalls how Thomas Russell was one of the number [which we may be sure included herself],

> . . . who in the days of Wilberforce abstained from the use of slave labour produce until slavery in the West Indies was abolished, and at the dinner parties to which he was so often invited and when confectionary was so much used he would not taste anything with sugar in it . . .
> I am both ashamed and sorry to think that Belfast has so far degenerated in regard to the Anti-Slavery cause.[14]

And again : America

> . . . considered the land of the great, the brave, may more properly be styled the land of the tyrant and the Slave . . . Belfast, once so celebrated for its love of liberty is now so sunk in the love of filthy lucre that there are but 16 or 17 female anti-slavery advocates, for the good cause paying 2/6 yearly, not one man, tho' several Quakers in Belfast, and none to distribute papers to American Emigrants but an old woman within 17 days of 89.[15]

There she was—the little frail, bent, figure—standing by the gangway with her leaflets as the jostling crowds made their way on board : it was the only service she could still render to the cause of liberty, that dominating passion of her life. References to her abhorrence of slavery continue till her letters cease.

In spite of a delicate childhood Mary remained physically active and mentally alert long after others of her age were showing signs of decline, so that when she left the Ladies Committee at the Poorhouse no one thought of her as old. But she had outlived her generation. Away back in 1829 her dear sister Margaret had died, and six years later John's successful career ended. He had become a rich man. He and his sons sailed their yachts in all the fashionable regattas in Ireland and on the Clyde, and it was on one such expedition that he died at Ardrossan. As well as conducting his own flourishing cotton business he belonged to the company that operated the first passenger steamship sailing between Belfast and Glasgow. His large family were all able and attractive. One of his sons, another Francis, inheriting his father's artistic taste, became a noted art collector. An ardent admirer of the Pre-Raphaelites he was known to D. G. Rossetti, who wrote of him as

" the mighty McCracken ", and he owned at one time Rossetti's " Ecce Ancilla Domini ", Holman Hunt's " Scape Goat " and Arthur Hughes' " Ophelia ", besides paintings by Wilson, Turner and others. Ann, the eldest of the family, married a Scottish doctor—they lived in Paris for some time and in a letter of 1831 describing her visit to the Hotel Dieu—the Hospital of the Sisters of Charity—she says :

> All the patients looked so comfortable with their clean sheets and white quilts, I could not help thinking how gratified my Aunt Mary would have been to see so many sick people so comfortably lodged.[16]

No doubt she knew that Aunt Mary was, just then, busily engaged with the Ladies' Committee at the Poor House. Eliza, the second daughter—so like Aunt Mary in a hundred ways and yet neither seemed aware of the resemblance—the adorable Eliza, married Robert James Tennent, later Member of Parliament for Belfast, and their younger daughter became the mother of Captain Henry Harrison [died 1954] the friend and life-long vindicator of Charles Stewart Parnell.

John's children travelled much and far, often in search of health, and to some death came tragically early. One son—Henry Joy—who seems to have inherited, as well as his uncle's name, all his commanding charm and outstanding good looks, died within a year of his young wife, leaving behind a baby daughter eventually to be the mother of Sir Henry Reichel, first Principal of the University College of North Wales at Bangor.

One gets the impression however that these lively nephews and nieces had moved far away from the world of the uncle and aunt who lived close by ; then, as to-day, the normal difference between generations was accentuated by abnormal changes in standards and behaviour.

With Atty Bunting, the ties of affection remained lasting and strong. From Dublin he wrote constantly to Mary Ann relating every detail concerning the harassing preparation of his third and most ambitious volume on

Ancient Irish Music. The bitterness with Dr. McDonnell had been set aside, and on Bunting's frequent visits to Belfast, when he stayed with Mary and her brother Francis, the old collaborators met, and through Atty were brought into touch with his circle of brilliant friends in Dublin. On one occasion at least, to Mary's great delight, Atty brought with him his two pretty daughters, one of whom met and married Mr. R. Macrory of Belfast. Very shortly afterwards, in 1843, Edward Bunting died. His third volume, published in 1840,* had been enthusiastically received, but years of research meant a heavy drain on an organist's salary, and his family were left with little support. Once again Mary Ann exerted herself in a familiar cause, and, in conjunction with others, used all her influence through Sir James Emerson Tennent, to secure for Mrs. Bunting a Civil List pension. They were, however, unsuccessful. What memories Atty's death would recall! — the Harpist's Festival, Wolfe Tone's departure, Thomas Russell, and much, much else — he had shared so intimately in the family life. The care that she and her mother had lavished on the self-opinionated, difficult boy and young man had been most generously repaid in love and gratitude, and she was proud of his success. The loss was all the more poignant for exactly 12 months earlier Francis, her last remaining brother, had died.

All through life, however, Mary had been making and keeping friends, and by this time Dr. R. R. Madden was to be counted among them. A few years previously, having started the formidable task of writing *The Lives of the United Irishmen*, he had come to Belfast seeking help and information from Mary McCracken, and thus a long friendship and correspondence was begun. Now, as a consolation to herself, and in reply to Dr. Madden's note of sympathy, Mary sent him a letter describing the circumstances of her brother's death, which gives an affectionate picture of the kindly, considerate Francis, "the last of the Volunteers":

*Entitled *The Ancient Music of Ireland* and dedicated to Queen Victoria.

After you left Belfast [she wrote] his strength declined slowly and visibly, but his patience and gentleness continued till the last. About ten days or less before, his sail-making apprentices asked permission to visit him which was granted, they came in a body, he received them cordially, shook hands with them all and ordered each a new pair of trousers of his best manufacture. On Friday 16th Dec. he wrote a note on business, also a certificate on the back of one of his apprentices indentures, both without spectacles; but had suffered for some days from extreme exhaustion which rendered him restlesss but not fretful. On Sunday 18th he suffered much from difficulty in breathing and at one time the phlegm had nearly choked him, the two following nights he breathed quite freely. Monday 19th was the last day he came to the drawing room, on that day after being dressed he was obliged to lie down for three or four hours before he could come further. On Wednesday night he breathed with much difficulty and in the morning wished to rise in the hope of finding ease. He was accordingly raised, wrapped in a blanket and placed in his easy chair until his bed was made to which he was glad to return; he complained no more but seemed to breathe with somewhat less difficulty, his last words were in prayer. About an hour it might be before he breathed his last he still appeared sensible and on the bed clothes being raised off his chest lest the pressure might be painful he drew in his hands, crossing them on his breast and closing his lips and eyes ceased to breathe without a struggle. Such a peaceful transition from this to another (and I think a better) world robs death of half its terrors, filling the mind with a sacred awe that raises it above the trifling concerns of this world to fix it on that which has no end. Another cause of thankfulness on the present occasion is that my dear Maria's health has not suffered by her long attendance and want of rest, as I feared it would, particularly as for the last few nights she never went to bed and exerted herself beyond her strength in assisting her uncle as his weakness increased, her quickness of thought and action leaving nothing for another to do, but she said her strength increased with the necessity of making use of it and while she is spared to us I possess a treasure for which I can hardly be sufficiently thankful. In all the various trials I have experienced I have always been sensible that I had many blessings demanding my utmost gratitude to the Great Dispenser of events, and I trust I have been and still am grateful.

And then, never allowing personal affairs to interfere with duty, she continues:

> I saw our worthy friend James Hope two days ago. He is extremely anxious about your forthcoming volumes respecting the North lest there should be any inaccuracies or anything admitting of misinterpretation, there is something of the latter he said respecting Newell's death . . . he wishes you would let him have either the proof sheet or manuscript to look over previous to being published . . . I hope in eight or ten days I shall have leisure to make a more thorough search among my old papers to see if I can find anything interesting, and I shall give you all I can recollect of Russell's letters and conversation, to make you acquainted with his character.[17]

Once again financial difficulties had to be faced. Francis, by his will, had made ample provision for Maria, but there was difficulty in disposing of the Ropewalk and little remained for his sister. She and Maria gave up the house in Donegall Street, improved and made so comfortable by Francis; six years of their lease had yet to go, and the "ill-tempered landlord" required a sum of £200 to relieve them of their obligations, the rent being £60 per annum. There was much sympathy in the town for the valiant little old lady, and she was deeply touched when the Vicar of Belfast, the Rev. A. C. Macartney [one time a member of the "Gentlemen's Committee"], ascertaining from a friend that she was in difficulty, spoke to some of her brother's acquaintances and collected from them the required sum.

> It was handed to me, [she wrote] in a letter with the names of each and the sums subscribed by them, the letter saying it was a loan to be paid at my convenience, but the latter was out of delicacy lest I should scruple to accept it, and I was told they had intended to have given a testimonial to my brother's memory, and it was considered the best way

> they could do so in assisting us . . . One gave £20, 17 £10 each and three £5 each, making up the £200 with £5 costs.[18]

The old meticulous accuracy still lively.

This was more than a merely friendly gesture. The Reverend Arthur Chichester Macartney represented the political structure against which the United Irishmen had struggled; it was his father, an Antrim magistrate, who had issued the warrant for Orr's arrest. Yet here he was—the Vicar of Belfast—taking trouble, not only to assist a noted survivor of '98, but to offer that assistance with such consideration that her proud spirit would not feel hurt or patronised. This generous, courteous act speaks volumes: it illustrates how the violent idealism of the United Irishmen, translated into other channels, could be understood and appreciated; how the McCrackens' singleness of purpose was respected by everyone; and how old animosities were being forgotten.

Some time after her uncle's death Maria, now in middle life, married William McCleery, a widower with a young family of two daughters and two sons. As well as a distant relationship there must have been a long and close friendship between the two families, for the second of Maria's step-daughters was called Mary McCracken McCleery, the eldest was Anna. Perhaps indeed Maria's husband was a son of that Wm. McCleery mentioned in Tone's diary as one of the original United Irishmen. It was a foregone conclusion that Maria would bring her aunt to the new home; it was a happy arrangement and Mary Ann lived with the McCleerys for the remainder of her life. In the short sketch of Mary McCracken's life written after her death by her step-niece Anna McCleery[19] there are glimpses of a happy and contented old age. To the end she greatly enjoyed the company of her friends, delighting in a large party round the tea table and, though a little deaf, "with a beaming face and happy smile could join in the mirth."

She was still extraordinarily active. In her letters to Dr. Madden there are constant references to "my out of door avocations "—the Industrial School, visiting the sick, and collecting subscriptions; she thinks it better "to wear out than to rust out"[20] and finds it a hardship to be restrained from exertion, but submits, not wanting to "fret Maria."

> Old as I am, [she wrote in her 88th year] and much as I have suffered and tho' conscious that my faculties are much impaired by age, I still feel it a duty, a pleasure and a privilege to continue in thankful trust and confidence in the giver of all good who has favoured me with such unusual health at such an age to go on in my endeavours as far as is in my power, which occupies all the daylight at the present season and therefore the previous part of this was written by candlelight and at intervals. My health has improved so much latterly that I cannot be sufficiently thankful for it and consider it a call to duty, a year ago when I had been out for three or four hours collecting for some of our charities I suffered so much pain below the small of my back [that] for near the half of the way in returning I had to press my hand with all my might on the bone for relief, but now I can walk home nearly as fast as I did 30 years ago without the slightest pain, but only a sleepiness which I indulge after dinner in my easy chair, and after tea I have other interesting occupations and sometimes whenever I have leisure Maria reads to me as I hear her the best, and besides I take up enough of the young people's time in walking as I am not allowed to go out alone.

All this consoles her for

> . . . not hearing so well and not seeing so well as formerly which is tiresome for others as well as to myself. I regret so much the loss of memory, but must think more of what I enjoy and am allowed to retain than of what I have lost, but [the old impatience at frustration] I am much inconvenienced on meeting people whose countenance I perfectly remember but cannot recall their names . . . We are very happy in the girls, we think they are superior to any we meet with and all who know them love and esteem them, were they Maria's own daughters she could not love them better."[21]

The comrades of '98 were not forgotten. In her letters to Dr. Madden she refers frequently to the Hope family. Jemmy Hope died in 1853, and she and old Israel Milliken—a former United Irishmen, now crippled with rheumatism and just able to get to his easy chair by the fire—arranged for the erection of the headstone in the little burying-ground at Mallusk, Co. Antrim, Dr. Madden being called upon to write the inscription. Mary kept in touch with Robert, Jemmy's surviving son, now living in the Toll-house at the Malone turnpike. Previously he had been employed by Mr. Smyth the printer and publisher, and Mary was sorry to hear from him that Robert had lately "acquired that unhappy propensity which has been the great bane of this country." She would call and try to "convince him of the benefits of total abstinence" and perhaps if Dr. Madden would write to him it might lend weight to the argument. She treasured her connection with Robert Hope "for his father's and mother's sake as well as for his own, and I think also highly of his wife." His eldest brother Henry Joy McCracken Hope had died as a young man.

There were others, too, whose interests she considered as her own, and she had long been the channel through which sums of money were regularly transmitted to families in the neighbourhood of Belfast by relatives who, after '98, had sought refuge in America.

One by one the old associates and friends had died, but there was still Eliza Templeton. All that life had held of joy and sorrow had been shared from childhood by the two old ladies. Eliza was still, in 1859, able to visit Mary Ann, and I have not been able to discover which of them had to bear the last inevitable parting.

Even at eighty-seven the sympathetic interest in people and events continued. With young James McCleery, Maria's eldest step-child, who had been "such a cause of vexation", she corresponded regularly. He had been bundled off to an uncle in America where, she tells Dr. Madden, he was giving satisfaction and earning a salary of 800 dollars. She then mentions her affection for the two girls [p. 301]. William, the youngest of the family, wanted to be an engineer and had entered the Belfast Academical Institution at fourteen. His masters said that " if he had but moderate industry he could accomplish whatever he should undertake " but alas ! he was " very playful and not industrious " and, though everyone hoped he would win a scholarship, " another of twenty-five years was the successful candidate. This, Maria thinks, will be of much use to him, he is very affectionate and fond of his mother and I trust will do well. Now I have given you a full account of our family and would be glad you would make me acquainted with yours as I take an interest in all that concerns you, and all that has once gained a place in my heart continues there still."

The same letter contains this also :

> We have got a model school and a nunnery* in Belfast both well worth coming to see. I have visited both and was quite delighted with them, they are such spacious buildings and the nuns are so pleasing in their manners—but I think with the same desire to be useful they could be more so if at perfect liberty. I could not bear to have my mouth shut going through the streets so that I could not take the part of some poor ill-used animal.[22]

Astonishing for her age !

In every letter a revealing touch slips in, for instance—the chance mention of the inflamed eyelids :

> . . . which [were] rather painful especially when I closed my eyes, so that when awake in bed I tried to keep them open. But after using zinc ointment for nearly two years the trouble has nearly left me and all these circumstances are matters for great thankfulness.[23]

Again : she is quite ashamed of a long letter, but

> I had not time to write another. I fear I am often very apt to make too great a display of what I have done and am doing, and that I am too much occupied with self, which I am not so sensible of at the moment, but when I am

*The Sisters of Mercy—the first convent to be established in Belfast.

> overpraised which is frequently the case, I feel quite ashamed that I am too full of myself—may I beg you will not thus put me to the blush in future.[24]

All the struggles had ceased—the irate letters to Eliza Templeton were more than half a century old, the Poorhouse children no longer needed her care—and such trifles as crippling rheumatism and failing faculties were borne with a new and patient serenity.

This long sequence of letters to Dr. Madden dating from about 1840 to 1859 and written when she was between seventy and ninety years of age, often, as she says, " by candlelight ", filled her declining years with a sense of purpose and usefulness, and secured for posterity treasured information which otherwise would have been lost. No detail in the tangled story of the United Irishmen was too small for her consideration—complete accuracy, she repeatedly urges, is so important, for one inaccurate statement casts doubt upon the whole, an observation which some subsequent recorders of the period would have done well to ponder. James Hope, Israel Milliken, Lady Emerson Tennent and anyone else who could supply information were written to, or visited, regarding the Bonds, Neilsons, Hamiltons and other Northern personalities of Ninety-Eight; her letter about Betsy Gray is the only bit of documentary evidence concerning that County Down heroine.[25]

Harry's memory was of course her paramount concern and much of Dr. Madden's memoir of Henry Joy McCracken was written, as he gratefully acknowledged, by Mary Ann herself. Dear as his memory was, it is characteristic of her that no sentimental trifles were allowed to sway her life-long prudence with regard to the spending of money. Money could be lavished where necessary, as in the defence of Russell or the care of destitute children, but it must not be squandered needlessly, and she dismisses as sheer extravagence Dr. Madden's suggestion that, for the second edition of the memoir, a better engraving of Harry's portrait should be procured; in spite of one " trifling defect " she affirms it is a most striking likeness, which anyone who knew him would instantly recognise. One correction, however, must be made in the text—" Young's Night Thoughts " was *not* a favourite book of Harry's as was stated, but of her mother's. [See p. 178.][26]

Next comes Thomas Russell, and again Dr. Madden acknowledges his debt. Everything she could remember was noted down, perhaps unconsciously, as much for her own contentment as that Dr. Madden should " be acquainted with his character." Indeed, fearing that she had been indiscreet, a second letter followed swiftly on the heels of one long missive, begging him not to mention all the details she had given, as some of the people concerned were still living and might be embarrassed. The story of Russell's love for Bess Goddard and of Miss Simms' secret affection for him is recounted, but only by inference do we gather the depth of her own abiding devotion. After more than sixty years she sees again in her mind's eye the beauty of his countenance—" his mouth was the most beautiful, particularly when he smiled, I ever saw ; and so perfectly truthful, as if so truthful himself that he never suspected deceit in others ": [27] and with, in all probability, a little smile of indulgence, she recalls his one and only failing and her own stern standards :

> Notwithstanding that he was remarkably religious, he frequently broke the third commandment by exclamations, a bad habit at that time prevalent, but not in general by Presbyterians,* and which surprised me in one of his character, and I had a great inclination to speak to him on the subject, but the stateliness of his manner prevented me.[28]

In this connection she constantly and bitterly, reproaches herself that " contrary to my dear sister's advice " she had lent Russell's papers to Charles Teeling and Samuel McSkimin, for in spite of repeated entreaties they had never been returned.

And so the letters go on. Frequently she pulls herself

*Russell, though a member of the Established Church by birth, had become a Presbyterian during his stay in Belfast.

up for " these tedious details which are a great fault of mine ", and, humourously advises Dr. Madden not to waste his time on them, but instead to hand her letters to his wife who would sort out the passages of importance. Detailed they undoubtedly are but nothing that Mary McCracken wrote was ever " tedious." One thing leads to another; she corrects a statement about her father's vessel, and remembers with pride his reputation for speedy voyages, disadvantageous though they were to his pocket, for " he got but half the sum when ashore." There was, too, his typical challenge to a certain Captain Moore whom he passed one calm day on going through Garmoyle, the deep pool in Belfast Lough. " What are you doing there " shouted McCracken. " Waiting for a wind " replied the other. " I am going to look for one " said her father, who, on returning to Belfast, having discharged one cargo at Liverpool and taken on another, was amused to find Captain Moore and his vessel still sitting in the pool of Garmoyle, which part, adds Mary Ann, " is called Moore's Hole to the present day."[29]

Only very occasionally is there a despondent note:

> The world seems in a sad state of wickedness just now, I cannot know how to account for it, considering all the efforts that are and have been made for many years past for the moral, religious and intellectual improvement of the civilized world, and particularly in the U.S. of America, the diabolical system of slavery is increasing and progressing, and the worst of it is that so many professing to be most pious Christians uphold and apologise for the system and wont allow a line to be published in their religious tracts reflecting on slavery. Surely that is quite inconsistent with all the teachings of Him whose followers they profess to be, but perhaps a crisis is near and it may be sooner than we expect that the eyes of the oppressors may be opened.[30]

In one letter she mentions the great changes that have happened during her lifetime—" discoveries in nature, inventions in art, almost like magic." The streets of the town were now lit by gas, the open Farset river in High

Street had been covered over, the port vastly changed since the days of her father's sailing ship, and the old Market House, so full of memory, had been demolished. She would not now have to drive to Lisburn in a chaise for, since the 1830's, one of the first railroads in Ireland connected it with Belfast; and all her old interest in mechanism must surely have been rekindled as she sat before that curious thing, a camera, for one of the earliest professional photographs [see plate facing p. 288]; she may even have wondered what David Manson's inventive mind would have thought of it. The little thatched two-storeyed houses opposite the Exchange, where Samuel Neilson had carried on his extensive drapery business, had long since been pulled down, and "Bankmore", the McCleery's house with its garden and orchard, till lately on the outskirts of the town, was even then almost submerged by the tall warehouses spreading out behind the White Linenhall. Indeed the Belfast of the '50's was becoming so like the modern city of to-day that we are amazed to read from her own pen, so late as 1859, of a case of small-pox: "a cousin of Mr. McCleery's who boards here got it he did not know how", and she wonders if Dr. Madden is aware of a most effective measure to prevent the face from being marked, for which at ninety years of age she writes the directions.[31]

But the writing is not so firm, she begins to repeat herself a little, though still the old habit of accuracy asserts itself—"Pray date your letters in the inside." By degrees she becomes less active, she is confined to the house: "In the autumn of 1865 [writes Anna McCleery], she had an attack of bronchitis from which she recovered, but mind and body had become weak. She faded peacefully and gently away, apparently contented and happy, without weariness or pain, until, after some hours of unconsciousness she breathed her last on the 26th of July, 1866, having completed her 96th year on the 8th of the month."[32]

So ended a life fuller than most of historic incident, fuller than most of self-sacrificing labour.

More than a hundred years earlier her grandfather, Francis Joy, had written :

> Happy, thrice happy are they who having the Sting of Death removed are arrived in safety and happiness beyond the dangers and troubles of this present State.

and her own verdict was :

> This world affords no enjoyment equal to that of promoting the happiness of others, it so far surpasses mere selfish gratification from its not only being pleasant at the time but from affording agreeable recollections afterwards.[33]

Mary Ann McCracken, the last of Francis Joy's grandchildren, lies buried within the shadow of the Poorhouse. She has bequeathed to her birth-place a legacy of unusual nobility and courage.

BIBLIOGRAPHY

Belfast Politics, 1794.
Belfast News-Letter : files in Linenhall Library, Belfast.
Belfast Monthly Magazine, 13 vols., Belfast 1808–1814.
Beckett, J. C. *Irish Parliament in the Eighteenth Century*, B.N.H. and P.S. 2nd series, Vol. IV.
Benn, George. *History of Belfast*, vols 1 and 2.
Bunting, E. Prefaces in Vol. I, Vol. II, Vol. III, 1797, 1809, 1840.
Butterfield, H. *George III, Lord North and the People.*
Curtis, E. *A History of Ireland.*
Drennan Letters. Public Record Office, N. Ireland.
Dobbs, Francis. *Irish Affairs* 1779–1782.
Fitzhenry, E. *Henry Joy McCracken.*
Fox, C. M. *Annals of the Irish Harpers.*
Fry, Eliz. & J. J. Gurney. *Report to the Marquess of Wellesley, Lord Lieutenant of Ireland*, 1827.
Gaffikin, T. *Belfast Fifty Years Ago.* 1870.
Grattan's Memoirs.
Green, E. R. R. *The Lagan Valley.*
Green, E. R. R. Cotton Industry in Northern Ireland, *U.J.A.* III Series Vol. 7.
Horner, J. *Linen Manufacture in Europe.*
Hayden and Moonan. *A Short History of the Irish People.*
Hamilton, Thos. D.D. *History of the Irish Presbyterian Church.*
Hammond, J. L. and Barbara. *The Bleak Age.*
Historical Collections relating to the Town of Belfast. 1817.
Hyde, H. M. *Castlereagh.*
Jacob, R. *Rise of the United Irishmen.*
Joy MSS. Linenhall Library, Belfast.
Kernohan, J. W. *History of Rosemary Street Presbyterian Church.*
Latimer, W. T. *Ulster Biographies relating to the Rebellion of* 1798.
Landreth. H. *Pursuit of Robert Emmett.*
Londonderry, Marquis of. *Memoirs and Correspondence of Viscount Castlereagh.*
Lecky, W. E. H. *History of Ireland in the Eighteenth Century.*
Longfield, A. *Notes on Linen and Cotton Industry in Northern Ireland.* B.N.H. and P.S. 2nd series, Vol. IV.
Madden, R. R. *The United Irishmen, their Lives and Times.*
Madden R. R. *Antrim and Down in Ninety-eight.* Cameron & Ferguson edition.
Madden Papers. T.C.D.
Maxwell, C. *Dublin under the Georges.*
Maxwell, C. *Country and Town in Ireland under the Georges.*
Millin, Shannon. *Sidelights on Belfast History.* 1932.
Monaghan, J. J. *Social and Economic History of Belfast*, 1790–1800. Thesis, Queen's University, Belfast.

Monaghan, J. J. *Social and Economic History of Belfast*, 1800–1825. Thesis, Queen's University. Belfast.

Monaghan, J. J. The Rise and Fall of the Belfast Cotton Industry. *Irish Historical Studies*, Vol. III, No. 9.

MacDermott, F. *Theobold Wolfe Tone.*

McDowell, R. B. *Irish Public Opinion.* 1750–1800.

MacDonagh. *The Viceroy's Post-Bag.*

McCall. *Ireland and her Staple Industries.*

McSkimin. *Annals of Ulster.*

Northern Star—files in Linenhall Library, Belfast.

O'Byrne, Cathal. *As I Roved Out.*

Paine, Thos. *Rights of Man.*

Porter, J. L. *Life and Times of Henry Cooke, D.D., LL.D.*

Roberts, W. *Life and Correspondence of Hannah More.*

Strain, R. W. M. *History and Associations of the Belfast Charitable Society.* Thesis, Queen's University, Belfast.

Tone, T. W., Life of, edited by his son. Washington, 1826.

Teeling, C. H. *History of the Irish Rebellion.*

Ulster Journal of Archaeology, II series—various articles.

Whitney, J. *Elizabeth Fry.*

Wollstonecraft, Mary. *The Vindication of the Rights of Women.*

Young, R. M. *Historical Notices of Old Belfast.* 1896.

Young, R. M. *Ulster in* '98.

REFERENCES

Abbreviations

McCracken Letters	McCracken letters in the Madden Papers, Trinity College, Dublin.
Joy MSS	Joy MSS, Linenhall Library, Belfast.
Historical Collections	Joy, Henry. Historical Collections relating to the Town of Belfast. 1817.
Old Belfast	Young, R. M. Historical Notices of Old Belfast. 1896.
B.C.S.	Belfast Charitable Society. Minutes of Committee.
Ladies Committee	Belfast Charitable Society. Minutes of Ladies Committee.
Tone	Life of Theobald Wolfe Tone, edit. by his son. Washington, 1826.
United Irishmen	The United Irishmen, their Lives and Times. R. R. Madden.
Lecky. Irel.	Lecky, W. E. H. Ireland in the Eighteenth century.
U.J.A.	Ulster Journal of Archaeology.
Irish Harpers	Fox, C. M. Annals of the Irish Harpers.
B.N.H.P.S.	Belfast Natural History and Philosophical Society.
P.R.O.N.I.	Public Record Office of N. Ireland.
B.P.L.	Belfast Public Library.
L.L.B.	Linenhall Library, Belfast.

CHAPTER 1, p. 13—p. 20.

[1]McCracken Letters.
[2]*Historical Collections*, p. 79.
[3]Joy MSS.
[4]*Ibid.*
[5]Benn. *History of Belfast*, p. 247.
[6]*Old Belfast*, p. 175.
[7]Benn. *History of Belfast*, p. 437.
[8]*Historical Collections*, p. 89.
[9]*Belfast Telegraph*, 13.11.1906. " Old Irish Paper Mills " by " Belfastiensis ".
[10]Joy MSS.
[11]*Ibid.*
[12]*Old Belfast*, p. 180.

CHAPTER 2, p. 21—p. 36.

[1]*Historical Collections*, p. 90.
[2]Joy MSS.

[3]Marshall, J. J. *Old Belfast.*
[4]Craig, M. J. *Dublin, A Social and Architectural History.*
[5]Joy MSS.
[6]*Historical Collections*, p. 118.
[7]*Ibid.*, p. 118.
[8]*Ibid.*, p. 119.
[9]*Ibid.*, p. 114.
[10]B.C.S. quoted R. W. M. Strain, The History and Associations of the Belfast Charitable Society. Reprint from *Ulster Medical Journal*, May, 1953, p. 33.
[11]*Ibid.*, p. 34.
[12]B.C.S.
[13]*Ibid.*
[14]B.C.S. quoted R. W. M. Strain, *The History and Assoc. of the B.C.S.*, p. 57.
[15]*Ibid.*, p. 57.
[16]*Old Belfast*, p. 193.
[17]Joy MSS.
[18]Owen, J. D. *History of Belfast*, p. 150.
[19]*Ibid.*
[20]*Historical Collections*, p. 138.
[21]*Ibid.*, p. 140.
[22]*Ibid.*, p. 141.
[23]*Ibid.*, p. 146.
[24]*Ibid.*, p. 148.
[25]Joy MSS.
[26]Millin, Shannon. *Sidelights on Belfast History*, p. 82.
[27]*Ibid.*, 85.
[28]*Historical Collections*, pp. 225 and 233.
[29]Joy MSS.
[30]P.R.O.N.I.
[31]*Ibid.*
[32]Joy MSS.

CHAPTER 3, p. 37—p. 42.

[1]*Belfast Telegraph*, 26.11.1898. "Joy Family" by "Belfastiensis".
[2]*United Irishmen.* 2nd series, vol. II, p. 390.
[3]*Belfast News-Letter*, 23.12.1803.
[4]*Old Belfast*, p. 175.
[5]*Ibid.* p. 269
[6]*U.J.A.* 2nd series, vol. X, p. 71.
[7]Fitzhenry, E. C. *Henry Joy McCracken*, p. 30.
[8]*Belfast News-Letter*, 23.12.1803.
[9]B.C.S., 27.9.1817.
[10]*Historical Collections*, p. 241.
[11]Biggar Papers. B.P.L.

CHAPTER 4, p. 43—p. 58.

[1]Benn. *History of Belfast*, p. 451.

[2]Information about David Manson has been collected from *U.J.A.*, 2nd series, vol. XIV; *The Belfast Monthly Magazine*, vol. VI; and from Manson's "*Plan for the improvement of Children in Virtue and Learning without the Use of the Rod*".

[3]Manson, D. *Plan for the Improvement*, etc.

[4]*Belfast Monthly Magazine*, vol. VI, p. 127.

[5]*U.J.A.*, 2nd series, vol. XIV.

[6]Hamilton, Eliz. *The Cottagers of Glenburnie*, *Edinburgh* 1810, p. 284.

[7]Benn. *History of Belfast*, p. 300.

[8]Quoted. Maxwell, C. "*Dublin under the Georges*", p. 269.

[9]Quoted. Maxwell, C. "*Country and Town in Ireland under the Georges*", p. 225.

[10]Quoted. Benn. *History of Belfast*, p. 422.

[11]*Historical Collections*, p. 328.

[12]Drennan Letters, Nos. 239 and 564.

[13]*Old Belfast*, p. 191.

[14]*Ibid.*, p. 188.

[15]*Ibid.*, p. 188.

[16]Roberts, W. *Life and Correspondence of Hannah More*, vol. III, p. 133.

[17]McCracken Letters.

[18]*Irish Harpers*, p. 12.

CHAPTER 5, p. 59—p. 77.

[1]Berwick. *History of Ireland*, Belfast 1815, p. 204.

[2]*Historical Collections*, p. 274.

[3]*Ibid.*, p. 239.

[4]Berwick. *History of Ireland*, p. 207.

[5]*Historical Collections*, p. 295.

[6]Hamilton, Rev. T. *History of the Irish Presbyterian Church*, pp. 111–2.

[7]*Tone*, p. 41.

[8]*Historical Collections*, p. 293.

[9]Kernohan, J. W. *History of Rosemary Street Presbyterian Church, Belfast*, p. 00.

[10]*Historical Collections*, p. V.

[11]*Ibid.*, p. 330.

[12]*Ibid.*, p. 334.

[13]*Ibid.*, p. 347.

[14]*Ibid.*, p. 351.

[15]*Ibid.*, p. 351.

[16]*Tone*, p. 21.

[17]*Ibid.*, p. 26.
[18]*Ibid.*, p. 27.
[19]*Ibid.*, p. 30.
[20]*Ibid.*, p. 34.
[21]*Ibid.*, p. 35.
[22]*Ibid.*, p. 36.
[23]*United Irishmen,* 3rd series, vol. II, p. 142.
[24]*Tone*, p. 51.
[25]*United Irishmen,* 3rd series, vol. II, p. 190.
[26]*Ulster Magazine*, January 1830. "Sketch of Thomas Russell".
[27]Drennan Letters, No. 449.
[28]*Tone*, p. 149.
[29]*Ibid.*, p. 141.
[30]*United Irishmen*, 2nd series, vol. II, p. 395.
[31]*Tone*, p. 145.
[32]*Ibid.*, p. 172.
[33]*United Irishmen*, 3rd series, vol. II, p. 153.

CHAPTER 6, p. 78—p. 85.

[1]Quoted. *Irish Harpers*, p. 97.
[2]*Ibid.*, p. 99.
[3]*Ibid.*, p. 100.
[4]*Ibid.*, p. 147.
[5]*Irish Harpers*. p. 137
[6]*Ibid.* p. 194.
[7]*Belfast News-Letter.*
[8]*Tone*, p. 155.
[9]Quoted. *Irish Harpers*, p. 196.
[10]Bunting, E. Preface to 1840 collection.
[11]Drennan Letters, No. 685.
[12]*Ibid.*, No. 685*a*.
[13]*Ibid.*, No. 698.
[14]Quoted. *Irish Harpers* p. 29.
[15]*Ibid.*, p. 304.
[16]*United Irishmen* 3rd series, vol. II, p. 155.

CHAPTER 7, p. 86—p. 106.

[1]*Tone*, p. 221.
[2]*Ibid.*, p. 222.
[3]Joy. *Belfast Politics*, Belfast 1794, p. 141.
[4]*United Irishmen*, 1st series, 2nd edit., p. 234.
[5]Drennan Letters, No. 434.
[6]*Historical Collections*, p. 395
[7]*Ibid.*, p. 363.
[8]*Ibid.*, p. 365.
[9]*Ibid.*, p. 365.

[10]*Ibid.*, p. 365.
[11]Drennan Letters, No. 461.
[12]*Ibid.*, No. 463.
[13]*Belfast Politics*, p. 171.
[14]*Old Belfast*, p. 181.
[15]Drennan Letters, No. 449.
[16]*Ibid.*, No. 389.
[17]*Ibid.*, No. 396.
[18]*Ibid.*, No. 396.
[19]*Ibid.*, No. 351.
[20]*Historical Collections*, p. 418.
[21]*Ibid.*, p. 459.
[22]Curtis, E. *History of Ireland*, p. 376.
[23]Drennan Letters, No. 426.
[24]Madden. *Antrim and Down in* '98, p. 108.
[25]*Ibid.*, p. 92.
[26]*Ibid.*, p. 98.
[27]*Ibid.*, p. 149.
[28]*Old Belfast*, p. 182.
[29]B.N.H. and P.S. 2nd series, vol. IV. Longfield, A.: "*Notes on Linen and Cotton Industry in Northern Ireland*"
[30]State Paper Office, Dublin.
[31]McCracken Letters.
[32]Drennan Letters, No. 495.
[33]*Ibid.*, No. 391*a*.
[34]*Tone*, p. 271.
[35]Drennan Letters, No. 397.
[36]*Ibid.*, Nos. 410 and 411.
[37]*Ibid.*, No. 411.
[38]*Ibid.*, No. 513.
[39]*Ibid.*, No. 435.
[40]*Ibid.*, Nos. 519 and 552.
[41]*Ibid.*, No. 544*b*.
[42]Quoted. Hayden and Moonan: *A Short History of the Irish People*, p. 425.
[43]*Historical Collections*, pp. 432–3.
[44]*Ibid.*, p. 433.
[45]*Old Belfast*, p. 191.
[46]*Tone*, p. 127.
[47]*Ibid.*, p. 128.
[48]*Ulster Magazine*, Jan. 1830.

CHAPTER 8, p. 107—p. 124.

[1]Drennan Letters, No. 605.
[2]*Ibid.*, No. 605.
[3]*Ibid.*, No. 618.
[4]*Ibid.*, No. 628*a*.

[5]*Ibid.*, No. 598.
[6]*Ibid.*, No. 610.
[7]*United Irishmen*, 1st series, 2nd edit., p. 365.
[8]*Historical Collections*, p. 441.
[9]Drennan Letters, No. 629.
[10]Tennent Papers. Belfast Museum and Art Gallery.
[11]Drennan Letters, No. 700.
[12]Wollstonecraft: *Vindication of the Rights of Women.* Everyman edit., p. 161.
[13]State Paper Office, Dublin.
[14]Marshall, J. J. *Old Belfast.*
[15]Drennan Letters, No. 452.
[16]*Ibid.*, No. 258.
[17]*Ibid.*, No. 452.
[18]McCracken Letters.
[19]Drennan Letters, No. 641.
[20]*Ibid.*, No. 636.
[21]Young, R. M. MSS. Belfast Museum and Art Gallery.
[22]Drennan Letters, No. 639.
[23]McCracken Letters.
[24]*Ibid.*
[25]*Ibid.*
[26]*Ibid.*
[27]*Ibid.*
[28]*Ibid.*
[29]*Ibid.*
[30]*Ibid.*
[31]*Ibid.*
[32]Monaghan, J. J.: "*Social and economic History of Belfast,* 1790–1800 p. 355." Thesis. Queen's University, Belfast.
[33]McCracken Letters.
[34]*Ibid.*
[35]*Ibid.*
[36]*Ibid.*

CHAPTER 9, p. 125—p. 164.

[1]McCracken Letters.
[2]*Historical Collections*, p. 463.
[3]Drennan Letters, Nos. 649–677.
[4]*Ibid.*, No. 651,
[5]McSkimin. *Annals of Ulster*, p. 38.
[6]*Shan Van Vocht*, vol. IV, No. 3.
[7]Drennan Letters, No. 651.
[8]*Ibid.* Nos. 595–596.
[9]McCracken Letters.
[10]*Ibid.*
[11]*Ibid.*

[12]*Ibid.*
[13]*Ibid.*
[14]*Ibid.*
[15]*Ibid.*
[16]*Ibid.*
[17]*Ibid.*
[18]*Ibid.*
[19]*Ibid.*
[20]*Ibid.*
[21]*Ibid.*
[22]*Ibid.*
[23]*Ibid.*
[24]*Ibid.*
[25]*Ibid.*
[26]*Ibid.*
[27]Drennan Letters, No. 652.
[28]McCracken Letters.
[29]*Ibid.*
[30]*Ibid.*
[31]*Ibid.*
[32]*Ibid.*
[33]*Ibid.*
[34]*Ibid.*
[35]*Ibid.*
[36]*Ibid.*
[37]*Ibid.*
[38]*Ibid.*
[39]*Ibid.*
[40]*Ibid.*
[41]*Ibid.*
[42]*Ibid.*
[43]*Ibid.*
[44]*Ibid.*
[45]*Ibid.*
[46]*Ibid.*

CHAPTER 10, p. 165—p. 192.

[1]McCracken Letters.
[2]*Ibid.*
[3]*Ibid.*
[4]McSkimin. *Annals of Ulster*, p. 64.
[5]Quoted. Lecky. *Irel.*, vol. IV, p. 414.
[6]*Ibid.*, p. 413.
[7]Madden, R. R. *Antrim and Down in* '98, p. 104.
[8]*Ibid.*, p. 122.
[9]*Ibid.*, p. 107.
[10]Drennan Letters, No. 710.

[11]Approx. 21,000, of whom 7,000 were Defenders. *United Irishmen*, 2nd series, vol. II, p. 435.
[12]*Ibid.*, p. 435.
[13]McCormick, J. *Irish Rebellion of* 1798. Dublin 1844. p. 256.
[14]*United Irishmen*, 2nd series, vol. II, p. 440.
[15]*Ibid.*
[16]*Belfast News-Letter*, 12.6.1798.
[17]*Historical Collections*, p. 483.
[18]Drennan Letters, No. 718.
[19]Octogenarian. *Belfast Sixty Years Ago*. Edited J. J. Marshall. p. 10.
[20]*United Irishmen*, 2nd series, vol II, p. 448.
[21]*Ibid.*, p. 481.
[22]McCracken Letters.
[23]*Ibid.*
[24]*United Irishmen*, 2nd series, vol. II, pp. 485–6.
[25]*Ibid.*, p. 487.
[26]*Ibid.*, p. 488.
[27]*Ibid.*, p. 490.
[28]*Ibid.*, p. 491.
[29]*Ibid.*, p. 493.
[30]*Ibid.*, p. 493.
[31]*Ibid.*, p. 494.
[32]*Shan Van Vocht*, vol. IV, No. 3.
[33]*Historical Collections*, pp. 489–90.
[34]Octogenarian. *Belfast Sixty Years Ago*. Edited J. J. Marshall. p. 10.
[35]*Ibid.*, p. 30.
[36]State Paper Office, Dublin.
[37]*United Irishmen*, 2nd series, vol. II, p. 497.

CHAPTER 11, p. 193—p. 226.

[1]McCracken Letters.
[2]Biggar Papers. B.P.L.
[3]*United Irishmen*, 2nd series, vol. II, p. 497.
[4]Lecky. *Irel.*, vol. V, p. 101.
[5]Drennan Letters, No. 758*a*.
[6]*Ibid.*, No. 810.
[7]*Ibid.*, No. 822.
[8]*Ibid.*, No. 911.
[9]*Ibid.*, No. 734.
[10]*Tone*, vol. I, p. 148.
[11]Quoted. Lecky. *Irel.*, vol. IV, p. 414.
[12]McCracken Letters.
[13]*Ibid.*
[14]*Ibid.*
[15]*Ibid.*

[16]*Ibid.*
[17]*United Irishmen*, 2nd series, vol. I, p. 247.
[18]McCracken Letters.
[19]Drennan Letters, No. 882.
[20]*Ibid.*, No. 943.
[21]*United Irishmen*, 3rd series, vol. II, p. 183.
[22]*Ibid.*, p. 202.
[23]*Ibid.*, p. 199.
[24]*Ibid.*, p. 202.
[25]Drennan Letters, No. 986.
[26]State Paper Office, Dublin.
[27]State Paper Office, Dublin. Letter to Bernard Coile.
[28]McCracken Letters.
[29]Landreth. *Pursuit of Robert Emmet.*
[30]McCracken Letters.
[31]*United Irishmen*, 3rd series, vol. II, p. 226.
[32]*Ibid.*, p. 331.
[33]*Old Belfast*, p. 190.
[34]In the family of Mr. Jos. W. Hammond, Dublin.
[35]*Old Belfast*, p. 191.
[36]McCracken Letters.
[37]Drennan Letters, No. 1057.
[38]McCracken Letters.
[39]*Ibid.*
[40]*Ibid.*
[41]*Ibid.*
[42]*Ibid.*
[43]*Ibid.*
[44]*United Irishmen*, 3rd series, vol. II, p. 258.
[45]Drennan Letters, No. 1086.
[46]*United Irishmen*, 3rd series, vol. II, p. 264.
[47]Drennan Letters, No. 1065.

CHAPTER 12, p 227—p 240.

[1]McCracken Letters.
[2]*United Irishmen*, 3rd series, vol. II, p. 278.
[3]McCracken Letters.
[4]*Belfast News-Letter*, 23.12.1803.
[5]*Irish Harpers*, p. 254.
[6]Mrs. R. M. Beath's collection.
[7]*Irish Harpers*, p. 48.
[8]Mrs. R. M. Beath's collection.
[9]*Annals of Irish Harpers*, p. 66.
[10]*Ibid.*, p. 561.
[11]B.C.S.
[12]*Irish Harpers*, p. 50.
[13]*Ibid.*, p. 65.

[14]Drennan Letters, No. 962.
[15]*Belfast News-Letter*, 10.5.1805.
[16]Drennan Letters, No. 1150.
[17]*Belfast Monthly Magazine*, vol. 6, p. 341.

CHAPTER 13, p. 241—p. 256.

[1]Drennan Letters, No. 1391.
[2]Tennent Papers. Belfast Museum and Art Gallery.
[3]*Old Belfast*, p. 276.
[4]McCracken Letters.
[5]*Old Belfast*, p. 193.
[6]*Ibid.*, p. 193. This letter is not complete.
[7]Ulster Since the Union. Belfast Broadcasting Corporation, 1954.
[8]*Old Belfast*, p. 192.
[9]McCracken Letters.
[10]B.C.S.
[11]*Ibid.*
[12]*Ibid.*
[13]*Ibid.*
[14]*Ibid.*
[15]Ladies Committee I (a very small volume).
[16]*Ibid.*
[17]B.C.S.

CHAPTER 14, p. 257—p. 287.

[1]*Belfast News-Letter.*
[2]*Ibid.* 2.3.1827
[3]*Ibid.*, 13.3.1827.
[4]Gurney and Fry. *Report on the Prisons of Ireland.*
[5]Ladies Committee.
[6]B.C.S.
[7]Ladies Committee.
[8]*Ibid.*
[9]*Ibid.*
[10]*Ibid.*
[11]Quoted. Bayne Powell: "*Housekeeping in Eighteenth Century England*".
[12]Ladies Committee.
[13]B.C.S.
[14]Ladies Committee.
[15]B.C.S.
[16]Ladies Committee.
[17]*Ibid.*
[18]*Ibid.*
[19]*Ibid.*
[20]*Ibid.*

[21]*Ibid.*
[22]*Ibid.*
[23]*Ibid.*
[24]*Ibid.*
[25]*Ibid.*
[26]*Ibid.*
[27]*Ibid.*
[28]*Ibid.*
[29]*Ibid.*
[30]*Ibid.*
[31]*Ibid.*
[32]*Ibid.*
[33]*Ibid.*
[34]*Ibid.*
[35]*Ibid.*
[36]*Ibid.*
[37]*Ibid.*
[38]*Ibid.*
[39]*Ibid.*
[40]*Ibid.*
[41]B.C.S.
[42]*Ibid.*
[43]Ladies Committee.
[44]*Ibid.*
[45]*Ibid.*
[46]*Ibid.*
[47]*Ibid.*
[48]*Ibid.*
[49]*Ibid.*
[50]*Ibid.*
[51]*Ibid.*
[52]B.C.S.
[53]Ladies Committee.
[54]Report of Ladies Industrial School. P.R.O.N.I.
[55]Ladies Committee.
[56]B.C.S.
[57]Drennan Letters, No. 1396.

CHAPTER 15, p. 288—p. 308.

[1]McCracken Letters.
[2]*United Irishmen*, 2nd series, vol. II, p. 498.
[3]McCracken Letters.
[4]*Old Belfast*, p. 196.
[5]McCracken Letters.
[6]*Ibid.*
[7]Ladies Committee.
[8]Report Ladies Industrial School.

[9]*Old Belfast*, p. 195.
[10]*Belfast News-Letter*, 1766.
[11]*Dublin Mercury*, 1768.
[12]*Historical Collections*, p. 163.
[13]*Old Belfast*, p. 269.
[14]McCracken Letters.
[15]*Ibid.*
[16]Tennent Papers. Belfast Museum and Art Gallery.
[17]McCracken Letters.
[18]*Ibid.*
[19]*Old Belfast.*
[20]McCracken Letters.
[21]*Ibid.*
[22]*Ibid.*
[23]*Ibid.*
[24]*Ibid.*
[25]Madden, R. R. *Antrim and Down in* '98, p. 243.
[26]McCracken Letters.
[27]*Ibid.*
[28]*Ibid.*
[29]*Ibid.*
[30]*Ibid.*
[31]*Ibid.*
[32]*Old Belfast*, p. 197.
[33]McCracken Letters.

INDEX

D.

E.

F.

G.

H.

I.

J.

N.

O.

O'.

P.